NEVER JUST A GAME

NEVER JUST A GAME

PLAYERS, OWNERS, AND AMERICAN BASEBALL TO 1920

ROBERT F. BURK

The University of North Carolina Press Chapel Hill & London

Library of Congress
Cataloging-in-Publication Data
Burk, Robert F.
    Never just a game : players, own-
ers, and American baseball to 1920 /
by Robert F. Burk
       p.   cm.
    Includes bibliographical references
(p.) and index.
    ISBN 0-8078-2122-5
    1. Baseball—Economic aspects—
United States—History—19th century.
2. Baseball players—United States—
Economic conditions. 3. Industrial
relations—United States—History.
I. Title.
GV880.B87   1994
338.4'3796357'0973—dc20
                                      93-22719
                                          CIP

98 97 96 95 94   5 4 3 2 1

FOR MY FATHER,

who took me to my first baseball game

CONTENTS

ILLUSTRATIONS

Photographs courtesy of the National Baseball Library,
Cooperstown, New York

PREFACE

 Baseball is a game many of us have played as children and adolescents. When age, waning physical capabilities, and adult responsibilities require us to give up active participation in it, we cling vicariously to the action through spectatorship. As fans, we witness professionals perform the game's refined skills, and we project our hopes, frustrations, and passions upon them. We see them as blessed, paid handsomely to play a game when we consider the opportunity to play to be payment enough. Because we see baseball as an escape from the "real" world of toil, we resent the slightest hint of complaint or greed on the part of our heroes. To be sure, professional baseball provides to spectators and players alike sport's nonthreatening outlets for emotional exuberance, individual expression, competitive fervor, and communal dedication to team and city. But for those who operate professional franchises, and for those employed by them in the sport, baseball has never been "just a game." As one of the most visible of entertainment industries, baseball claims a past marked from the beginning not merely by on-field heroics and blunders but also by bitter off-field struggles between players and management over prestige, power, and profits. Central to its labor history have been repeated battles over who would have access to its opportunities, how its profits would be divided, and, encompassing these concerns, who would control its operations.

Just as baseball descended from earlier bat-and-ball games of the colonial era, its antebellum inventors were the inheritors of a unique cultural tradition. They created baseball clubs as one of many forms of urban male voluntary association, as a secularized offspring of the congregational fellowship of their ancestors. When challenged by the sons of other ethnocultural stock, they first resisted encroachments and heralded their sport as the embodiment of traditional, "true" Americanism. Then, when clubs began to recognize the commercial possibilities of their ballplaying activities, the economic impetus for having the best playing talent and winning the most victories eroded these early walls of exclusion. At the same time, however, this drive accelerated both the trend toward refinements in the rules of the game to ensure that it was open only to those of the highest skill level and the growing segregation between on-field performers and nonparticipant officers who aggregated managerial power to themselves. Justified publicly on the basis of preserving the traditional virtues and upright character of the sport from those who might corrupt it, the skill refinement of on-field performers and the removal of management authority from players' hands also served the materialistic objectives of those who increasingly wielded that authority.

As the game spread throughout the Northeast, the most proficient clubs formed intercity cartels and marketed their entertainment business by means of professional leagues. Officers and stockholders saw that their franchises possessed remarkable growth potential but that their existing administrative machinery needed augmentation by an overarching federal structure if the industry's promise was to be realized. The model they chose, similar to that of a political party in its geographic layers of local chapters, state and national associations, and delegate conventions, proved to lack the centralized power and single-mindedness of vision necessary to prevent factionalism and parasitic competition for journeyman playing talent. Under the guidance of a Chicago captain of industry, William Hulbert, one collection of franchises in the largest attendance markets established a far more comprehensive cartel, dedicated to financial solvency through the brutal application of capitalistic principles. To avoid mutually destructive competition, member clubs pledged to honor each other's territorial rights to particular cities and to band together to crush outside challengers. To control labor costs by eliminating competitive bidding for player services, the "reserve clause" bound each franchise's playing employees indefinitely to their "owner" in a unique form of industrial-age serfdom. Cartel management collectively retained the right to control, or even to deny completely, access to employment on the basis of sex, age, religion, ethnicity, and race; and players seldom resisted, whether from their own prejudices or from fear of losing job security.

Enjoying an ability to dictate labor relations that owners of few if any other businesses could match, baseball's barons also adopted paternalistic and intrusive conduct regulations for the player force and increasingly relied upon mid-level overseers, in the form of captains (appropriately relabeled "managers") and umpires, to implement those regulations on their diamond-shaped versions of shop floors. The owners guarded with equal zeal their prerogatives over equipment specifications, park dimensions and features, and playing and scoring rules, ensuring that they could manipulate through such workplace control the statistical measures of productivity upon which they then based their salary offers. As other leagues of franchises in weaker markets emerged, the dominant "majors" even subordinated them, in exchange for extended territorial protection, into an expanding source of cheap replacement labor that further undercut players' economic leverage. The architects of the Gilded Age baseball industry, in short, anchored their hopes for success in the ability to seize and maintain comprehensive, monopsony control over the means of production—none of which was more important than labor.

Unfortunately for the baseball cartel, every method employed to compel management solidarity in labor policy for the sake of mutual profit and order—whether muscle-flexing by a dominant "hub" franchise magnate, interlocking stock ownership between clubs, or arbitration of management disputes by an executive commission—would falter. Undermining the cartel's efforts in this regard was the fact that baseball, as a skilled-labor-intensive entertainment business, could not emulate heavy industry and replace its workers with machines and cheaper unskilled labor. In baseball, the player *was* the game: he was the producer of runs and victories, and his act of production was the gate attraction. The more skilled the performer, the costlier his services but also the more appealing the performance. From the 1870s through the 1910s, the sport's broadening spectator popularity and the dramatic upsurge in the urban population facilitated internecine franchise competition and the rise of challenger "outlaw" leagues and trade wars, which triggered boom-and-bust cycles, franchise bankruptcies, and mergers similar to those in other industries.

While the owners struggled to impose order, players repeatedly availed themselves of opportunities temporarily to regain greater economic leverage by playing off one suitor against another in search of the best deal in pay and occupational control. Their successes, however, would prove as short-lived as the trade wars. For although the owners' ability to exploit ethnocultural and racial differences within the work force (a tactic common to American industry) remained limited in the period before 1920 because of the relative homogeneity of the player force, other weaknesses—including individual players' acquisitiveness, the differing economic status of stars and journeymen, job security conflicts between veterans and rookies and between major leaguers and minor leaguers, and the brevity of playing careers—undercut players' attempts to create enduring collective-bargaining institutions that could guarantee them a strong voice in industry councils. Nor did the players have enough managerial expertise, collective economic resources, or solidarity to create their own alternative, worker-controlled league. By 1920, owners would still hold the upper hand in the labor-management tug-of-war, but without having secured a satisfactory long-term solution to their labor problem.

In the preparation of this study of American baseball's early labor history, a story I hope in the future to carry to the present day, so many individuals have offered their hospitality, help, and counsel that I cannot name them all. But particular thanks are due to chief librarian Tom Heitz, research librarian Bill Deane, photo collection manager Patricia Kelly, and the rest of the wonderful staff of the National Baseball Library at Cooperstown, New York. Their enthusiasm for their subject, even as they battle limitations of space and financial resources, is contagious and merits the strongest support from the baseball industry. My hosts in Cooperstown during the summer of 1990, Rose and David Edwards, made me feel as if I were a member of the family, and they will always have a special place in my heart. The Green Educational Foundation provided crucial financial support for the research phase of the project. My appreciation also goes to David Sturtevant, Lorle Porter, Charles Drubel, and Doug Harms of Muskingum College, who read and critiqued the manuscript in its early stages. To them, and to all the others who subsequently reviewed the text, I am grateful for the errors they caught, and I absolve them of any blame for those that may remain. Once again, Judy Woodard gave generously of her time and labor in the preparation of the manuscript. At the University of North Carolina Press, special thanks are owed to executive editor Lewis Bateman and assistant managing editor Ron Maner, whose constant encouragement and professionalism are qualities sadly becoming too rare in the publishing business these days.

Finally, I owe unique debts to three other individuals. The first of these is to Dr. Harold Seymour, whose pioneering work in baseball history made the field respectable for intellectual carpetbaggers such as myself. The second is to Bill James, a fellow Kansan who has done more than anyone to reenliven contemporary baseball research, and who continues to show that statistics do not always have to lie. And finally, I am indebted to Patricia Geschwent, who has prodded and sustained me for the last eleven years. My one wish is that this modest volume, and whatever success it may enjoy, will finally convert her into a baseball fan.

NEVER JUST A GAME

ONE

FROM CONGREGANTS TO CONTESTANTS

The origins of American baseball, and of its labor history, are best found not in a single town, or in the mind of a single inventor, or on a single date. Nor are they to be found in a particular social model, whether it be industrialization, urbanization, or that newer hybrid, modernization. Although the earliest ball games can be traced back to far distant rural societies, for the more immediate ancestors of our "national pastime" we must turn to a distinctive people, inhabiting the preindustrial villages and hamlets of Stuart England, and to the regional culture and folkways they introduced to North America in a series of migrations beginning in the 1620s. For although the game of baseball had many distant ancestors and was influenced by a variety of factors, it claimed one primary cultural midwife—the Puritans of colonial New England. Early base ball games of varying types and with varying numbers of participants reflected basic folkways of the Puritans. Subsequent custodianship of baseball by their descendants shaped the rules, patterns of organizational control, and class and ethnocultural makeup of the sport in the eighteenth and early nineteenth centuries. By the antebellum era, "respectable" Yankees' fear of socioeconomic and ethnocultural "declension" in the ballplayer ranks led to both the elevation of playing-skill requirements and, increasingly, the removal of club management responsibilities from players' hands.[1]

The Puritan sporting activities that eventually evolved into antebellum baseball embodied, in the words of historian David Hackett Fischer, the "combination of order and action, reason and emotion, individuality and collective effort" of an idealized community of saints, or a perfect congregation of the elect. Following the exodus of some 21,000 English dissenters to Massachusetts in the initial eleven years of that colony, the children of this migration exploded in numbers to 100,000 by 1700 and over a million by 1800. Within a century and a half they spread far beyond the borders of the Bay Colony to northern and southern New England, eastern New Jersey, Long Island, upstate New York, and northern Ohio. Wherever they went, they took with them as part of their cultural tradition the playing of ball games, and it is no historical accident that antebellum baseball first flourished in these same areas of the North. "Barnball" or "cat" ball games for small numbers of participants became very popular among New England boys. But given the Puritans' overriding emphasis on preserving the internal unity and harmony of their modest, godly communities of husbandmen, artisans, and tradesmen, a larger-scale form of ballplaying that could accommodate anywhere from twelve to twenty players per side—"town ball"—grew rapidly in popularity in the eighteenth century.[2]

It has been argued that colonial Puritan strictures against popular amusements in general stagnated the life of baseball among adults and thereby necessitated the game's spontaneous reinvention in antebellum New York City. But that argument, much like earlier claims regarding the Puritans' sexual practices, overstates a prudish stereotype, extends it well into the eighteenth century, and ignores everything about the ball games that was utilitarian to the Puritan creed. Ministers did issue strictures against "idle recreation," "Popish" or pagan activities, and play on the Sabbath; one divine, for example, decried "Morris-dancing, cudgel playing, and baseball," among other activities. They also attempted to restrain the more informal types of ballplaying among their young, who they assumed lacked the maturity to exhibit instructive and self-improving teamwork rather than exuberant individual display. But the very need to proscribe some boundaries upon ballplaying, without issuing absolute prohibitions, testified to the popularity of base ball games in New England communities. If accommodated to Puritan priorities, ball games were ritual occasions for community and spiritual socialization, the display of fellowship and skill, and the acting out of life's tests of harmony and piety by sober, respectable men. Because the games, when strictly controlled by rules and conducted by mature, "manly" congregants, did not undermine the "New England way," they did not carry the same stigma of immorality as the "rough-and-tumble" blood sports of the "meaner" classes or the more ostentatious avocations of English Anglican elites. They could be devices for a godly community, through recreation, to "improve the time," not merely to "pass" it or "kill" it.[3]

The unusual strength of nuclear families among the Puritans, and the deeply rooted congregational culture of their villages, ensured that even as New Englanders made the transition from Puritan to Yankee and oriented their lives toward worldly success, they continued to hand down from generation to generation their associational traditions and activities. As their descendants fanned out across the Northeast, they accordingly carried baseball to new homes. But if baseball in its various local forms flourished in the Yankee North, access and receptivity to it among non-Yankee ethnocultural groups remained sharply limited, despite the dramatic upsurge of immigration in the 1700s from North Britain (the Scotch-Irish) and the German provinces of Central Europe. The depth of baseball's Puritan/Yankee roots, in other words, ensured the survival of such sporting activities until a more propitious time for popular expansion and commercial exploitation but also raised barriers to the arrival of that time and acted as a restraint upon the subsequent extent of ethnocultural transformation when it did occur.

By the time of the American Revolution, members of secular Yankee male associations, based in institutions such as militia companies, inns, and schools, included ballplaying in their fellowship activities. Soldiers at Valley Forge played in the harsh winter of 1777–78 despite the hardships. Following the Revolution, a Princeton undergraduate referred in his diary to a pastime called "baste ball," pursued covertly on the college grounds in 1786; a children's book published in Worcester, Massachusetts, in 1787 included an illustration of ballplaying; and Daniel Webster took part in ball games at Dartmouth College in 1797. Brown, Williams, and Harvard students were known to enjoy the diversion by the early nineteenth century. Oliver Wendell Holmes, father of the celebrated jurist, scribed a classic description of his participation as a Harvard undergraduate in 1829, and William Alcott a decade later reminisced that among youthful sporting "addictions," "our most common exercise was ballplaying." Some twenty years before the Knickerbockers of the 1840s, a local variant of baseball called "the New York game" was being played by Yankee migrants to the Empire State. Famed Whig political operative Thurlow Weed belonged in 1825 to a fifty-member Rochester association that included baseball among its activities; and in the same year a Delhi, New York, newspaper carried notice of a baseball challenge issued by a Hamden team. As early as 1833, Philadelphia was home to the Olympic Town Ball Club. It may even be true, in a particularly ironic twist, that the once-reputed but since-discredited "founder" of baseball, Abner Doubleday, codified a set of rules before 1840, well ahead of Alexander Cartwright of the Knickerbockers.[4]

What, then, was the significance of the emergence of the Knickerbocker Baseball Club in 1842 and the establishment by member Cartwright of the "Knickerbocker rules"? To begin with, the presence of the Knickerbocker Club in New York City was an example of the geographic spread of the game beyond New England by migrating Yankees and a sign of the continuing power of the associative ideal among such northerners in the form of urban voluntary organizations. In the more congested yet impersonal spatial and economic setting of the antebellum city, these new institutions of association, like their Puritan forerunners, gave Yankee men of middling respectability a sense of place and promoted their collective physical, emotional, and spiritual improvement in the face of internal and external corruptions. Antebellum Yankees sought to preserve the essence of traditional values and rituals within voluntary associations adaptable to the city's unique environment. After playing ball together on a vacant Manhattan lot since at least 1842, the members of the Knickerbockers were forced to seek new grounds, so they formed a dues-paying club in 1845 in order to rent for $75 a year the Elysian Fields, a playing ground in Hoboken, New Jersey, accessible by ferry across the Hudson River.

The Knickerbockers of antebellum New York City are most noteworthy, however, because, through a combination of promotion and luck, their rules emerged as the standard guidelines for the sport of baseball. Apart from altering the rules by which they played—and the fact that they met in a room of Fijuz's Hotel, owned by one of their number, instead of a church or town meeting hall—the Knickerbockers echoed ethnocultural patterns of the past, resembling their Puritan ancestors and other Yankee aggregations. Of the forty-six known surnames of members of the 1845 Knickerbockers and its two early contemporaries in the city, the "New York" and "Brooklyn" clubs, nearly 75 percent (34 names) reflected pre-colonial English ancestry. Many of the names, such as Cartwright, Fisher, Miller, Smith, and Tucker, bespoke ancestral roots in medieval English trades, or, as with Brodhead, Marsh, and Vail, made literal reference to family topography of origin. Five other surnames suggested earlier Norman French or Huguenot roots, also consistent with the great migration of seventeenth-century Calvinists to New England. In contrast, only two names were Dutch in origin, two Irish, and three German.[5]

Yankee by religious and ethnic roots, the Knickerbockers also illustrated the truncated system of class orders of their Puritan ancestors. A study of fifty club members from 1845 to 1860 reveals the presence of seventeen merchants, twelve clerks, five brokers, four professionals, two insurance salesmen, one bank teller, one sugar dealer, one hatter, one cooperage owner, one stationer, one U.S. marshal, and several "gentlemen." Alexander Cartwright, the originator of the club's pioneering playing rules and field geometry, combined the talents of a bank teller, surveyor, and volunteer fireman. His elder brother claimed proprietorship of a bookshop in the city. Of those members identifiable for the 1845–50 period alone, a majority of forty-four worked in white-collar occupations, with slightly over one-third engaged in commercial and financial entrepreneurship, about one-fourth functioning as professionals (doctors or lawyers), and another two-fifths employed in lesser white-collar trades or clerical positions. Of the handful who were more affluent, Benjamin C. Lee (whose father was also an honorary member), claimed a $20,000 estate in 1845, and J. Paige Mumford, another "gentleman," was the son of a well-known merchant who had fallen upon hard times by 1845.[6]

Such a truncated (if not quite "upper-class" in most cases) membership of Yankees suggests that the Knickerbockers and similar emerging clubs in New York, Brooklyn, and other northern cities also resembled New England congregations and Yankee voluntary associations in their methods of membership selection. As in Puritan churches of an earlier day, which had required testimony from members in support of applicants' elect status before permitting them admission to the community of saints, early baseball clubs functioned as decentralized, member-run associations that decided among themselves who would or would not join their fellowship. Members chose officers from their number, and those officers found themselves, like earlier New England ministers and public officials, in the ambiguous posture of being both of the membership/electorate and apart from it insofar as they were expected to exemplify superior virtues and principles. Administrative functions resided in a president, vice-president, secretary, treasurer, and three directors, chosen after the fashion of a town meeting by the membership. They met separately about once a month during the playing season and exercised such responsibilities as arranging for facilities, determining a practicing and playing schedule, securing club equipment and attire, picking the active players and team captains for each outing (whether intra- or interclub), and acting as conduct judges and issuers of disciplinary sanctions for violations of club rules.

The Knickerbockers and their contemporaries viewed as supremely important the maintenance of "manly," upright fellowship, harmony, and decorum. For them, excellence in performance meant exhibiting character as well as skill. But most on-field competition took place within individual clubs rather than between clubs and varied greatly in seriousness—from practices to "friendly" contests to "social games" to outside "matches." Additionally, a member's duties to his associates and to the principles of manly fellowship went far beyond the playing field and playing season. Games of any type were but one aspect of the entire responsibilities of a member, which included participation in meetings, elections, postgame banquets, and off-season activities such as balls, suppers, and skating parties. A club, in other words, represented a select fraternity of like-minded men, a voluntary association of sober, respectable Yankees dedicated to healthful recreation, fellowship, and public virtue. Attendance, propriety, and cooperation were expected and demanded; selfishness, loutishness, and truancy were punished; and more violent disruptions of comity were excoriated.

In the way of a religious congregation, the Knickerbockers used dues, fines, and punishments to help maintain their exclusiveness, finance their activities, and define their purposes. Also as in congregations, violations of certain rules concerning decorum and behavior were more common than others, as club members tested the boundaries of group discipline while avoiding any challenge to the association's basic integrity. Individuals paid annual dues of $5.00, plus a $2.00 initiation fee. Switching allegiance to another club meant forfeiting the dues. Early fine schedules proscribed penalties of fifty cents for disobedience, twenty-five cents for either expressing one's views before an umpire's call or questioning the call afterward, and six cents for each instance of the use of profanity. The latter fine reflected both a desire to reinforce proper decorum and a recognition of the greater frequency and modest significance of the offense in question. Given the greater responsibilities and expectations placed upon captains, the club assessed fines of $1.00 per incident upon them for neglecting their duties or prematurely leaving the field. Truancy on the part of players and captains alike became increasingly common, however, arising from conflicts between club responsibilities and work or health demands, despite efforts to accommodate work schedules by designating Mondays and Thursdays as "play days." One miscreant explained, "I have been too weak to run and to achey [sic] to strike a ball," while another lamented that his business had demanded "every moment of [his] time thus far in the season." It has been suggested that one reason the Knickerbockers did not play interclub matches for five years after 1845 was the frequent truancy of members from practices and meetings.[7]

Under the Knickerbockers' operating rules, for internal matches the club selected teams of nine men, including a captain. Outsiders, particularly if they were members of another recognized club, could be asked to fill in if necessary to have eighteen players. The Knickerbockers firmly observed the nine-man team standard and ranked its members from a "first nine" to a "muffin" team, based upon social status, the judgment of officers, and acknowledged skill level. Such ranking, however, also proved most compatible with the creeping competitive urge to identify and field the best team for interclub contests. Players "warmed up" before games by fielding balls hit to them, but did not take "batting practice." The early terminology of the sport identified particular areas of the field, in keeping with Cartwright's design, distinguishing between the "outfield" (with its left, center, and right subsections) and "infield" (including the positions of first, second, and third base and shortstop). But the players occupying these positions at any given time had not yet been defined specifically as "shortstops" or "left fielders," and their attire did not include positional indicators such as numbers; a participant was a "baseballist," or an "artist," not a narrow position specialist by name, even though in practice assignments to particular spots were growing more frequent. This nondifferentiation reflects most members' status in trades that had not yet been superseded by task-specific, component wage-labor work. Baseball's preindustrial artisan origins and its practicioners' placement of priority on controlled, nonviolent exercise are also evidenced by the fact that the sport emphasized manual and mental versatility and dexterity in the field, as well as moderate running, rather than raw hitting power or pitching trickery.[8]

With continuing local variations in rules, organizational details, and disciplinary sanctions, the number of baseball clubs in New York, Philadelphia, and other northeastern cities mushroomed in the late 1840s and early 1850s, following the patterns of Yankee migration and commerce. In New York and Brooklyn, the Knickerbockers were followed by the Independent Club, the Excelsiors, the Eagles, the Putnams, the Eclectics, and many more. Newark and Long Island alone claimed eleven or more ballplaying associations by 1854. In the metropolitan area the Knickerbockers, Gothams, Eagles, and Empires dominated Manhattan, and the Excelsiors, Putnams, Eckfords, and Atlantics became the best-established quartet in Brooklyn. As the number of clubs proliferated, teams assumed more distinctive local identities, with patriotic names, symbols, and colors resembling those of militia companies. The Eclectics, for example, sported dark blue flannel pants, white shirts trimmed in blue, red belts, and white caps with blue stars. The Charter Oaks of Brooklyn featured white pants, white caps with blue peaks, and black belts emblazoned with the team name. The shift to distinctive team attire reflected some concessions to practicality of play but perpetuated the earlier preoccupation with projecting collective harmony and outward respectability.

A concern for harmony and respectability notwithstanding, as the number of teams and interclub matches expanded, so too did reports of on-field lapses of decorum and discipline within and between teams; such lapses ranged from swearing and fighting on the field to betting, indecent anecdotes and songs, and public drunkenness off it. The perceived loss of "order" in the game as well as its modest geographic and social spread in the urban Northeast were signals of a more fundamental, however subtle, shift in the game's focus for its participants. Traditionally, intraclub activities and fellowship had been emphasized, with the secondary aim of displaying, and verifying, to oneself and one's immediate brethren, a presupposed social and spiritual worth within a relatively stable local order. Now the players' emphasis was shifting toward ballplaying in interclub contests as a means to preserve a public status under siege or to accumulate a greater measure of outer worth, both materially and spiritually. The emerging ethic, whether held by a middling Yankee craftsman or shopkeeper fearful of declension or by a lower middle-class worker or immigrant seeking respectability, was less communitarian, more competitive.

Such gradual changes in ballplayers' basic values and purposes were fundamentally the product of two sets of forces—one spiritual, the other material. The first of these, a long-term consequence of the Second Great Awakening, was the erosion among Yankees of traditional notions of predestination and spiritual election. The belief that upright, virtuous behavior merely reflected an essentially fixed spiritual status yielded before a "softer" Protestantism that allowed greater leeway for individual and collective striving for betterment and preparation for salvation. The new ethic encouraged Yankees to view their individual and collective outside activities as a means of protecting a status among others that could be lost, or of securing a new status that could be gained, through engagement with the outer world. Materially, the shift reflected the intensifying economic pressures and insecurities of a changing urban occupational structure and a growing ethnic mixture within the limited spatial confines of the antebellum "walking city." Yankee petty proprietors, artisans, and clerks sought to protect themselves from the declension of the factory system, while those in the more respectable new echelons of specialized manual labor, whether native-born or immigrant, sought to obtain the same social standing that their white-collar "adversaries" intended to preserve.

Increasing expressions of concern by "traditionalists" within the sport, and by reporters of similar cultural background who were beginning to cover it reflected the realization that the ballplaying fraternity was losing its exclusiveness. By the mid-1850s, mirroring the shifting production structure and social mobility patterns of antebellum cities and the influx of Irish and German immigrants, the game was becoming both less Yankee and less preindustrial in its personnel and guiding spirit. If efforts at total exclusion of non-Yankees were destined to fail, the alternative response by those holding sufficient prestige and power within the clubs was to accelerate the segregation of management from player personnel and functions. If a more heterogeneous playing fraternity could not be counted upon to display traditional values on the field or to police itself, lines of cultural exclusion from the ballfield would be upheld if and where possible. But where they could not, an increasingly centralized and segregated managerial hierarchy would regulate player *behavior* while vigilantly guarding its own reins of power from intrusion. At the same time, reflecting the growth of the "acquisitive ethic" among all "types" in the sport—whether Yankee or newcomer, player or nonplay-ing duespayer and "stockholder"—ball club participation became based less and less upon the desire for fellowship and more and more upon the financial rewards and status to be gained.[9]

Baseball by the 1850s simply could not be maintained on the same basis as it had even a decade before. The Knickerbockers, for their part, tried to hold the line through the device of scheduling matches only with clubs that used (and thereby could afford to pay the fees of) the Elysian Fields. But by comparison to other urban sports, baseball was too cheap to play (with equipment too easily made or bought and replaced) and too adaptable in various forms to the spatial constrictions of the city to remain exclusive for long. A comparatively more fluid class structure made efforts at social exclusion far from foolproof, particularly within such less continuously intimate, secondary associations as ball clubs. Some immigrants, and certainly many more second-generation Ameri-cans, could pass for upright Yankees on the basis of their conduct, occu-pational success, or intermarriage. Barring that, they could form their own baseball clubs. The nationality-conscious fears of a post-1848 flood of Europeans drowning out traditional Americanism, ironically, itself en-couraged baseball's growth in popularity among non-Yankees. In con-trast to English rounders, cricket, or other competitors that had continu-ing ties to an Old World nationality, American baseball attracted Irish and German "outsiders" who saw it as both a form of New World accom-modation and a repudiation of the alternative games of traditional ethnic enemies.

By the mid-1850s, urban communities of Irish immigrants and their offspring in particular were contributing increasing numbers of players and clubs. Of 228 identifiable members of clubs in Newark, Jersey City, and Orange, New Jersey, in the late 1850s, about 7 percent were first-generation Irish; in Orange by itself, the figure exceeded 1 member in 5. These totals do not even include members born in America of Irish descent, for whom data is not available. Specific clubs became noted for their high proportion of Irish manual workers, including the Washington Club of Hoboken (mainly laborers) and the Columbia team of Orange (predominantly hatters). Such a drive for participation and acceptance was shared by native-born urbanites whose access to the game had been limited not by ethnicity but by past class, family, and geographical bar-riers. Now access by these aspiring manual workers also could not be easily policed in the name of order. Whether native or immigrant, those entering the Yankee middle-class world of baseball clubs sought to emulate the behavior of their immediate "betters" by rejecting the less respectable working-class "bachelor subculture" of blood sports and by cultivating a sense of respectability through their adoption of patriotic labels—derived from place-names, the names of famous individuals, or appropriate character traits—for their own nines.[10]

From the ranks of an occupationally and ethnically shifting blue-collar lower middle class, then, the baseball fraternity steadily received more entrants. The Eckford Club of Brooklyn, named after Scottish shipbuilding mogul Henry Eckford, featured shipwrights and mechanics. The New York Mutuals, born of the Mutual Hook and Ladder fire company, soon became the sporting possession of the Tammany Hall political machine. Policemen stocked the Manhattans, while the Phantoms sprang from an association of barkeepers, and the Pocahontas Club from dairy company employees. The Metropolitans originated in an association of schoolteachers, and the Baltic, Jefferson, and Atlantic clubs based themselves in food tradesmen, especially butchers, with more flexible afternoon work schedules than other manual craftsmen. Data for New York City compiled by Melvin Adelman indicates a subtle "downward" shift in the occupational status, if not necessarily the income level, of the player force by the mid-1850s. A smaller percentage of members, especially "actives," than before came from the ranks of white-collar entrepreneurial and professional categories, and a higher proportion was drawn from skilled manual workers and lower white-collar clerks. Similar studies of New Jersey nines by George Kirsch verify that skilled manual workers by the late 1850s increasingly outnumbered their nonmanual counterparts, and the combined number of manual workers and lower white-collar clerks constituted over 60 percent of the total identifiables.[11]

It is important not to exaggerate the breadth of the "opening up" or "declension" (depending on one's perspective) of baseball's class structure, even though significant changes were occurring. Of the skilled craftsmen who made up ever-larger percentages of active participants on the field, most still came not from factory-organized or "sweated" trades but ones in which workers still retained a comparatively high degree of control over their work schedules and rhythms. While the on-field participation of professionals and entrepreneurs dropped, this did not mean that the sport had become accessible to the working poor or to large segments of the working class in general as we would usually define it. The Eckford Club's employees, for example, ranked among the best-paid manual laborers in the city, with incomes comparable or superior to those of clerks. The blue-collar share of the player force rose notably higher in Brooklyn, reflecting its more "plebeian" character, than in New York City, where as late as mid-decade the white-collar proportion remained at the high level of 87 percent. But over the next five years, the skilled blue-collar share in New York City nearly tripled to almost one-third of the total. In the combined metropolitan area, while more than three-quarters of identifiable club members had been "white-collar" in the first half of the 1850s, in the latter half the percentages of skilled blue-collar and lower white-collar clerical participants converged and totaled over three-quarters of the membership. Over the same five years, Newark, Jersey City, and Orange, New Jersey, clubs claimed a blue-collar average of 36 percent of their membership, with a high of nearly 74 percent in the Orange nines. Among five Newark clubs, the blue-collar share ranged from less than one-quarter to well over half, and in all but one aggregation it claimed the largest share of any occupational grouping.[12]

As the number and occupational diversity of clubs grew, so did the frequency and spectator popularity of interclub matches, which converted the ballfield from a place of ritual fellowship to an arena of contest pitting neighborhoods, ethnic and religious groups, parties, companies, and occupational classes against each other. Game schedules began to stretch at both ends of the outdoor season into March and November. By 1856 the New York metropolitan area alone featured a playing "season" of fifty-three games. Two years later, the metropolis claimed approximately 50 adult clubs, as well as 60 youth auxiliaries and feeder clubs. New Jersey likewise claimed at least 130 active clubs by late in the decade, including 36 in Newark and 42 in Jersey City alone. Teams secured additional playing fields to accommodate the demand, including the Capitoline Grounds in Brooklyn, a field in Englewood, New Jersey, the Reed House facility in Harlem, Hamilton Square in Manhattan, the Excelsiors' facility in South Brooklyn, Wheat Hall in East Brooklyn, and a field on Long Island. Brooklyn, once dubbed the "city of churches," appropriately assumed a new identity as the "city of baseball clubs." Hoboken, the "stronghold of lager beer," now became known as a citadel of baseball too. Two-to-four-hour matches, beginning in mid-afternoon to accommodate players' work schedules, drew 5,000–10,000 spectators.

Baseball had become a serious matter of victory or defeat, of gain or loss, in which hardened specialists now were required. The growing popular fervor for baseball within an expanding proportion of the middling classes found display in workingmen's nines practicing at 4:00 or

The New York Knickerbockers and Brooklyn Excelsiors with umpire, 1858. The pose presents the idealized antebellum baseball image of a fellowship of respectable amateur sportsmen.

5:00 A.M. to prepare for matches. With increasing frequency, clubs devoted their practices primarily to preparing their best nines—not usually their higher-status members—for interclub contests. By the latter half of the 1850s, while high white-collar proprietors and professionals still made up one-fifth of New York–area players who had seen action in at least one contest in the last five years, they constituted but 13 percent of "actives"—those seeing duty in at least four first-team games in a year or ten contests within five years. By contrast, nearly half of all actives among New York metropolitan nines at the time were skilled blue-collar employees. When the Excelsiors lost a match in difficult weather conditions to the Atlantics, writers attributed the outcome to the fact that the Excelsior playing force of clerks and proprietors simply lacked the outdoor hardiness of their blue-collar rivals. Another sign of the pursuit of individual and collective fame and gain was the emergence of all-star and championship contests. The first "all-star game," between New York and Brooklyn squads, occurred in 1858 at Long Island's Fashion Race Course, with 1,500 fans paying fifty cents each to attend.[13]

With continued improvement and expansion of antebellum transportation and communication, the interior urban centers of the Northeast and Midwest received more ballplaying ambassadors and imported the New York game. In upstate New York, Syracuse, Cazenovia, Canandaigua, Batavia, Troy, Albany, and Buffalo clubs organized local teams. In 1860, the Brooklyn Excelsiors launched a two-week tour of six matches with nines from western New York, won all of the matches handily, and then returned to play the Atlantics in the first "national championship" before a crowd of 8,000. By 1857, the public square of Cleveland, Ohio, already provided the setting for daily contests. Chicago soon boasted of the prowess of its teams. Detroit sponsored the Franklin Club; and even before it gained statehood, the Minnesota Territory claimed a team. South of New York, Washington, D.C., gradually gained attention for its nines, which often drew players from the ranks of the city's government clerks.

Given New York's supremacy as the North's commercial, transportation, and immigration hub, and given the success of the Knickerbocker rules in dominating play within Gotham's metropolitan area, baseball's outward march was also the march of standardization of playing rules and organizational patterns. New England towns and cities, possessing a better claim as the game's original custodians than New York, nonetheless found their versions of playing rules pushed aside by the New York game. The Massachusetts game stubbornly persisted, like the congregational ideal itself, in spite of its impractical retention of "soaking" (recording an out by hitting a runner with a thrown ball), ten-to-fourteen-man squads, stakes instead of bases, and one-hundred-run requirements for victory. Several teams endured under the traditional rules in Boston, but the improved rules were introduced there in 1857 with the arrival of a New York watchcase maker and former Gothams player. Soon the city's Tri-Mountains converted to New York rules and withdrew from the Massachusetts Association of Base Ball Players. By 1860, even Philadelphia's Olympic Town Ball Club succumbed to the new orthodoxy, after twenty-seven years of playing by the "traditional" rules.

At the same time that baseball officers and press boosters celebrated the game's impressive growth and claimed for it the title "national pastime," many of them also issued jeremiads on the social and moral declension of the sport. Newspaper accounts cited increasing rowdyism and gambling by players, spectators, and even umpires, and near-riots triggered by gangs and pickpockets. By 1860, a riot blamed on one team's working-class Irish fans forced the early suspension of a Brooklyn championship match. Increased fines by clubs of up to fifty cents per incident for profanity, disobeying the captain, or challenging the umpire did not lessen the on-field problems. Concerns about moral and social declension were not unique to baseball and were directed at many other urban institutions of the 1850s, including fire and police companies and political party organizations. According to the New York *Clipper*, Gotham's leading sporting publication, baseball's gambling problem was but a symptom of the larger "spirit of faction" generated by the swelling "foreign element of our immense metropolitan population."[14]

Baseball's tradition-minded boosters, however, were far from ready to give up on the game. Their own consciousness of nationality was a major reason for their insistence that America lay claim to its own "national pastime," and their tendency to discount any evidence of Old World paternity for baseball. They heralded the game, despite its corruptions, as the truly representative American (i.e., Yankee) sport, a "democratic" contest in which two teams of respectable men tested themselves against each other in a "natural" setting in orderly, fair, manly competition. They also hoped that the game's virtues could make the sport, through the "reforming" agencies of its clubs, a source of cultural instruction, moral uplift, and order—a "redeeming" institution—for an increasingly chaotic urban society. Press spokesmen dubbed teams "missionary organizations preaching the new gospel of health," "the greatest safety valve of society," and an "important and valuable adjunct to the church." The Detroit *Free Press*, praising the accurately named Early Risers (whose members practiced before 7:00 A.M. because of their work schedules), claimed baseball occupied "their leisure time in healthy exercise counteracting the growing tendency to visit saloons and other places of resort with which the city abounds, thus saving them from early immorality." In a similar vein, *Porter's Spirit of the Times* credited baseball with promoting "patience, fortitude, self-denial, order, obedience, and good humor."[15]

But could baseball clubs redeem the American city and at the same time achieve a national stamp of recognition as had the German Turnvereins, unless the Old World "corruptions" of the immigrants were screened out? How could the Yankee distinctiveness of baseball be restored and maintained? The more extreme nativists in baseball, as in the larger society, assumed that exclusion could be accomplished as a simple consequence of morphology. German immigrants were presumed to be naturally stocky, jovial, self-disciplined but lumbering sorts physically unsuited to baseball, while the Irish were depicted as subhuman simians in their brute strength, emotional and violent excesses, and childlike immaturity. But what if in physical features and overt behavior "Paddy" failed to embody the more easily isolated caricature? How, then, to guard against a more subtle acceleration of baseball's social and moral declension and preserve avenues for its emerging "reforming" and acquisitive roles?

It was such concerns, including the budding awareness among club officers of baseball's commercial potential, that gave rise to a hierarchical formal governance structure and a regulatory mentality by the eve of the Civil War. Already within the clubs, the higher socioeconomic classes claimed a larger and larger share of offices as their participation as on-field actives dropped. According to one study of club officers in New York City from 1856 to 1860, only 16 percent were blue-collar workers, and this figure amounted to but half their actual share of the total baseball membership. Brooklyn's skilled manual workers were likewise underrepresented in club offices, although not so disproportionately, constituting 30 percent of the membership but less than 24 percent of officers. Representing the other side of the coin, only about one New York and Brooklyn nonofficer member in eight claimed a higher white-collar professional or proprietary occupation. Equally revealing was the fact that the higher the official level in baseball's emerging governance structure of the 1850s, the greater the socioeconomic gap between officials and grass-roots members.[16]

It is in the context of this growing stratification of the governance of baseball, driven by fears of player declension and visions of profits, that the creation of the National Association of Base Ball Players should be seen. Although member clubs, like political parties of the era, still emphasized the ideal of local player/member self-rule, the reality was becoming quite different. Over a dozen clubs in 1857 sent delegates to Smith's Hotel in New York City and elected Dr. D. L. Adams as the association's first president. More importantly, they established a committee to administer and exercise control over member clubs' playing rules (one result was the adoption of the Knickerbocker rules as the official standard of play). By the next year, when the presidents of the Knickerbockers, Gothams, Empires, and Eagles summoned delegates from all of the "organized" clubs in the metropolitan area, twenty-two teams responded, and their representatives formally created the National Association on March 10, 1858. A committee appointed by the delegates assumed the task of formalizing an administrative structure by drafting a constitution and bylaws. Although the first National Association could but tenuously claim its title, given that New York state clubs outside the metropolitan area, to say nothing of clubs outside the Empire State, had not been invited, it gradually opened itself to state and then regional expansion. Its national delegates and officials, in turn, were chosen not directly by club members but by an intervening level of state association delegates. The delegates and officers of National Association conventions were, on average, even more Yankee and elitist in background than local club officials. *Porter's Spirit of the Times* alluded indirectly to this fact when it lamented the National Association's decision to exclude junior clubs (those with members under the age of twenty-one) from representation, an action the paper attributed to a "clique of men" supposedly concerned with their own money, status, and fitness.[17]

The National Association established standardized requirements for member clubs and, in so doing, shifted control of the sport upward. Officials at the national level now would set playing and off-field rules and requirements, while individual club officers assumed the unenviable burden of implementing the new guidelines and policing the compliance of club members. To belong to the national body, a club had to have at least eighteen members. This membership requirement, combined with the rising imperative to achieve victory through a featured first nine, made governance by a larger number of nonplaying but dues-paying "stockholders" more likely for clubs belonging to the association. With such changes, local administrative power shifted. Club applications for National Association membership, due at least thirty days before the group's annual convention in order to allow for a careful review, also could be screened through the requirement of a two-thirds vote of approval by the national delegates, while late applicants, if otherwise acceptable, could be given a probationary status until the following year. Each member club, regardless of the size of its membership, claimed two national delegates and two convention votes. The association initially charged club dues of $5.00, although it later reduced them to the formality of a $.50 charge.

Within the National Association and the sporting press, debates intensified between those labeled in some quarters as "traditionalists" and others dubbed "modernists." Actually, the main principals in both camps usually shared a "traditionalist" Yankee heritage as well as the hope of restoring within and between clubs a shared set of values and rules of conduct—a renewed sense of mutual heritage, collective harmony, and order. They differed, however, on whether it could best be achieved by turning back the clock and returning to an ethnoculturally purer, decentralized, and amateurish fraternity of sportsmen—thereby forsaking the full capitalist possibilities of the sport—or by adopting administrative structures and rules to enforce a particular cultural ethic upon an increasingly heterogeneous, acquisitive, and competitive playing force. In keeping with the latter course, among the first regulations of players' conduct adopted by the National Association were limits on their ability to move from one club to another, bans on direct financial compensation for their individual services, and regulations of ethical conduct. Now before a player could participate for a new team in an interclub match, he had to prove a thirty-day tenure with his new club. The association, besides banning individual play for pay, also barred players, umpires, and scorers from betting on contests.[18]

Under the enforcement procedures laid out by the national body, a nine-member Judiciary Committee received the cases stemming from the new regulations. Clubs submitted charges against accused violators to the National Association's secretary, and the panel ruled on the cases within ten days of their arrival. Rulings of the Judiciary Committee could be reversed by a two-thirds vote of the annual convention following the decisions. Encouraged by the National Association's lead, state and regional panels further elaborated punishments and procedures down the line. As a result, "throwing a game" now required a player's formal expulsion from his club, barred other member clubs from securing his services, and even prevented member clubs from playing matches against nonmember teams containing such players. Another "sad-but-necessary" crackdown against individual and team social misconduct came in 1859, when the association banned postgame banquets and refreshments hosted by home clubs on the grounds that these traditional expressions of fraternal fellowship had degenerated into mere extensions of on-field rivalry and rowdy behavior.[19]

Other on-field rules changes forced a heightened level of specialized skill and physical and mental dexterity and reflected the twin desires of club operators for both a more appealing product and greater labor control. Just as limits upon player mobility and mercenary behavior could promote a less willful, more upright and stable player fraternity, it was reasoned, so too might heightened skill specialization weed out those who were undisciplined, immature, or physiologically ill-suited by age, class, or ethnicity. Among the rule-based skill changes, the association barred fielders from using their hats or caps to record outs. The "fly rule," which required catching a batted ball, whether foul or fair, in the air rather than on the first bounce for an out, became a lively issue of delegate debate until its adoption in 1864. Some opposed it as a departure from the sacred past; modernizers defended the proposal as a way to improve the quality of play and of the players. Proponents of the change claimed it would make the sport more "manly," and, again exploiting the nationalistic angle, insisted that it would show American sportsmen capable of as much skill as English cricketers (who employed a fly catch rule). In general, by the end of the 1850s, clubs were increasingly characterized by positional specialization on the part of individual players and continuing refinements in the skill requirements for each position.[20]

The growth of position and skill specialization carried with it, however, long-term implications that were unforeseen, if not necessarily unwelcome for baseball officials' purposes. It did not eliminate big, "slow-footed," or "muscle-bound" participants. As teams competed for victories and honors, they found that particular physical "types," though perhaps less well suited for multipositional duties, might actually be better suited for some stations. Catchers, even if they stood thirty feet behind the batter, still benefited from having a "barrel-chest" that could withstand the punishment of the position, as did third basemen also. Gangliness could become a positive virtue in a first baseman, as could straight-ahead running speed in an outfielder. Strength could certainly have its uses for a batter, particularly when wielding a mahogany bat up to forty-four inches long. Nonetheless, the players occupying infield positions—particularly those in the middle of the diamond that required refined hand-eye coordination, mental concentration, and physical dexterity—were still seen as the truest exemplars of the traditional baseballist ideal. Lingering associations of ethnicity with physical and mental attributes in turn shaped patterns of positional specialization by ethnic group as well as physiology. And these patterns in turn influenced subsequent opportunities for captainships, nonplayer offices, and other avenues of upward mobility within baseball.

The clearest impact of rules changes and team policies encouraging greater skill specialization, however, was to lessen dramatically the ability of first-generation immigrants to become club ballplayers. On top of the constraints of time and physical endurance of a working-class life that tended to obstruct an immigrant's access to ballplaying, the unlikelihood of his having played the game as a youth (and therefore of having picked up its "inside" skill and subtle strategy) in the Old World, further reduced his chances of success. Even at its peak in the 1850s, first-generation immigrant participation in clubs probably accounted for at most 10 percent of total membership, divided about equally between English and Irish arrivals, with a sprinkling of Germans. After the 1850s that percentage plummeted, creating a long-term pattern in which those who were not American by birth were effectively excluded from the sport, although their American-born children would not necessarily be. The children, if not precluded by class and racial barriers, might still succeed where their fathers had failed, by playing the sport and absorbing its myriad refinements in their youth and on junior teams.[21]

Accompanying changes in umpiring rules also signaled the gradual abandonment of the ideal of a self-regulating, decentralized ballplaying fraternity in favor of a player force supervised from above and no longer controlling its own workplace. In the early 1850s, clubs still had utilized a system in which each side selected one of its number to serve as an umpire. Both men positioned themselves at a desk or table on the third-base side, while a third man, chosen with the approval of both teams, sat "solitary and alone," with top hat, frock coat, and cane, as the final arbiter in case of disagreement between the other two. Although the first two individuals' presence evoked images of an adversarial advocacy process, what it more tellingly conveyed was the blurring of distinctions between player and umpire. Disputes between elected arbiters were noteworthy for their infrequency, again displaying the essence of good-spirited fellowship and gentlemanly contest. Abandonment of the "two-advocate" system in 1858 actually signified the emerging separation of umpiring personnel and their responsibilities from the player force as well as the centralization of on-field administration of the rules governing contests and conduct in response to the declension of decorum and good faith by players and spectators alike. In a related development, clubs endeavored to maintain attendance at games by middle-class women in order to convey a continuing image of respectability to ball-playing and to discourage through the female presence additional unseemly male displays.

What the sport's new governors in the National Association were groping for was an administrative structure for American baseball that, if it could no longer recreate the old congregational norms, could impose a standardized set of playing rules and codes of behavior that would offer instruction, uplift, and improvement to player and spectator alike. Outdistanced rivals such as the Massachusetts Association of Base Ball Players and similar town-ball devotees, still numbering at least seventy-five clubs by 1860, resisted outright surrender but continued to lose ground. The National Association expanded to fifty-three clubs by 1860 and, more importantly, by that date extended its administrative reach beyond New York City to the upstate region as well as to neighboring New Jersey and Pennsylvania. Reflecting the popularity of the National Association version of the game, the New York sporting press began carrying game summaries and box scores, and enterprising boosters compiled rudimentary performance statistics on teams and even individual players. *Beadle's Dime Base Ball Player*, a new guidebook edited by the English-born sportswriter Henry Chadwick, sold 50,000 copies. Pressing its advantage and adjusting its games to urban spectators' time constraints, the National Association replaced its twenty-one-aces end-point for games with first a seven-inning and then a nine-inning standard. More than ever before, as the decade concluded, the lament of "The Baseball Fever" rang true:

> Our merchants have to close their stores
> Their clerks away are staying
> Contractors, too, can do no work
> Their hands are all out playing.[22]

Even before the opening shots on Fort Sumter, baseball had drifted away from its moorings as a cultural embodiment of the congregational life of New England Puritanism. It had become more ethnically and occupationally diverse; more attuned to the public pursuit of, rather than the private display of, social worth; and, in an effort to preserve the fundamental virtues and values of the past amid such changes, more hierarchically administered and regimented. In the process, the narrowing proportion of members actively engaged in playing the games already had found their control of the clubs eroding in favor of nonplaying, usually wealthier, members, investors, officers, and delegates. As baseball continued to expand geographically and grow in popular favor in the 1860s and early 1870s, these developments offered club operators the promise of making it a lucrative business. Accordingly, issues of player-versus-management control within the industry, and the labor confrontations they would trigger, assumed an ever more prominent place in baseball's continuing evolution, with the stakes of the outcome escalating for both sides.

 **TWO**

A National
Game and Its
Journeymen,
1860-1875

By 1860, baseball's practitioners had carried the game far beyond its traditional New England home. Competing nines could be found in the towns of the Old Northwest, the river cities of the Mississippi and its tributaries, and the southern seaboard. Baseball had even reached the West Coast, with none other than the gold-rushing Alexander Cartwright as its bearer to San Francisco. No longer was the sport confined to New Englanders or transplanted Yankees, either; it now enlisted players and teams from the ranks of second-generation Irish and Germans, along with Scotch-Irish descendants and a sprinkling of immigrant English cricketers. Adjusting to the changes in on-field composition, clubs now featured a stratified occupational hierarchy that separated management personnel and responsibilities from ballplaying performers. The expansion of the game west of the Appalachians and the adjustment, however uneasy, to a more diverse playing force reinforced baseball's claim as the "national game." As such, it began to accumulate its own equivalents of Parson Weems stories linking it to famous national personages. According to one such account, even the slugging Republican presidential nominee, Abraham Lincoln, put off receiving a group of convention delegates dispatched to inform him of his selection until, in his words, "I make another hit." Although no corroboration for the story exists, as president, the rail-splitter from Illinois, accompanied by his son Tad, attended contests between teams of government clerks in the capital.[1]

But while the game's expansion and "official" acceptance evoked pride within the baseball fraternity, the pride was paired with concern. Geographic migration, continued ethnic and class diversification, player specialization, and creeping commercialism all led to a growing sense among traditional adherents that the game had been uprooted from its natural geographic and cultural "soil," and that they had lost control over the sport's processes of change. More profit-minded modernists, in turn, worried that the widened choice of employer with which geographic expansion provided players would cause them either to lose their gate attractions to higher-paying suitors or bankrupt them if they did succeed in retaining their charges. Would the game's players so completely lose any sense of geographic and ethical roots that they became completely amoral individualists, unbeholden to a club, a community, or the integrity of the game, interested only in the highest payment from the highest bidder? Would baseball teams become little more than traveling collections of wayward young men with all the ethical standards of gypsies and vagabonds?

Even before the guns opened on Fort Sumter, the highest-caliber players had started to test their bargaining power in a sport whose commercial possibilities the clubs had only begun to tap. If club revenues were increasingly tied to victories in interclub competitions, and such results required the best performers, would not those with the requisite playing skills and willingness to migrate play rival organizations off against each other for the best deal? Players such as Jim Creighton, whom the Brooklyn Excelsiors paid under the table, became known as "revolvers," for whom clubs bid against each other. Competition for victories and profits intensified the growing ethnocultural divisions within the sport and reflected conflicts and tensions between rival urban communities of Yankees, English, Irish, and Germans. Would clubs be able to cooperate in the crafting and implementation of strategies to curb player wanderlust, and their own hunger for victories and profits, for the sake of collective club stability and survival?

The Civil War, accordingly, did not trigger either the geographic or the socioeconomic diversification of baseball and did not itself cause the competitive rush for profit by players and club officers alike. But it did accelerate the processes of change in some ways, adding new terminology to the baseball work force and tailoring it in new ways. While Union troops encamped in myriad locales along a thousand-mile front, they served as evangelists for the national game. Soldiers played to while away the time in training, as diversion against boredom between engagements, and even as captives in prison camps, with the New York servicemen most renowned for their skill. Confederates who had learned the game before Sumter, or now absorbed it from their Yankee enemy, also played ball in growing numbers. Meanwhile, the manpower drains of war thinned out clubs and club members in the Northeast, rewarding those organizations best positioned to bid ruthlessly for available on-field talent and thereby prevail at the gate. Jim Creighton, ironically, became a civilian "casualty of war" in 1862, when he died following a cricket accident. At home, the war accentuated the competitive spirit and combativeness of players and clubs. Drawing upon war terminology, pitcher and catcher (or sometimes just the pitcher) were dubbed a "battery," and successful nines were expected to display the efficiency and esprit de corps of a military unit, in spite of the players' varied backgrounds and the mercenary ways clubs assembled them into teams. Like those of the warring armies, the "weapons" of baseball performers were increasingly standardized, with the National Association adopting requirements for the weight, measurements, and composition of both bat and ball in 1861. Uniforms, too, became more "uniform," projecting a national unity of baseball sportsmen, while distinctive team colors, insignia, and details signified a public fealty to locality and sublimation of individualism by players that did not always correspond to reality.[2]

In baseball's old heartland of the Northeast, clubs found themselves under siege for the first three years of the war. Desperate to retain spectator interest and money, some of them in the winter of 1861 even resorted to such stunts as playing on ice skates. According to different estimates, the number of surviving National Association clubs dropped approximately 60 percent from late antebellum levels and by 40 percent in the New York City area. By 1864 only thirty teams in the association,

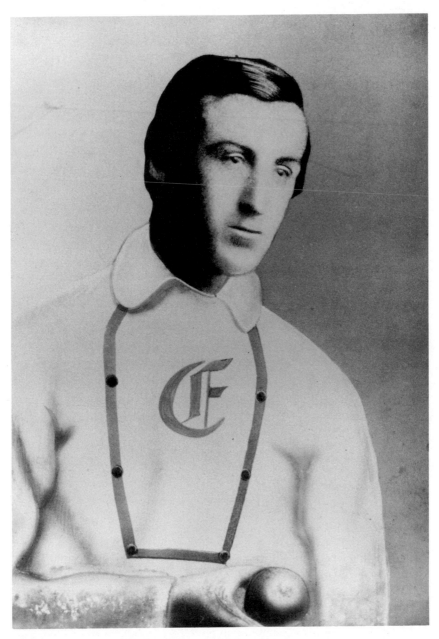

Jim Creighton, baseball's first famous revolving player

from three states and the District of Columbia, sent delegates to the national convention. As a sign of the continuing specialization of on-field performance designed to dazzle spectators, the delegates succeeded, after five previously unsuccessful efforts, in adopting the fly catch rule. The pressures upon clubs and players did not destroy the sport, but they did serve to weed out less commercially minded aggregations and further encouraged the most talented players, already "professionals" in income and commitment to the game, to accept a life of portable labor and loyalties. The migratory impulse accelerated from 1864 on as Union successes encouraged both a partial return to normality on the home front and the arrival of baseball's martial ambassadors in remote areas of the conquered South. Clubs that could attract the lion's share of playing talent with financial promises, and back them up with the gate receipts that the talent then generated, survived if not prospered. A wartime championship challenge match between the Brooklyn Atlantics and the Eckfords drew an estimated 15,000 attendees, or "kranks." In a patriotic gesture not often repeated during the war, the two clubs vied only for a silver ball rather than a cash prize, with gate proceeds donated to the U.S. Sanitary Commission.[3]

More typical, however, was cutthroat competition between clubs and grounds owners for fan income. But if club directors and grounds operators were becoming sports impresarios in the crucible of wartime competition, and baseball teams were becoming middle-class entertainment franchises, their top-line players, in keeping with these trends, were assuming the life of touring professionals for hire, much like theatrical troupers. Like trained actors, top baseballists played specific roles, or positions, in tandem with others, and to be a superior player required ever more extensive practice and coordination. In the antebellum era, when players had not seen baseball as a profitable livelihood, once- or twice-weekly practices had sufficed. Now the refinement of both individual and team skills required far greater commitment in order to acquire the commensurate rewards of professionalism. That meant time away from one's other job and—for players who had them—from family and home responsibilities. The increasingly vigorous nature of on-field competition, along with the requisite personal sacrifices, continued to shrink the age parameters of the active player force to young men in their twenties. Young adults of such age were most likely to combine peak physical skills with the fewest conflicting responsibilities. This trend, too, reinforced the troublesome image of the emerging baseball professional as physically but not emotionally mature, as adventurous but rootless, in a sport which increasingly called upon him to travel far from home, whether employed in-season or barnstorming between seasons.

The northern populace might not have noticed or been especially alarmed at the increasingly transient nature of wartime baseball, since in so many other ways normal civilian life had been similarly uprooted. But it did not bode well for those who wanted a return to a nostalgic version of prewar baseball normality, to a restored order in which players "knew their place," when in 1863 star Al Reach entertained lucrative bids from competing clubs for his negotiable services while other fighting-age northerners were making the ultimate self-sacrifice for the Union. The leading bidder in the effort to lure Reach from the Brooklyn Eckfords was Baltimore's Arthur Pue Gorman, machine politician and later U.S. senator. Although Reach abandoned his former club for the sum of $1,000 a year, he did not choose Gorman's nine, but instead the Philadelphia Athletics, on the basis that their games would be closer to his Flushing, Long Island, home. The Athletics did not stop with Reach, also acquiring the services of three other players at an under-the-table rate of $20 a week.[4]

More traditionalist clubs and members in the National Association, repelled by the growth of team commercialism and illicit individual play-for-pay, fought for a return to an already severely eroded amateurism. The Knickerbockers, long the embodiment of antebellum Yankee traditionalism, at first refused to accept gate receipts or even to play in contests against teams that did. But faced with a dwindling number of comparably "pure" opponents, the New York nine's own financial needs forced them to participate in contests with more commercially minded clubs, although they still refused to accept a share of the gate for themselves. Even this "concession to concessions" proved too much for at least one Knickerbocker player, James Whyte Davis, who resigned in protest. The personal stands of Davis and like-minded individuals, however, merely contributed to the process of segregating amateurism from various gradations of team and individual professionalism. As a net result, the amateur-professional split was another respect—in addition to ethnicity, class composition, and geography—in which baseball's image as a homogenizing, unifying force sustaining Yankee communitarian values was brought into question. With war's end, could the sport be counted upon as one, in the words of the Reverend C. H. Everett, "whose regulations are calculated to prevent the ill-feelings engendered

Knickerbockers team photograph, 1864, displaying the separation of club management from on-field personnel that was the norm by the Civil War

by other games, and one, moreover, which serves to attract our young men from places of bad repute, and to supply in place thereof the right kind of recreation and exercise?"[5]

The importance of "binding the nation's wounds" presented an additional rationale for a "reconstructed" baseball as a national sporting institution that could help restore respectable behavior, fellowship, and unity both to America's war-scarred sections and its contentious urban neighborhoods. One wartime trend in the clubs' playing-labor composition, amid the instability and turmoil of geographic and ethnic expansion and commercial competition, did seem reassuring to those nostalgic for the antebellum past. Although the game's actives continued to grow more ethnically heterogeneous, with more second- and third-generation Irish and Germans, Scotch-Irish players, English cricketers, and Yankees contributing to the mix, the occupational class declension that had characterized the player force of the 1850s at least temporarily abated. Whether due to the unequal class impact of military enlistments, a shrunken number of clubs and therefore more selective membership decisions, or other competing economic opportunities and demands, teams in baseball's home region saw the proportion of skilled and semi-skilled blue-collar actives on their rosters decline—if clubs in New York City and Brooklyn were typical of others in the Northeast—and the percentage of players of white-collar, proprietary, clerical, and professional background rise modestly. At the same time, management ranks continued to reflect the upward class shifts of the 1850s and the segregation of on-field from off-field personnel, with club officers generally claiming higher socioeconomic status than active players, and delegates to the National Association claiming still higher standing.[6]

Hopes of a further restoration of the participation patterns and values of the "Yankee game" within the player force soon evaporated in the years following Appomattox. There was no return to earlier standards of amateurism, ethnic and geographic homogeneity, and class stability; instead the pace of the unsettling changes of the past two decades reaccelerated. One manifestation was the even more exaggerated competitive commercialization and materialism displayed by clubs and individual players. As one commentator observed of baseball, "From a simple pastime it has become a systematic business with hundreds of persons who, either as players or directors of nines, derive their entire revenue during the summer months from the profits of the games played by their respective clubs." Within two years of the end of the war, the seven or eight most successful clubs in the Northeast shared about $100,000 in gate receipts. The New York Mutuals alone garnered around $15,000. Even the Knickerbockers offered up the first "ladies day" promotion in 1867. Despite a modest rise in fees, an estimated 200,000 spectators attended games the following year.[7]

Nor was it just in the Northeast that baseball mania was catching hold among spectators. Reaching beyond their usual capital attendees of government clerks and officeholders (including Andrew Johnson on occasion), the Washington Nationals set out on an 1867 midwestern tour that included matches in Columbus, Cincinnati, Louisville, Indianapolis, St. Louis, and Rockford. Despite the Nationals' losing only to Rockford and its star player, Albert Spalding, gate receipts failed to cover salaries and travel expenses, forcing club backers to cover an additional $3,000 of costs by journey's end. While barnstorming ventures by other clubs proved more lucrative, even they showed the growing tension between the financial need for team notoriety and on-field victories, dependent upon superior talent, and the spiraling costs of acquiring and providing for the same. The imperative of victory was well illustrated by the Unions of Morrisania during their tour of western New York state, in which they were accused of cheating by permitting only their own traveling umpire to work their games.[8]

Given the expanding profit potential for the most successful teams and, despite marginal financial prospects for the rest, an ever-increasing number of far-flung clubs, players found even more opportunities than during the war for "leveraging" their refined playing skills. Such leverage lay not just in negotiations with rival clubs for covert salaries, still barred by National Association rules against professionalism, but also in illegal fixes and gambling arrangements with those whose "sporting interest" in the outcomes of games extended beyond the realm of gate receipts. Besides prohibiting pay and gambling, the National Association had tried for years to police the interclub migration of players by requiring a thirty-day "residency" with a club before granting a journeyman his playing eligibility. Even though such rules had been ignored by players like Creighton and Reach, some observers still preferred to believe that stars "revolved" only because of abusive treatment from their former club and assumed that ethical pride, team loyalty, and residential stability mattered more to a star player than the prospect of immediate monetary gain.

The postwar years saw such illusions shattered, much as they saw the erosion of the popular national faith in honest politics and government during Reconstruction. The number of violations of player compensation and mobility rules and the number of creative methods used to circumvent the regulations both mushroomed after 1865. Albert Spalding of the Rockford Forest Citys garnered a deal for $40 a week to join the Chicago Excelsiors, although the Excelsiors concealed the true nature of the offer by hiring him for a fictitious grocery clerk job. In 1867 George Wright deserted the New York Gothams in favor of the Washington Nationals, who claimed to be paying him not for his baseball services but for a government clerkship listed at the address (238 Pennsylvania Avenue) of a public park. William Fischer received a new suit of clothes, board money, a cover job, and a $115 advance but then spurned the Philadelphia Athletics, who were not used to such rejection, for a better offer in Chicago. By the late 1860s, one estimate placed the "average" professional player's salary at between $600 and $900 for two-thirds of a year; another estimate, while probably high, put the figure at $1,000–2,500 by 1869. Such pay was especially impressive in an era in which even white-collar clerks and skilled craftsmen, to say nothing of unskilled and semiskilled laborers and tenders, could not expect to earn $500 in a twelve-month period.[9]

Particularly prominent for their ethical "flexibility" in procuring playing talent from other clubs, concealing their players' real employment, and consorting with gamblers were the New York Mutuals, headed from 1860 to 1871 by the notorious political boss of Tammany Hall, William Marcy Tweed. Tweed attempted in one instance to lure Cincinnati second baseman Charlie Sweasy to the Mutuals despite the existence of both a prior gentleman's agreement and an actual written contract held by Cincinnati. The New York boss's payroll could rarely be matched by any rival organization, for he could draw not merely upon directors' contributions but also upon the tax revenues of the city of New York for financial sustenance. Mutuals players claimed employment in the street and coroner's departments, with team pay, according to one estimate, totaling $38,000 per year. With so little "honor among thieves" in the directorates of rival clubs, it is no surprise that players similarly sought to maximize their share of the game's returns—money which, after all, their on-field labor generated. Given that fact, it was only natural that a trio of Mutuals players were at the center of the most widely publicized hippodroming scandal of the Reconstruction era. In a September 28, 1865, game with the Eckfords, observers accused players Ed Duffy, William Wansley, and Thomas Devyr of "laying down" in exchange for bribes. Despite an investigation by the National Association's Judiciary Committee that produced a ban on Duffy, the Mutuals unilaterally reinstated Devyr for the 1868 season while charges were still pending against him. After the Mutuals defeated the Union Club, W. J. Herring, a Union executive and a Judiciary Committee member, arranged Devyr's banishment, only to be overruled by the National Association's delegates in general convention, 451-143. The emboldened Tweed then reinstated Duffy also, but this action led to his club's expulsion from the New York state association. Undeterred, the Mutuals simply "persuaded" the National Association to circumvent the state organization and to reinstate Wansley as well for the next season.[10]

Next after the Mutuals, the Haymakers of Troy, New York—another boss-ridden club with ties to a Democratic Irish political machine—could claim the dubious distinction of being baseball's most corrupt organization. The Haymakers' chief officer was John Morrissey, an Irish immigrant, former 1858 heavyweight boxing champion, one-time congressman, and active state senator. Foreshadowing his subsequent career as proprietor of a lucrative gambling house, Morrissey deployed his players "like loaded dice and marked cards." Charges of hippodroming followed the Haymakers wherever they traveled. But given the weariness induced by barnstorming train and coach travel and the growing presence of reporters covering "upsets" as well as expected victories, even in the absence of clear proof of fixing, such charges surfaced with disturbing regularity. When the Washington Nationals defeated a Chicago Excelsiors squad touted as the "champions of the West" after first losing to a much inferior Rockford nine, press accusations of a "laydown" in the earlier contest provoked Gorman and other owners to demand a public retraction. When evidence of player malfeasance could be produced, as in the case of the Mutuals, however, the National Association's enforcement officers found their disciplinary powers effectively neutralized by the accused club's refusing to attend their scheduled hearings, getting sanctions overturned by the full convention, or simply ignoring them.[11]

Without denying the growing existence of cheating by money-hungry players, it is conspicuous that the prime targets of baseball corruption charges were teams popularly linked with non-Yankee, especially Irish, urban political machines and spectator followings. *Wilkes' Spirit of the Times* described a particular bit of fan unruliness at a match as resembling "an Irish fight at a fair," and its protagonists as "bull-necked, low-browed, crop-haired brutes who degrade humanity so much in our cities." The emerging baseball fiction of the day, written mainly by New England Victorian literati for a respectable middle-class audience, featured proper Brahmin heroes and suitably coarse Irish antagonists described as gang members, "blackguards," and "brutes." The fears expressed in these characterizations reflected the fact that baseball, whether in the Northeast, the Midwest, or the South, was now visibly the province of non-Yankees of varying degrees of cultural acceptability. In postwar New Orleans, for example, in addition to middle-class occupation-based clubs of telegraphers, firemen, and postal workers, Ku Klux Klanners and Regulators sponsored nines, as did German-American associations called the Schneiders and Landwehrs, Irish aggregations such as the Feinan Baseball Club, and the Boston and Pickwick business firms, which sponsored black teams.[12]

Postwar claims of baseball player "declension" also drew upon shifting occupational and class lines, which paired accelerating ethnic heterogeneity with a decline in the on-field presence of white-collar players. If the patterns within New York and Brooklyn clubs were typical, the five years after the Civil War saw a return to higher proportions of skilled manual workers in the player force, following a modest dip during the war. Of occupationally identifiable New York–area players on National Association clubs for the 1866–70 period, 62 percent claimed a manual craft background, compared to but 36 percent from white-collar and professional ranks. Other areas claimed lower blue-collar percentages— Chicago nines apparently had but half the proportion and Newark a 45 percent blue-collar share—but the *trend* was toward a higher manual-worker share of the on-field labor. A sign that among the active players the best were likely to be of a blue-collar background is the fact that of twenty-eight New York area actives who later joined the National Association of Professional Base Ball Players, fifteen were of manual-craft heritage, mostly young mechanics and products of blue-collar-based junior clubs. In contrast, at the level of the National Association convention, the proportion of skilled blue-collar representation measured only one-fourth of the total number of delegates.[13]

Such retention of white-collar control at the national convention level meant little, however, if individual clubs and players could effectively flaunt the National Association's authority and if a growing proportion of the delegate population itself felt little kinship to past traditions of amateurism and Yankee custodianship. And how could the National Association's judicial enforcement machinery work if, as in 1867, the organization had only $1,021.76 in its treasury? The need for member clubs to generate income by scheduling matches with the very clubs that most blatantly violated standards of amateurism, and who because of it attracted the best talent and offered the largest gate attraction, meant that real power resided with the Tweeds and Morrisseys despite the bitter aftertaste of such realities to National Association traditionalists. One club, for example, upon losing a player to the Mutuals, resorted to the publication of a pamphlet on the matter in the hopes of publicly shaming that club into returning its performer—without success. But in the broader sense, too, the former guardians of Yankee moral values and participatory traditions in baseball were finding their avenues of influence dwindling to being the self-appointed literary and journalistic consciences of the sport.[14]

The loss of cultural control over the sport and those who played it by Yankee traditionalist clubs and their representatives was not merely a product of shifting lines of ethnic and class participation but was a result of profound geographic migration. The war had played an important role in that transformation by weakening the club networks in the Northeast while sowing the seeds for club expansion, and player migration, elsewhere. The number of clubs in the National Association jumped from 91 to 202 in 1866, with 73 in New York, 48 in Pennsylvania, and 26 in New Jersey, while the number of states with clubs in the organization grew to seventeen. *Wilkes' Spirit of the Times* claimed the next year that over 2,000 baseball clubs featured over 100,000 participants, and by November 1867, the National Association included 175 junior clubs in addition to the adult nines. On the West Coast, the growing number of clubs in and around San Francisco had led to the formation of a state association in 1866. But it was to the Midwest in particular that the organizational nexus of baseball was shifting. In the Queen City, as Cincinnati styled itself, the Cincinnati Base Ball Club, composed mainly of law-office clerks, followed the Live Oak Club in 1866, and by the next year the city hosted a twenty-four-team tournament and spawned a state affiliate to the National Association. St. Louis witnessed a comparable baseball boom. Des Moines, Iowa, claimed nine clubs by 1867, and the Iowa State Base Ball Association emerged the same year, as did a similar entity in Minnesota. A year earlier, midwestern organizational power already had begun to concentrate in regional form with the Midwest Association of Base Ball Players.[15]

At the 1867 convention, the National Association further centralized delegate voting by limiting teams to proxy representation by their state association if the state held more than nine member clubs. As a result, only 11 men representing eight state and regional aggregations wielded over two-thirds of the 700 floor votes, with 150 others casting the remaining ballots. As a sign of the burgeoning strength of midwestern delegate votes in the hands of powerful state bosses, four representatives—from Illinois (110 votes), Ohio (88), Wisconsin (52), and Indiana (42)—controlled over 300 tallies. The geographic shift of power within organized baseball truly became unmistakable in 1868. That year, Ohio captured not only the presidency of the United States in the person of Ulysses S. Grant but also the presidency of the National Association of Base Ball Players in the person of George F. Sands of Cincinnati. Reflecting the new voting power of midwestern delegates, a Wisconsinite gained the vice-presidency, while the new national secretary hailed from Rockford, Illinois. Yankee traditionalist delegates, finding their influence waning, grumbled that the new powers, blamed repeatedly for encouraging player revolving from eastern clubs, were "adopting the unscrupulous tactics of the New York politicians."[16]

In a sad irony, the representatives of machine-based, more ethnically diverse clubs in both the Northeast and Midwest, having forced grudging respect through their blunt exercise of political power, now used their clout to adopt a policy of racial exclusion from the association's player force to suit their own social prejudices. Before and during the Civil War, free blacks had formed successful baseball clubs despite white ethnic hostility, particularly from the Irish. After the war, in the District of Columbia, some Freedmen's Bureau clerks played for the black Washington Mutuals, and another government clerk, Charles E. Douglass, the son of Frederick Douglass, participated on the Alerts. In Chicago, the Chicago Blue Stockings drew members from the ranks of black hotel and restaurant waiters. In Philadelphia, the Pythians' players were middle-class blacks, two-thirds of whom had been born in the city, while one-fifth had been born in Virginia or South Carolina, with a far larger percentage of mulattoes than the general black population. Nonetheless, when they sought membership in the Pennsylvania state association in the fall of 1867, the governing body rejected their petition. When the issue reached the full National Association two months later, the association similarly judged black membership unacceptable and adopted a formal ban on the inclusion of black players and clubs. Organization spokesmen claimed that even raising the question of black affiliation in public sessions risked a "rupture being created on political grounds" and a damaging "division of feeling" within the association.[17]

In similar fashion, the ascendant midwestern and machine-based northeastern clubs usually deployed their forces to champion growing competitive commercialization and player professionalization in the sport. By contrast, the voices of traditional amateurism were usually found in select, older Yankee aggregations. They echoed the concerns of reporter Henry Chadwick, who often served as their public voice, that the new breed of Reconstruction era players would never again "play with the same kinds of feelings or for the same objects as they used to." Although a few clubs advocated a complete return to antebellum amateurism, most grudgingly acknowledged that for their own survival they could not eliminate club play for gate money. At best they could remove the stigma of hypocrisy, and perhaps the temptation for players to accept bribes and fix games, by "legalizing" and then regulating open, individual professionalism. The *New England Base Ballist* admitted that existing National Association rules against player pay were unenforceable and argued that open professionalism would eliminate "ringers" and remove nonworking ballplayers from urban machine public payrolls. Players would then cease being "as corrupt aldermen and assemblymen," who collected under-the-table bribes from the highest bidder.[18] With such reforms, National Association clubs might once more count upon the fealty of member players, and in a more amalgamated, secular context, they could restore the primacy of Protestant work ethic values of individual sacrifice, teamwork, and moral uprightness.

Whether these hopes of moral regeneration of the sport's playing labor and public image were realistic, such rationalizations were now functionally necessary for virtually all top-level clubs, since even the most "amateur" of them typically featured paid players who, either in place of or in addition to direct compensation, were exempted from club dues and operating fees. In the New York metropolitan area, the 1868 season had opened with a contest between handpicked nines of professionals from New York City and Brooklyn clubs before a paid crowd of over a thousand spectators. When the season ended, the 1868 National Association winter meeting saw its Rules Committee conclude that the antipay regulation was a "dead letter" and recommend the formal recognition of separate classes of amateur and professional players. Only two years before, in a last gambit for amateurism, the association had threatened the expulsions of clubs that employed players for pay. Now the threat was lifted. At the same time, the delegates sought to limit the possibilities for revolving, in the event that open acceptance of play-for-pay did not sufficiently eliminate players' motivation to jump clubs, by increasing the club "residency requirement" for playing eligibility to sixty days. Predictably, and ominously, representatives of the New York Mutuals opposed the change and argued for a reduction of the probationary period prior to eligibility to but ten days.[19]

The 1869 playing season offered the first test of whether or not clubs featuring overt professionals could adequately harness their charges' individualistic, acquisitive instincts, as well as their own parasitic competition for player services. It was with particular interest that the individual and collective fortunes of the first all-professional team, the Cincinnati Red Stockings, were followed. The Red Stockings' embrace of professionalism had been spawned partly by civic and regional pride, as a result of the club's humiliating 53-10 loss (its only loss of the 1867 season) to the Washington Nationals. Financial pressures also had intervened at the end of 1868, with the team suffering a $600–700 operating deficit, compounded by the necessity of picking up an additional $1,000-a-year obligation and a $6,000 balance on the Union Grounds lease it had previously shared with a cricket club. At the same time, local rivalry with the Buckeye Club had led each team over several years to increase the number of paid ballplayers on its squad. By 1869 the Red Stockings' backers had opted to go for broke in their market by financing an all-professional unit through stock issues, with a combined payroll of season-long contracts totaling nearly $10,000.

The man tapped by team backers to captain the assemblage of talent was Harry Wright, the immigrant son of an English professional cricketer and a veteran both of that sport and baseball in New York. Following a career that included playing for the Knickerbockers, Wright had arrived in Cincinnati in 1865, lured as an instructor for the Union Cricket Club at a $1,200 salary. After the 1867 season he had been retained by the Red Stockings at the same salary as a playing captain. At age thirty-four in 1869, Wright was a decade older than most of his players, including his younger brother George. The team he led was an assemblage of outside mercenaries, with only one man on the squad's ten-member playing roster a Cincinnati native—first baseman Charles Gould—and Indianapolis native Cal McVey the only other player not from the East. The elder Wright, a center fielder, and his brother, a shortstop and fellow veteran of New York baseball, received the highest salaries on the team. One account placed their wages at $1,200 and $1,400 respectively, although George later claimed they were actually $2,000 and $1,800. Pitcher Asa Brainard followed with $1,100, trailed by third baseman Fred Waterman at $1,000; second baseman Charlie Sweasy, first baseman Gould, and catcher Douglas Allison at $800; and left fielder Andrew Leonard, right fielder McVey, and substitute Richard Hurley at $600 apiece. Most claimed clerical or skilled manual backgrounds, and their off-season jobs ranged from Captain Wright's jewelry trade to engraver (George Wright), insurance broker (Brainard), hatter (Sweasy and Leonard), bookkeeper (Gould and Waterman), piano maker (McVey), and marble cutter (Allison). With the lowest-paid team member earning $800 for an eight-month season (March 15–November 15), all earned 15 percent to 70 percent more than the most highly paid manual craftsmen of the day. It was Wright's task to ensure that his well-paid "boys" deliver a comparably high level of individual and team performance and assume the regimen and self-discipline of the true professional.[20]

If, as historian Steven Gelber has written, baseball "replicated and legitimized the social and intellectual environment of the work place," Wright's approach to piloting the Red Stockings illustrated an early infiltration of management techniques from shop-floor industrialism into baseball's methods of on-field player control. Given his paternalistic managerial approach to his duties, which included those of a traveling secretary as well as a field director, it seems especially fitting that he arranged for his players to travel via Pullman car during their eastern road trip. With his more distant, superior relationship to his players underscored by the age differential (Asa Brainard, the next oldest member, was but twenty-seven), Wright insisted that his charges adopt a no-nonsense, professional attitude toward their craft. His players wore more practical flannel knickers, woolen stockings, and caps instead of cumbersome pantaloons and flat-brimmed hats. His frequent practice sessions, rigidly scheduled, drilled his men in game situations, strate-

The undefeated Cincinnati Reds of 1869. Besides their fame as the first overtly all-professional team, their residences (all but two came from far outside the Queen City's region) underscored the growing journeymanship of ballplaying employment.

gies, and even the use of hand signals. He honed their specific component skills with the aim of converting them into a "nicely adjusted machine" rather than perpetuating the more casual hitting, throwing, fielding, and fraternization of an earlier era. Suggesting the more intrusive aspects of such segregated, centralized, direct oversight of players' lives by the captain/manager (and reflecting his employers' great stake in the team's success), Wright enforced team rules mandating "gentlemanly and temperate behavior at all times," including healthy eating habits, abstinence from alcohol and tobacco, and a disciplined off-season regimen.[21]

Wright's on-field results were impressive. The Red Stockings went undefeated in 1869, with the only blemish on their record a tie with the Haymakers, which resulted when the men of Troy walked off the field in the sixth inning, as they had been instructed to do, in order to protect local gamblers' bets on them. On an eastern tour, the Cincinnati nine drew an estimated 200,000 fans, many of whom hoped that their host clubs could put the Queen City's upstart mercenaries in their place. The Red Stockings also tacked on a West Coast trip, backed by local boosters back home. Despite the on-field record, however, in other respects the Cincinnati club had failed to resolve the conflicts between player salaries and club profitability that had plagued other nines. After all, if an undefeated team could still barely show a profit for its labors, what did that say for other clubs' prospects? The next season the Red Stockings finally lost a game, to the Brooklyn Atlantics in eleven innings, before a crowd of 9,000 fans who payed a fifty-cent admission charge. For their action in restoring eastern pride, each Atlantics player garnered $364.

For the Cincinnatians, the aftermath of defeat proved grim. The club lost several more contests and showed no profit. In August, the president and club secretary resigned. Within the club, accusations surfaced against the team's best-paid players, charging them, despite Wright's stern hand, with behavior "destructive of the subordination and good feeling necessary to the success of a nine." Faced with outside bidding for their players' services, club officials blamed "enormous" salaries paid to "growlers and shirkers" for a "heavy levy" that had been assessed upon the nonplaying members and stockholders of the club. Amid charges of "jealousies" between players, and of players' "extravagance and dissipation," the Cincinnati organization concluded that their strategy of paying players but limiting the total payroll to $6,000–8,000 could not guarantee a profit, and they opted instead to develop their "amateur talent." The Wrights, McVey, and Gould quickly jumped to a new club in Boston, also called the Red Stockings, while the rest of the squad joined the Washington Olympics.[22]

Clearly no individual club, even one as skillfully guided on the diamond as Cincinnati, could in isolation quell the demons of player greed and wanderlust or insulate team harmony and discipline from outside temptations. Still, others, driven by civic boosterism and the vision of baseball riches, were willing to continue trying. In Chicago, backers of the White Stockings copied the Cincinnati example, raising $20,000 in subscriptions for an all-professional club and advertising openly for players in newspapers and the sporting press. But in the view of more and more team executives and directors, a new governing structure exclusively for the top professional clubs, providing oversight to a more manageable number of teams than the unwieldy National Association served, was essential in arriving at the proper balance between player compensation and club finances and between player choice of employer and interclub competitive equality.

When the National Association's delegates met at the end of 1870, both the advocates of professionalism and the champions of amateurism were ready for a parting of the ways. Both believed that only a smaller association with a more homogenous membership and outlook could hope to provide the necessary regulatory framework, whether in order to discipline a professional work force or to restore and shelter an amateur fellowship. Illustrative of the loss of faith in the National Association's oversight powers was the fact that, despite widespread player revolving, the Judiciary Committee received no formal complaints for adjudication from offended clubs. With fewer than thirty actual delegates in attendance, the convention received and rejected by a 17-9 vote a resolution sponsored by amateur clubs in the New York area, notably the Knickerbockers and Excelsiors, condemning professionalism. The individual sponsor of the antiprofessionalism resolution, Brooklyn dock builder and Eckfords delegate Frank Pidgeon, warned his listeners in the language of artisan republicanism that to embrace professionalism meant not just competition between clubs but also the eventual loss of worker independence and the imposition of wage slavery. Unchastened, the convention majority, controlled by some twenty top professional clubs, adjourned the gathering sine die.[23]

Each faction proceeded to form its own governing association the following March. The devotees of amateurism, seeking to restore baseball's prewar "state of grace," created the National Association of Amateur Base Ball Players, which, after struggling for four years, collapsed. Executives of ten leading professional clubs, for their part, announced the existence in 1871 of the National Association of Professional Base Ball Players (NAPBBP). Clubs represented in its original membership were the Philadelphia Athletics, Washington Olympics and Nationals, New York Mutuals, Troy Unions, Boston Red Stockings, Rockford Forest Citys, Cleveland Forest Citys, Chicago White Stockings, and Fort Wayne Kekiongas. When the last-named club collapsed in the middle of the first season, the Brooklyn Eckfords replaced it. Although the formal constitution of the new association mirrored the old except for the absence of language opposing professionalism, the NAPBBP was even less an association of baseball *players* than its predecessor. Delegates represented not only far fewer teams but also an even narrower managerial class within them. Such a pattern was but an extension of trends that dated back to the creation of the old National Association, of course, but it reflected the organizers' stern determination that the reins of control in their emerging industry not be shared with their playing employees. Among the club officers, shareholders, and directors who served as delegates, only one active player remained—Harry Wright of the Boston Red Stockings, whose managerial functions already outweighed his fading playing skills in importance.

Despite its claims to a more efficient structure, the new professional association did not arrange fixed schedules for its clubs. Clubs themselves arranged the schedules of their playing tours, and the championship was determined by which team won the most three-out-of-five series against association rivals in the sequence of tours. If more than one team prevailed in an equal number of series, the club with the best winning percentage was recognized as champion. Usually eastern teams made two western road trips during the course of a season, and western clubs reciprocated with two trips east. However, each season some clubs threw the makeshift schedule, and the revenue projections based upon it, into chaos when financial woes or greed for home dates induced them to make but one road trip or even none. Member clubs also were still allowed to schedule as many games (basically exhibitions) as desired against inferior teams from outside the association. The Boston club in 1871 won all thirty-two of its matches against such opposition, despite extending some competitors five outs per inning to equalize the odds.

The players of the NAPBBP displayed the changes in, and the limits of, the class, age, and residence patterns that geographic expansion and commercialization had wrought in the nation as a whole. Virtually all still hailed from either modest white-collar or skilled manual-labor backgrounds and thus were neither rich nor poor. Their nonbaseball pursuits included work as proprietors of newsstands, bars, billiard halls, haberdasheries, and sporting goods stores; public and clerical employees such as firemen, policemen, municipal utility workers, and low-level city bureaucrats; and manual craftsmen, including hatters, stove repairers, bricklayers, brush makers, engravers, and tailors. According to one study of New York–area residents on National Association clubs, 17 out of 34 came from skilled manual trades. Baseball employment paid far better than such jobs but required a great degree of geographic mobility, as over half of the same group of players performed for teams outside their immediate home areas, and offered far less career longevity. A separate study of 29 players employed on New York–area professional teams reveals that their average age was 24 years, with a range in ages from 19 to 34. These figures are somewhat misleading, however, for only 2 players were above age 30, and 23 were under age 25. A larger survey of over 300 association professionals conducted by historian Steven Riess shows that, by place of birth, 83 percent of American-born players came from cities, with the most heavily represented being Philadelphia (39 players), Brooklyn (38), Baltimore (27), and New York (26). As a livelihood, in other words, baseball proved best suited to the young, vigorous, unattached, and mobile urbanite from a respectable, but not affluent, economic background.[24]

Given the travel and other physical and emotional demands of a journeyman baseball player's life, and the economic instability of clubs, short playing careers were the norm, with the average probably in the two-to-three-year range. However, if the results from the study of New York–resident professionals are typical of the player force generally, a clear distinction in career longevity already had developed between white-collar and blue-collar performers. Nine out of twenty-one blue-collar players played five seasons in the new association, as contrasted to only one white-collar player. One year or less was the most frequently recurring career length for the white-collar team members, while five years was the modal category for those veterans who were manual workers. On average, the blue-collar player's career was over a full year longer than that of his higher-status counterpart. When controlled for player age, the figures are even more striking. Of the thirteen white-collar participants in the professional association with New York residences, six retired from the game before their thirtieth birthday, while only five of the twenty-one blue-collar actives did so. If one compares the two sample groups of New York–resident players and players on New York–area teams, the greater youth of the latter also suggests that the mobile blue-collar player from New York often extended his career via his willingness to play for a nonhometown nine, making even more transient a working life already marked by long-distance road trips. Blue-collar players may also have stayed longer in the game because they possessed skills superior to those of their teammates and because they faced a narrow range of economic alternatives in industrializing cities with shrinking skilled-craft sectors.[25]

Whatever the occupational background of the player, baseball itself as yet provided very few nonplaying employment opportunities as his on-field career waned. Through the 1860s and 1870s, teams did not, for example, employ nonplaying coaches. In the pursuit of field captaincies, a veteran player with New York–area roots, particularly if of Yankee or English stock, enjoyed a distinct advantage. Of the twenty-three out of thirty team captains in the NAPBBP whose birthplaces could be identified, twelve came from New York. At least three others—Harry Wright, Al Reach, and Richard Higham—had been born in England but had emigrated to the New York metropolitan area. In contrast, 184 of the 250 players for whom exact birthplaces are known came from outside the New York–Brooklyn setting. A few ex-players found work as gatekeepers, policemen, or night watchmen for particular clubs. The fortunate few, most notably Albert Spalding and George Wright, were able to parlay successful careers and notoriety into lucrative sporting goods entrepreneurships. On the disreputable side, others occasionally translated more ignoble playing connections into later occupations as professional bookies and gamblers.[26]

Data on the national and ethnic heritage of the professional player force of 1871–75 is even sketchier than other data, and the conclusions that can be based on it more tenuous. But it is clear that the overwhelming majority of baseball professionals were American-born players rather than first-generation immigrants. The professionalization of the player force, measured in the refined on-field skills required of a successful performer, had succeeded in limiting access to the play-for-pay ranks almost completely to native-born Americans who had been able to hone their talents in a youth subculture of ballplaying. In Steven Riess's study, 233 of 319 players, or nearly 75 percent, were known to have been born in the United States, compared to only 28 (6.4 percent) who were foreign-born, with the birthplace of the remainder unidentifiable. From even more fragmentary information compiled by the former head of the

National Baseball Library, Lee Allen, of fifty players in this era whose ethnic heritage on both parents' sides could be traced, all but one claimed ancestry in the British Isles, Germany, or Holland. Nearly half, twenty-four, could be traced to "pure" English (whether Yankee, other colonial English, or more recent vintage), English-Irish, Scotch, or Scotch-Irish stock. Fifteen individuals, or 30 percent of the total, were of German or Dutch descent, with two of them also identified as Jewish. Ten players (20 percent) were Irish, and the remaining individual, a light-skinned Cuban third baseman for the Troy club, Esteban Bellan, was the only member of his nationality in nineteenth-century "major league" baseball. In short, the player force was made up of native-born players of Western European descent, most prominently of English, Irish, or German ancestry, who had learned the refinements of the game from youth and in many cases had "apprenticed" on junior clubs.[27]

Despite the obvious importance of acquiring the most promising, and reliable, young playing talent, professional clubs' methods of procuring it remained haphazard and extremely subjective. Clubs drew from junior teams and, to a lesser extent, from colleges or from other amateur nines they played or otherwise "heard of." No formal network of paid scouts, or "farm system" of feeder clubs existed. One of the most advanced clubs, the Chicago White Stockings, did send John Barleycorn to New Orleans in 1871, however, to examine talent on area amateur nines. Barnstorming exhibitions often provided opportunities for concealed scouting of other organizations' players. The Brooklyn Excelsiors sponsored their own junior club of some twenty to thirty players, aged fifteen to twenty, and the Mutuals since 1870 had sponsored parallel amateur and professional nines for "stashing" talent. But all too frequently assessments of prospects' ability were based upon a single sighting, or word of mouth, or performance at openly advertised one-time tryouts and were inflated or depressed according to the particular personality, ethnic, or character biases of the evaluator.

In marked contrast to the haphazard nature of player scouting and acquisition, the on-field performance of the journeyman professional ballplayer displayed ever-growing refinement, specialization, and sophistication. First basemen now "covered the bag" against base runners, who themselves more frequently employed sliding techniques to avoid tags. Clubs quickly learned the advantages of deploying a left-handed fielder at the position. Fielding in general, despite the absence of gloves, already had grown so refined under the fly catch rule that batters were instructed to hit down on the ball. Pitchers, considered the "cleverest" of players, now bent the rules by subtly bending their arms during their underhand deliveries. The unenforceability of the rule requiring straight-arm delivery forced the legalization of bent-arm pitching in 1872. Pitchers also changed speeds to confuse the batter and spun the ball off their fingertips to create curves (a trick especially well applied by former cricket bowlers). The growing importance of pitching led clubs to employ an extra hurler in their tenth roster spot and to begin substituting one pitcher for the other as another form of "change of pace." Catchers, forced to stand closer to the batter in order to thwart base runners, but more vulnerable to injury because of it, despite initial ridicule began to introduce "bird-cage" face masks. Some teams opted to carry an extra catcher instead of pitcher because of the injury risk. By 1875, St. Louis first baseman Charles C. Waitt introduced the first "glove," a skin-tight bit of apparel for either hand with the fingertips cut out and no padding, so as to prevent blisters without impeding throwing.[28]

As players more and more resembled fixed and task-specific, albeit highly skilled, shop-floor employees in their on-field roles, their cost-conscious bosses borrowed techniques from industry to better measure their charges' actual performance as a means of relating performance to pay. In response to such needs as well as the growing spectator hunger for information on their heroes, the sporting press provided a crude but growing array of "productivity" statistics. Victorian sportswriters tried to prod club officials into acknowledging that the "best" statistics measured not sporadic, dramatic displays but consistency of performance and, through that, dependability and team loyalty over raw individualism. As early as 1864, Henry Chadwick had championed a version of batting average as a criterion of hitting skill preferable to the number of home runs hit. Reflecting the game's early limitations on pitching techniques, the earliest pitching measurements assessed hurlers' control, not their runs allowed. Early statistics also crudely attempted to underscore a single player's contribution to team success, such as season totals for runs scored per average number of outs, or runs per game, without the ability to adjust these team-dependent numbers for the shortcomings of the rest of the lineup. Beginning in 1869, other statistics, such as average bases gained per hit, per game, began being compiled, and the decimal batting percentage, or batting average, made its formal appearance in 1870. The next year, the inaugural season of the professional association, *Beadle's Dime Book* began publishing annual batting averages, number of home runs, and other familiar statistics to the baseball public. As is still all too commonplace, however, such measures were not adjusted for the level of competition, differences in park dimensions, or other variables, leaving the comparative player performance assessments based upon them by krank and club executive alike still imperfect.[29]

The National Association of Professional Base Ball Players, the first attempt at an all-professional "league," proved a dismal failure and collapsed after five years. Its biggest shortcoming was its lack of effective power to promote competitive balance and mutual survival between clubs through the ability to curb players' freedom of economic movement. Given the resultant bidding wars for playing talent, and no real attempt to screen out clubs in inadequate markets or with insufficient financing—only a $10 initiation fee was required—association franchises failed at an alarming rate. From 1871 to 1875, twenty-five separate clubs participated at one time or another in the association, and eleven of them did not survive a single year. In 1872, five of eleven teams folded. In 1873, two of nine did so, and in 1875, four out of thirteen. In only one season, 1874, did the eight teams that started the season finish it. The more affluent and better-managed clubs engaged in their own cutthroat versions of survival of the fittest, hoarding the best players, paying the highest salaries, and using their leverage as the main attractions to hold up the weaker clubs for higher shares of the gate. Boston delegate Harry Wright, whose club narrowly lost the 1871 "pennant" and won the next four, demanded the establishment of a $.50 admission price, noting that theater shows of the day charged anywhere from $.75 to $1.50. Boston's fans might pay such fees to see their top-flight nine, but would other spectators in weaker markets? Wright also demanded for his club a 60 percent share of the gate or a $150 guarantee for league road contests—the rate he charged for outside exhibitions—arguing with some justification that cancellation of a home game with Boston by another club cost his organization $600–800.

Inadequate provisions to ensure a comparatively level financial "playing field" between clubs exacerbated operating cost problems—especially player salaries. Players recognized that despite regulations against revolving, the clubs' parasitic behavior toward each other's talent gave them, as free agents, continued bargaining leverage over their income, work conditions, and place of employment. In the matter of "jumping" or "not jumping," the player held considerable power. In early 1871, Ned Cuthbert, following his "sale" from the Philadelphia Athletics to the Chicago White Stockings, refused to play for his new employer without the approval of his family. The inflationary effect of such player leverage on salaries crippled profits for even the most "successful" organization. Boston's player payroll, $14,500 in 1871, jumped by over $6,000 within five years. Harry Wright himself pulled down $2,500 as field captain and club secretary. An established player, even if a substitute, could usually expect pay of at least $800 for three-quarters of a year, and starters $1,000 to $3,000 either as straight salary or, on cooperative nines, as a share of the gate taken off the top. A beginner received $75 a month if he lasted the season. With the average NAPBBP salary for the entire period of its existence probably in the $1,300–1,600 range, even a feeble club such as the New Haven Elm Citys found that in order to compete on the field and through some hope of victory attract adequate fan support it had to offer salaries averaging $1,600 a player, three or more times the average of a nonbaseball worker of the era.[30]

Salary costs, although the largest single item, were but one of the labor expenses of fielding a competitive nine. On road trips, clubs absorbed charges of $1.00 a day per player for room and board, and the same cost even at home for single players during the season. The Boston ledger, for example, included the costs of bachelors' rooms at a "Mrs. Parker's." One road trip cost the Red Stockings $1,161.03 but did take in $3,537.22. Indications that even Boston was not usually that fortunate include the fact that the club showed a profit of over $4,000 in 1873 but plowed all but $768 of it back into operating costs, that it showed figures of $833 and $65.20 for the following season despite a 52-18 record, and that, with a 71-8 mark in 1875, it still did not distribute the $3,261 earned as stockholder dividends but reinvested it in the club. Equipment and uniform costs soaked up additional revenue, and with players going through three uniforms each a year, Boston spent a not inconsiderable sum in paying $3.50 per yard for the cricket-flannel material from manager George Wright's own sporting goods establishment. Boston's official operating costs in 1875, which came to $34,505.99, included $20,685 in player salaries. The first champions of the professional association, the Philadelphia Athletics, netted but $150 from their 1871 triumph.

Grounds improvements used up additional revenue, making it even harder to afford the best available playing talent. The Chicago club, waging its battle with the bottom line, converted a dump site into its own 7,000-seat park rather than pay escalating rentals on expensive urban grounds. The new facility included separate sections for ladies and city politicians and a six-foot-high fence to keep rowdies and nonpayers out. The most zealous, and affluent, boosters could purchase a season ticket for the cost of $15. Unfortunately, the great Chicago fire destroyed a large section of the city, and with it the White Stockings' home season of 1871. With insurance payouts of but ten cents on the dollar, the team could not even afford to complete its road schedule. With the aid of a sporting publication, which provided the club with free railroad passes for the penniless, unattired squad, it fulfilled its obligation. Directors, in a noble gesture to their captain, dipped into their pockets for a $500 bonus at season's end, but earlier plans to boost the player payroll to $24,000 the next year to overtake Boston had to be shelved.[31]

Perhaps by coincidence, as player costs and other expenses escalated and club profitability waned, press mouthpieces for the clubs floated suggestions for rules changes to "speed up the game." Ostensibly intended to enhance spectator appeal, the moves also would likely have the effect of reducing players' offensive productivity statistics and giving owners more factual ammunition in salary battles. In 1872, the "wrist snap" delivery for pitchers was legalized. Between the 1873 and 1874 seasons, Henry Chadwick proposed that rules be tightened so as to do away with "fair-foul" hits—batted balls that began in fair territory and veered into foul ground in front of first or third base. Consideration of these rules changes, however "esthetically" appealing, nonetheless also displayed a continuing naiveté on the part of both club officials and sportswriters about the full range of economic consequences in taking such actions. For even if they perceived that rules reducing player batting statistics might help curb the higher salary demands that higher numbers fueled, subsequent experience would demonstrate that rules tinkering that reduced offense and scoring also frequently turned off spectators and diminished gate revenues.[32]

As the NAPBBP staggered through its final two seasons, its failures were all too obvious. In the midst of the 1874 season, the Boston and Philadelphia teams had barnstormed to England in hopes of recouping profits, only to lose an additional $3,000. Continued competitive imbalance (illustrated in 1875 by the fact that while Boston went 71-8, the Brooklyn Atlantics won only two games the entire season) and inequitable markets led to a fire-sale mentality on the part of losing clubs. Faced with bankruptcy, the Philadelphia Centennials, in one example, sold two players to the rival Athletics for $1,500. The Athletics, however, could not afford to finance the transaction out of club moneys, so directors were forced to pay for it out of their personal funds. Club officers' scrambles for survival also led to more backstage dealings with illicit bankrollers, gamblers, and game-fixers.[33]

The member clubs of the NAPBBP had inherited, and had refined further, intraclub management structures that segregated players from those who employed them and regulated their work lives. But they had failed to create an overarching governance structure that could effectively regulate their own competitive instincts for players, victories, and profits in order to provide for their mutual survival and prosperity. As a result, players had been able to exploit interclub management rivalries to gain higher salaries and greater freedom of movement, albeit at the cost of high rates of club failure and job instability. The irony was that the very trends club leaders had decried in the labor force since before the Civil War—growing ethnocultural, geographic, and social class diversity and an acquisitive individualism that destroyed fealty to team and community—had infected their own efforts at self-policing for the common good. But by the same token, the diversity and individualism of the player force had effectively blocked its reforging of a fraternal solidarity across clubs—a union—that could ensure the long-term survival of the material gains and the power to choose one's employer that individual players' acts temporarily had wrested. In the absence of such collective player power, how long would professional baseball management permit itself to remain feckless and divided?

 **THREE**

BARONS AND SERFS,
1876-1885

By the mid-1870s, population growth and an extensive railroad network in the metropolitan Northeast made a regional professional league (in effect a cartel of franchises), with a fixed season schedule, economically feasible. What was required from a capitalist's perspective was some individual or group with the financial ruthlessness to enforce interclub arrangements restricting competition and protecting markets and with a similar willingness to bring player-employees to heel. The difficulty lay in the fact that other entrepreneurs might envision the same opportunities, form rival leagues, and launch bitter struggles over the prime urban markets. This contest for the survival of the fittest, if carried out in baseball as it was in other industries at the time, would cripple the winner with debts at the same time that it destroyed the losers. The greatest sources of financial strain would be the escalated costs of retaining player services and the gate losses from players jumping to rival organizations that would be triggered by interleague and interclub trade war. In the aftermath, surviving owners would need to reimpose a frugal economic order upon their employees by cracking down on contract breakers, reining in players' geographic mobility, imposing cartelwide wage scales, and cutting individual salaries, as well as utilizing their administrative controls over the workplace, especially those over playing rules, to reduce player productivity statistics and justify further wage economies. Such severe crackdowns, however, would risk generating renewed player outrage in forms that might only add to the existing labor turmoil within the fledgling industry.

Professional baseball's first such empire-builder, bent upon securing in uncertain times both his own club's dominance and the league's collective stability through formation of a dominant cartel in the largest markets and the suppression of players' migratory opportunities, was William Hulbert. Hulbert, born in Otsego County, New York (the county in which Cooperstown is located), combined the drive for business dominance of the era's nouveau riche with a traditional Yankee craving for the respectability of well-established position. It was also fitting that Chicago, the transportation hub of Gilded Age industrialization as well as Hulbert's home since the age of two, provided the setting for his creation of a baseball business empire. The Windy City, more than any other midwestern metropolis, was the visible manifestation of the region's advancing raw economic power, civic boosterism, and determination to outshine its eastern predecessors. Chicago baseball displayed the same characteristics in microcosm. By the 1870s the city claimed over fifty teams, many sponsored by industrial concerns within a commercial league. Interclub competition for victories and prestige was so keen that, despite the expense, employers gave their playing charges time off to hone their skills.

Following his education at Belard College, Hulbert acquired a coal dealership and parlayed it into a position on the Chicago Board of Trade. Although he had never played baseball, he joined the Chicago White Stockings as a shareholder in 1870 in order to further cement his image as a civic promoter. From that vantage point, he had come to grasp baseball's possibilities as a money-maker in its own right and as part of an expanding network of associated enterprises, from transit companies, grounds firms, and hotels to sporting goods distributors. A driven

William Hulbert, owner of the Chicago White Stockings and founder of the National League cartel

power-seeker, in his forties at the time, Hulbert signaled his willingness to become a bigger player in the White Stockings' operation by becoming an executive in the club in 1875. Determined that his Windy City franchise should assume the dominant position in a more efficient and lucrative baseball empire, with the aid of player-captain Albert Spalding and Chicago *Tribune* sports editor Lewis Meacham, he plotted raids upon other clubs' talent to secure the White Stockings' dominance. At the same time, he engineered the collapse of the National Association and the triumph of his new aggregation, the National League of Professional Base Ball Clubs. In matters of on-field talent assessment, Spalding provided the baseball acumen that Hulbert lacked, while Meacham served as Hulbert's public relations defender and mouthpiece in the sporting press.

Hulbert's first move in his "palace coup" was to lure Spalding away from the Boston club. With his own career winding down, the star eagerly signed for a $2,000 salary as player-captain, plus the promise of 25 percent of the gate. In turn, Spalding served as management's agent in enticing fellow players, against National Association rules, to jump to the White Stockings in advance of the 1876 season. Among those secured were former Boston teammates Cal McVey, James "Deacon" White, and Ross Barnes and Philadelphia Athletics star Cap Anson. Yet another Philadelphia player, Ezra Sutton, committed to Chicago but reneged. While Spalding built up Chicago's on-field assets in preparation for Hulbert's break with the NAPBBP, Meacham laid out the public rationale. In October 1875 he explained that the sport's fiscal and corruption problems required a new "closed corporation" of sound teams that would only play each other in accordance with a limited, fixed schedule. The keys to the success of such a closed corporation would be the ability to secure and protect the largest and best home markets and to bring the player-employees under effective, comprehensive control. As partner Spalding later explained, "The idea was as old as the hills; but its application to Base Ball had not yet been made. It was, in fact, the irrepressible conflict between Labor and Capital asserting itself under a new guise. . . . Like every other form of business enterprise, Base Ball depends for results on two interdependent divisions, the one to have absolute control and direction of the system, and the other to engage— always under the executive branch—the actual work of production."[1]

Hulbert's player acquisitions and the promise of the Chicago population market gave his organizational insurrection a fighting chance for success. He was adamant in thinking that his Chicago franchise ought to serve as the hub of the new circuit. But he still needed partners in the form of clubs and officers in the top northeastern urban markets. Not wishing publicly to alarm potential allies who might be concerned that he would subordinate them in a new league to his own competitive interests, Hulbert maintained that his greatest incentive was to save the game from "its slough of corruption and disgrace." Hulbert's arguments resembled southern conservatives' justifications for undermining Reconstruction, and like their assurances, his own offers of baseball "redemption" cloaked deeper purposes. He lined up a "western front" of supporting interests in attorney Charles Foule of St. Louis (director of the Browns, vice-president of the NAPBBP, and a member of the association's Judiciary Committee) and fellow executives from Cincinnati and Louisville clubs. Following a December 17, 1875, meeting, they then approached eastern executives in Hartford, Boston, New York, and Philadelphia with the aim of creating a new, eight-team professional league. With Foule drafting the constitution, representatives of the clubs announced the existence of the National League of Professional Base Ball Clubs on February 2, 1876, in New York City. Having successfully sprung their surprise announcement upon the National Association and many in the sporting press, including the venerable Henry Chadwick, the National League's "founding fathers" in convention openly pledged themselves to the new entity and renounced their former allegiance to the NAPBBP. Within weeks, the old National Association collapsed.[2]

Although Hulbert and his right-hand man, Spalding, were the driving forces behind the new league, they were required to make certain concessions in order to ensure eastern participation. Four of the five men serving one-year terms on the board of directors that governed league affairs came from the East. The first president was not Hulbert, but insurance executive Morgan Bulkeley of Hartford, who served but one year before being replaced by Hulbert and moving on to a career as governor and then U.S. senator from Connecticut. Reinforcing the initial eastern image and sense of continuity with the old association were secretary-treasurer Nicholas Young, a Washington congressional clerk and former NAPBBP secretary, and ex-star Harry Wright, who served as recording secretary. In keeping with Hulbert's claim of moralistic motives, the National League banned Sunday games, liquor sales, and pool selling and gambling on club grounds.

Each club received exclusive territorial market rights from other league teams, with only one NL club allowed within a five-mile market radius. Member clubs were even barred from playing non-NL teams within the territorial confines of another league city. For any club expansion to occur, the petitioning club had to demonstrate a city market of at least 75,000 people, unless exempted from the requirement by a unanimous vote of league club representatives. As a symbolic demonstration of financial soundness, member teams had to post annual dues of $100, not just a one-time $10 fee, as in the old National Association. In league contests, visiting teams would receive 30 percent of the gate receipts in a playing season that stretched from March 15 to November 15 and featured ten games (five home, five away) between each club. Nonappearance at scheduled contests, or use of ineligible players, meant an automatic forfeit. Furthermore, these actions—as well as disbanding in mid-season or disobeying board rulings, the league constitution, or contracts—could, upon a two-thirds vote of member clubs, result in the expulsion of a franchise from the league. Each club was obligated to provide its own police for its grounds and to file a game report after each contest with league secretary Young.

Of these various provisions, the exclusivity of market guarantees represented the most obvious immediate departure from the old regime. But just as crucial were the new league's plans for its player-employees. Hulbert and his associates aimed at nothing less than a form of baseball indentured servitude, in which the ability of member clubs to raid each other's talent during a season and the player's rights of geographic mobility and choice of employer would be drastically reduced. Players would enjoy no representation in the governing institutions of the National League. Club executives merely dispatched contracts to their players, refusing to negotiate. Signed players had to obey their captain without right of refusal, and club management unilaterally assumed the authority to assess a player's attitude and effort and react accordingly. Clubs required players to obey sobriety regulations and to submit themselves to medical examinations conducted by doctors retained by management. Injury, illness, or insubordination—all as attributed by management—could cause unilateral dismissal without pay or notice. Clubs also could suspend player pay for shorter periods for what they dubbed "indifferent or careless play" or for "conspiring" against the club or "manifesting a disposition" to do the same.[3]

Any member club could still sign a player under contract to a particular team, so long as the player's services under the new contract did not begin until after his old one ended. Clubs that violated active contracts by enticing in-season jumping, however, were subject to expulsion by the National League and a boycott by the other teams. A released player could sign with another league franchise only if shown "honorably" discharged, and then only after a twenty-day period, allowing club representatives ample time in most cases to collude in order to reduce the number and size of offers to the player. Whether notified officially of improper conduct or not, if a released player went unsigned after the twenty-day probation, clubs considered him the same as expelled, and neither he nor overtly blacklisted men could be signed by a league franchise without that franchise risking expulsion or boycott by the rest. The ejected players thus could be permanently denied employment on the collection of teams that claimed the best, highest-paying markets, and even nonmember clubs could suffer boycotts of games from league nines for daring to bring a blacklisted player into their areas.

In keeping with the objective of holding down labor costs, the new league, citing the desire to speed up contests, adopted equipment and rules that effectively limited scoring and individual offensive statistics. The official ball, a National Association holdover, was a "dead" ball of hard rubber wrapped in wool and encased in stitched horsehide that only became deader with continual use during a game. Pitchers hurled underhand from a six-foot-square area, or "box," to a hitter who indicated beforehand whether he desired a high or low pitch. Nine inaccurate tosses constituted a walk, which allowed the batter to take base but statistically counted in his batting average as an out. Three swinging strikes constituted an out; if two swings were followed by a called strike, a fourth strike was required. Pitchers were allowed to snap their wrists in delivery, and some utilized bent-arm tosses in spite of rules against the practice (which was then legalized in December of 1877). Improved pitching, better fielding, the outlawing of the "fair-foul" hit, and prohibitions on player substitutions (except in the case of a pinch runner, selected by the opposing captain) after the fourth inning of a game speeded contests but also led to fan grumbling about dull, lower-scoring games.[4]

As might have been expected, given Hulbert's pains to stockpile players for his own club before announcing the new league's existence, the White Stockings dominated the circuit. In contrast, both the Philadelphia Athletics and New York Mutuals failed to complete the opening season and were summarily expelled. In Philadelphia's case, its owners' offer of an 80 percent gate share to St. Louis and Chicago if those clubs would play extra road dates in the City of Brotherly Love rather than insist on the completion of a western tour by the Athletics proved insufficient to stave off collapse. The Mutuals, in turn, were offered a $400 guarantee for two games in Chicago and three in St. Louis within one week's time to help them defray road expenses (albeit at the cost of tired, noncompetitive ballplayers), but when their owner refused, the club received the axe. Throughout the first six years of the National League, in fact, the number of games scheduled in a season fluctuated from sixty to eighty-five because of repeated club failures and canceled games. Probably no club made money in 1876, with Boston's recorded loss of $777.22 most likely small compared to the losses of most other clubs. Nonetheless, Chicago's entrepreneurs found ways to beat the odds. Spalding, besides his on-field salary as player-captain and team manager, operated a sporting goods emporium that served as "head-quarters for the Western Ball clubs." Despite some missteps—Spalding's experiment of topping his nine with caps of different colors by position in 1882 led to the team's ridicule as a "dutch bed of tulips"—Spalding's monopoly rights to produce the league's official baseball and its post-season publication, edited by Henry Chadwick, guaranteed Chicago financial success. As early as the start of the 1877 campaign, Spalding became a full-time executive.[5]

For other clubs and their officers, as the meager returns of 1876 showed, the National League had not yet adequately addressed the problems of interclub financial competition, market imbalance, and player cost and mobility. Press organs outside Chicago increasingly attacked the organization as a "star chamber" and a "monopoly" that served only Hulbert's interests at the expense of the other clubs and baseball generally. Hulbert lent further ammunition to the attacks by his assumption of the league presidency in 1877, his sponsorship of a rule barring managers from the players' bench during games (a clear slap at the Boston nine and their hands-on leader, Harry Wright), his continued opposition to lower admission prices despite pleas from midwestern club operators in weaker markets, and his similar refusal to allow Sunday ball and beer sales. Reflecting his own satisfaction with a fifty-cent admission fee in Chicago and his determination not to let the lesser element invade the ballparks, Hulbert favorably compared the National League's standard admission charge with that of comparable "proper" Victorian amusements such as the theater (between twenty-five and seventy-five cents) or public lectures (fifty cents). Hulbert's militance against alcohol and reduced admission prices led the St. Louis Browns to pull out of the National League in 1877 and prompted Cincinnati to think about following suit, since league prohibitions on grandstand beer sales forced Queen City patrons to journey "downstairs to moisten."[6]

The loss of teams in the Philadelphia, New York, and St. Louis markets, combined with the maintenance of fifty-cent admissions and morals restrictions, created opportunities for outside rivals to challenge the National League's professional monopoly and thereby drive up labor costs through competitive bidding. Although not a direct challenge to the National League's players or markets, the New England League formed around a group of Civil War–era amateur and semipro nines. Far more of a threat was the International Association of Professional Baseball Players, formed by St. Louis Red Stockings owner L. C. Waite and representatives of seventeen non-NL clubs, with famed curveball pitcher Candy Cummings as president. Featuring thirteen clubs, including three in Canada, before the start of the 1877 season and shuffling in ten others during that year, the league triggered more competitive turmoil and created additional bidding wars for player contracts. Over time, the rival league proved itself geographically and financially overextended, with its inadequate $10-per-club membership fee and absence of effective capitalization requirements responsible for many of its financial woes. But at first the International Association's twenty-five-cent admission fee threatened to undermine the National League's gate structure and drive an even deeper wedge between NL owners in inequitable markets.

Hoping to preempt the opposition from various quarters, Hulbert's league announced the creation of a thirteen-club League Alliance, a subordinate aggregation of teams affiliated with the National League. In exchange for $10 fees and promises to eschew raids on NL playing talent, Hulbert promised alliance franchises the security of reciprocal respect for their player contracts, territorial rights, and disciplinary sanctions. Initially the National League even appeared to hold out the hope of equal membership to alliance clubs through a suggested constitutional amendment. Under the proposal, one new club each year from the alliance might be admitted to the National League if it had accumulated the best record against non-NL opposition in a prior season played under NL rules. However, two negative votes from NL club representatives could kill any such expansion, and Hulbert himself supported the sanctity and soundness of maintaining an eight-team NL circuit. More clubs would only "dilute" talent, increase the number of high-stakes bidders for its services, and thus add to salary and travel costs. In the words of Hulbert's mouthpiece, the Chicago *Tribune*, League expansion was "rather too communistic even for these liberal days." The 75,000-person market requirement also effectively restricted expansion, although NL owners found ways around it when they desired. It was blatantly ignored in the cases of the Syracuse and Troy clubs, and met in the case of Worcester only by counting everyone within its five-mile territorial radius, not just the population within the city's actual limits.[7]

Once the National League extended its market range by deploying the alliance against the International Association, it manipulated its new partners in ruthless, self-interested fashion. NL assertions of territorial rights were extended to prohibit preseason as well as in-season games in alliance cities between NL and nonalliance outside teams and any games by the alliance with non-NL or nonalliance nines on grounds controlled by the National League. Alliance clubs were permitted two delegates each to National League meetings, but they did not have voting power. The National League in turn demanded that the alliance include only one club per market and insisted upon higher financial guarantees from alliance nines than it did from other clubs for games with its teams, in exchange for the security from raiding that NL owners offered. In truth, about the only real market protection the system provided alliance clubs was against the scheduling of games in their cities by NL teams against nonalliance nines, for under the arrangements two clubs in Hulbert's league could still play each other within alliance territory.

Despite its counterattacks, the National League found itself caught in a severe cost-profit squeeze in 1877, triggered by competition for fans and players with the International Association and a jump in salaries (see Appendix, Fig. 1). As one example, in the previous season Boston had accumulated over $30,000 in expenses, of which salaries claimed over $19,000. With player talent at a higher premium because of interleague bidding warfare, the figures rose in 1877 to $34,443.46 overall and $22,420 for salaries. The salary change represented a 16 percent jump from the previous year. Not surprisingly, Boston club losses also soared, from under $800 to over $2,200. St. Louis dropped $8,000, and despite its on-field prowess, even Chicago ended 1877 $6,000 in the red. The Cincinnati club, denied lower admissions and grandstand liquor sales needed to induce additional revenues, survived the full season only after owner Si Keck relinquished club control to an eight-member group in July. Ignoring the consequences for competitive balance and league health in the scramble to protect his own franchise, Hulbert took advantage of Cincinnati's peril to raid its talent after Keck's resignation had caused the formal release of his players from their contracts. After signing two Cincinnati players, Hulbert was prevailed upon to return one of them for the sake of the new ownership.[8]

The common knowledge that franchises were in financial trouble and struggling to meet their salary obligations encouraged individual players to seek "outside" money from disreputable sources and also induced owners to seek "escape hatches" from their prior contractual promises to players. Players faced a greater temptation to lay down in retaliation for double-dealing or to do so simply because of frustration at clubs' unwillingness to let them seek their highest compensation level in an expanded baseball labor market. Owners, after pledging bonuses for "good behavior and good work" to discourage interleague jumping, then imposed new levies in an effort to recoup the payments. The 1877 season saw the inauguration of a fifty-cent-a-day fee upon players for their board on road trips. Players also were required to purchase, clean, repair, or replace their uniforms out of their own money. Doubling the management payback, of course, was Spalding's ownership of the supplying firms. At first, the uniform expense could be covered in advance by a $30 deduction from the player's salary. But as costs of manufacturing the clothing rose, clubs no longer found the deduction adequate, and they increased the levies on their employees rather than conserve material by deleting such requirements as the one mandating neckties. Boston players John and James "Orator" O'Rourke made the payment of uniform fees the basis of a contract battle, signing only after friends put up their obligation for them.[9]

With much more at stake if a player became incapacitated and thus incapable of delivering on the club's "investment" in him, management now not only required players to submit to medical examination by a club-selected physician on demand but also required players to pay for such services. Club officials claimed the sole right to determine a player's fitness to play and therefore the team's obligation to fulfill salary obligations, a prerogative open to flagrant abuse. Chicago's Ross Barnes found himself docked one-third of his $2,500 salary for being incapacitated for three months. When he appealed the White Stockings' unilateral action, a court ruling upheld its legality. Violations of team discipline and moral codes provided another rationale for clubs not to fulfill contract salary and job security obligations for higher-priced charges. NL officials authorized umpires to fine players up to $20 per incident for using profanity.

President Hulbert, for his part, willingly presided over a "moral crackdown" on player conduct, though his evenhandedness remained subject to question. In the case of one of his own players, outfielder Paul Hines, he resorted to a public shaming tactic, condemning the young man's indifferent play in an open letter to the Chicago *Post* and threatening to tell his father on him. In contrast, Hulbert "threw the book" at Louisville pitcher Jim Devlin when his fading performance in the stretch run led to charges in the Louisville *Courier-Journal* that Devlin had "thrown" more than pitches. Three players on the team confessed to dealings with a New York pool seller, and four in all—Devlin (who received half of a total $300 bribe), George Hall, Al Nichols, and second baseman and captain William Craver—received lifetime expulsions. A desperate Devlin pleaded by telegram, "I am living from hand-to mouth all winter I have not got a Stitch of Clothing or has my wife and Child." In response, Hulbert quietly dispatched $50 but added, "Damn you, you have sold a game, you are dishonest, and this National League will not stand for it."[10]

Although the International Association's challenge inflicted pain upon the National League, the rival conducted its player raids in a more gentlemanly fashion than it might have. Following the National League's lead, the International Association "tampered" with players under current contract to other clubs by negotiating future deals, but the contracts its agents hammered out did not take effect until a player's existing obligations expired. Nonetheless, players were shrewd enough to use such "futures" bidding as leverage in their efforts to pry off-season compensation and salary advances from their current owners. Others cited "legitimate" economic hardship stemming from unexpected family crises or their own dissipation. But by the end of the 1877 season, although the National League was severely strained, the threat from the International Association already had been effectively repulsed. The rival's Canadian clubs all collapsed, and, reflecting the International Association's greater vulnerability to NL buying power in an open futures market, it attempted to protect its rosters by imposing an 1878 ban on in-season contract discussions with its players until October 1. Unreassured, four association clubs jumped to the League Alliance to obtain more reliable protection from NL raiding.

For its part, the National League found itself forced by franchise collapses to adopt three new clubs (Indianapolis, Milwaukee, and Providence) in order even to maintain a six-team circuit in 1878. Because of the financial strains caused by the International Association "war"—and made possible by the demise of the rival league as an effective talent bidder as that war came to a close—NL owners now imposed extreme budgetary economies, especially in salaries. Having extended bonuses to players in the off-season to forestall jumping and secure contract renewals, management now deducted these \$100–500 bonus payments from players' 1878 season incomes or treated them as loans by unilaterally deducting 6–8 percent interest charges from paychecks. Club officers and league officials colluded to restrain competitive intraleague bidding for released players and to encourage buying such free agents only at reduced wages. When Boston business manager Wright sought league permission to sign catcher Charles Snyder from the disbanded Louisville club, NL secretary Young consented but advised Boston to reduce its salary offer from the \$1,500 that Snyder formerly received to only \$1,280. Young maintained that no other clubs were interested in the player's services and that, if kept at the higher figure, Snyder would only waste the difference, being "not loaded down with brains." In a rare display of employer integrity, however, Wright offered Snyder the full \$1,500.[11]

In general, NL owners slashed payrolls in an effort to recoup the losses of 1877 (see Appendix, Fig. 1). Boston, despite Wright's individual act of generosity, trimmed its overall salary obligation to \$18,814 in 1878 and to \$15,759.92 by 1879. During 1878, the league publicly condemned the practice of paying out in salary more than clubs drew in earnings and expelled Milwaukee at season's end for its fiscal profligacy and debt. Faced only with a fizzling International Association (it folded in 1880) and a weak, one-season (1879) Northwestern League that charged twenty-five cents for admission and lacked a fixed schedule, Hulbert urged further payroll cuts in order for the industry "to be conserved in its best state." League secretary Young added that profligate, pay-squandering players still threatened to "kill the goose that laid the golden egg." Two of the league's three new entries—Milwaukee and Indianapolis—that had died at the end of the 1878 season were replaced by four more teams—Buffalo, Syracuse, Cleveland, and Troy—in order to restore an eight-team schedule in 1879. Only Chicago could claim a balance sheet in the black.[12]

With clubs still struggling financially, the National League announced on September 29, 1879, the most far-reaching change in the history of its labor relations—the adoption of the "reserve clause." Initially, officials declared that each team could henceforth reserve five players off its eleven-man roster for the year following their current contracts, even in the absence of a new signed contract. For those players affected, the adoption of the reserve clause meant that their ability to change employers between season contracts had been eliminated unless their "owners" agreed to permit a change via release. The club retained the power to unilaterally terminate a player contract with thirty days' notice or to assign a player to another team. If a reserved player attempted to override the clause by jumping to another team, all other league and alliance clubs were barred from employing him or even from playing a team with him on it upon pain of expulsion. The player would be subject to blacklisting and the threat of permanent banishment. In effect, for reserved players all contracts had now been standardized, and their bargaining rights had been eliminated on all issues except the level of their annual financial compensation. Even on that question, the player no longer had the practical leverage of interclub bidding, but could only resort to holding out from his present club in the hopes that fan clamor for his presence would pressure management into a more generous offer. Clubs, however, were not even required to notify the player of his reserved status. If a player did bolt to a non-NL/alliance organization, the weaker markets and resources of such clubs nonetheless would effectively exert management's desired salary discipline upon the entire player force.

The introduction of the reserve clause was the most significant step yet in a progression of moves to limit player independence and control, which had included the separation of players from mechanisms of workplace management, prohibitions upon in-season revolving, penalties against illicit forms of compensation, extensions of clubs' exclusive territorial rights, wars against outside competition, and ownership practices of collusion and wage-fixing. Its timing, however, also reflected the particular objectives at the end of the 1879 season of a majority of NL owners, led by the notorious penny-pincher Arthur H. Soden of Boston. Soden and his allies wanted the reserve for the obvious reason of limiting player mobility and therefore salary leverage. But they also desired to erect more effective barriers to the off-season raiding of their clubs' top talent by the few franchises with pockets deep enough to absorb higher salaries for the sake of championships and gate attendance—most notably Hulbert's White Stockings. The adoption of the reserve clause also demonstrated that the National League had succeeded in killing off its outside rivals to the extent that it did not fear that this new restriction on players' rights would drive them to other clubs and leagues. Instead, the reserve, the owners believed, would facilitate additional belt-tightening as well as maintain a more consistent level of on-field competitive balance.[13]

Defending the league's decision, president Hulbert incredibly insisted that it had been the players who had demanded the reserve clause in order to increase their job security. The Cleveland *Plain Dealer* of October 10, 1879, asserted that players need not fear for their livelihoods, since owners had compensated them in the past at levels higher than $1,000 a season, or $12 a game and $6 an hour. Club officials also claimed that the major impulse behind their action had not been financial retaliation against the players but rather a renewed desire to clean up the game's image. They pointed to the impression of compromised player integrity when performers played in a series against a team that had already contracted their services for the next season. But critics pointed out that the clause plunged those covered by it into an even more blatant wage slavery. As for the effects of the reserve on interclub competitive balance, those officers with stronger financial backing still did not lack for ways to use it in contractual dealings with fellow owners. The reserve to some extent also promised to impede opportunities for young players to break in with NL clubs, now that such clubs could more effectively "stockpile" veteran talent. For the veteran, besides the reserve's salary implications, the denial of freedom of mobility meant less opportunity to escape a moribund team for one with better championship chances or off-field merchandising opportunities.[14]

The impact of the reserve clause, in conjunction with the effect of already-introduced economies and the demise of nonalliance competition, was to extend reductions in player salaries into the early 1880s (see Appendix, Fig. 1). As expected, Boston's tight-fisted Soden led the way in payroll cuts and other forms of cost reduction. Clubroom upkeep, $1,626 in 1875, fell to $551 in 1880. Team travel expenses, $6,808 five years earlier, dropped to but $2,813. Boston's salaries tumbled 20 percent from 1877 to 1880, to an average of $1,377.50. When his players nearly mutinied, Soden, rather than restore the cuts, fired his manager Wright for failing to deal with the discontent firmly enough. An example of how Soden himself dealt with players was his treatment of Charley Jones in a dispute over $378 of back salary the player claimed for a late-season road trip. Fearing that prompt payment of the sum would lead to Jones's skipping the team in Cleveland and returning to his Cincinnati home, Soden not only refused to pay the amount in dispute but also fined his charge $100 and suspended him. When Jones then did flee to the Queen City, Soden had him expelled and blacklisted. Despite a Cleveland Common Pleas Court ruling in his favor, the National League refused to reinstate Jones, who after a two-year hiatus reentered "major league" baseball with the rival American Association.[15]

Although in isolated cases some owners gave raises or bonuses of

$100–200, more typical of the direction of salary offers was the case of Tommy Bond, who found his 1880 pay slashed from $2,200 to $1,500. According to subsequent figures released by Albert Spalding to show owner financial generosity in the later 1880s, the average salary of 16 selected ballplayers in 1881 fell to but $1,350, below even the Boston average of the previous year. The same individuals, according to Spalding's own numbers, earned only $25 more on average the next season. Such economies did gradually improve club finances, for although still only a minority of clubs made a profit in 1880, the number of clubs in that minority was larger than before. By season's end Hulbert could claim that the National League no longer included any "weak sisters." Typical was Detroit, which entered 1881 with a $5,000 balance and ended the year with $12,440. At the same time, however, the economies did nothing to help players prepare financially for life after baseball. Steven Riess's examination of 1871–82 professional ballplayers showed that fully 35 percent slid downward occupationally into blue-collar jobs after leaving baseball, with nearly all the rest merely maintaining a low white-collar status. Of twenty-six New York–area players researched, eleven showed some upward mobility, but the progress registered by seven of these was very modest, while thirteen remained at essentially the same occupational level and two declined. Owners, for their part, refused to assume any responsibility for their charges' between-seasons or postcareer struggles, asserting that more generous actions would be misplaced, as players would waste any money they received on gambling and dissipation.[16]

Recognizing that their employees had nowhere else to go, and desirous of maintaining an image of rectitude that would attract the more affluent, respectable Victorian customer, owners now intensified the disciplinary crackdown on their players at the same time that they squeezed them financially. Part of the process involved raising the professionalism and authority of umpires, while increasing their social separation from the player force. Umpires certainly did not have an easy task, subject as they were to physical threat, spikings, and verbal harassment from players and spectators alike. Lack of league disciplinary backing and low pay had resulted in rapid job turnover and temptations to bribery. When Billy McLean demanded a pay scale of $5.00 a game for umpires in 1876, the National League refused. But by as early as 1878 the league reversed itself, with the home team paying the umpires, and the following year it designated a regular staff of twenty approved arbiters from whom clubs could select to work their games. In 1881 umpires' on-field authority, and their segregation from players and spectators, was increased by new rules that allowed only a team's captain or his designee to address an umpire and disallowed reversal of decisions on the basis of player or bystander "testimony" after the fact. The National League's ban on all liquor sales in its parks in 1881 also drew inspiration in part from the desire to assist umpires in reducing fan rowdiness and violence. The next year, umpires received the power to order the ejection of hissing or hooting spectators from playing grounds. The National League also banished for life one of its arbiters, Richard Higham of Troy, for corruption.[17]

The owners' moral crackdown directly targeted players in a host of other ways. In 1879 they approved the application of shorter-term suspensions as a more flexible instrument than the blacklist for lesser individual violations of rules and etiquette. The following February, in "An Address to the Players," the National League established a formal "new system of discipline and penalties." "Drunkenness and bummerism" merited suspension without pay. Incapacitating illness or injury also meant "no pay for no services rendered." In management's view, player ethical shortcomings had made it necessary to "reach the pockets as well as the pride of a player." As a consequence, one player reportedly played five innings in an 1881 game with a broken wrist rather than forfeit his wages. Even if players did not receive formal lifetime expulsions, shorter suspensions could end up lasting a full season, or even into the next.[18]

Promising commensurate rewards for compliant, "earnest, deserving" men, the owners altruistically insisted that the new regimen "surrounds the player of morally weak tendencies with wholesome restraints." Players, however, often received no notification of their alleged transgressions until they got their envelopes with fine-reduced pay inside. And on-field blunders that were not the consequence of intoxication from "German tea" or other indulgences could still trigger punishments. With the league publication, the *Spalding Guide*, rating a sober player's worth at $1,200 but a drunk's at not half that much, clubs employed Pinkerton spies and inside informers to infiltrate and report on their charges. The blacklist, formerly a covert, internal document, became a formal public record in 1881. Of it Spalding claimed, "No piece of legislation was so well calculated to give good results since gross acts of intemperance and insubordination were subversive to discipline and good order." Specific grounds for blacklisting included "dissipation" and "general insubordination," and the punished player could not even appeal his sanction until the next annual winter meeting of NL owners. In the spring of 1882 Hulbert ordered the lifetime expulsions of ten players for chronic intoxication.[19]

It is doubtless true that some level of player policing was justified, given the proliferation of gambling and saloons in post–Civil War America. Some estimates claim that the years 1860–80 saw a 700 percent increase in liquor investments in the United States. But what may have been every bit as much an incentive for a highly publicized moral crackdown as actual player lapses was management's interest, by questioning player rectitude, in undermining popular sympathy for players and, with it, their sole source of bargaining leverage in a period of salary retrenchment and the reserve. Aiding management's efforts was the baseball public's willingness to equate the growing Irish player cohort with moral declension. Although the owners were hardly themselves a homogenous assemblage of moral exemplars, they were more than willing to exploit the Victorian prejudice that equated Irishness and corruptibility to explain and justify their tightening of restrictions on players. In order to shield their umpires from similar accusations, the National League almost always employed arbiters of Yankee or English origins to work their games.

Aiding the owners' efforts to exploit the popular equation of lushery and corruption with non-Wasp ballplayers, the playing force featured large numbers of Irish and German descendants (see Appendix, Fig. 2). Of some ninety-two players entering the National League from 1876 to 1884 for whom former baseball librarian Lee Allen identified parental ethnic heritage, 41 percent were of Irish stock. Non-Irish products of the British Isles made up an additional 34 percent. Players of varying Teutonic ancestry (mostly Germans, but with a few Dutch, Austrian, or Swiss as well), claimed a 21 percent representation. The remaining players likewise all claimed direct or indirect origins in Western Europe as descendants of Canadians, Frenchmen, or Swedes. Ironically, the Victorian fan's vicarious enjoyment of the aggressive, even "dirty," style of play attributed to the Irish, featuring the "stolen base," was central to the league's success. Whether or not owners really would have preferred a more dignified headliner, fans flocked to see the playing exploits of the roisterous Mike "King" Kelly. Kelly, whose various off-field indulgences contributed to his premature death at the age of thirty-six, even enjoyed the tribute of a popular song entitled "Slide, Kelly, Slide!"[20]

Meanwhile, the League extended its ongoing efforts to bring market conditions, including the cost of its player-employees, under greater control by attempting to calibrate playing and scoring rules. By sponsoring rules modernizations, owners searched for the elusive grail of a profit-maximizing formula for gate increases with the least salary escalation. Club owners recognized that changes to speed up the game could make their product faster-paced and more appealing to more customers—unless they also seriously diluted offensive excitement. They also knew that pitchers constituted, at most, only two men out of each team's eleven-man roster, while the rest earned their reputations and salaries primarily through their batting performances. In turn, offense drew spectators but pushed up the statistical productivity figures, and thereby the salary expectations, of the nonpitching majority of ballplayer-employees. Accordingly, the league's bosses frequently tinkered with the rules, accelerating games and manipulating offensive productivity levels in a manner comparable to that of an industrial production line (see Appendix, Figs. 3 and 4). Between the 1879 and 1880 seasons, the National League reduced the number of balls for a walk from nine to eight, which speeded up games modestly but dropped batting averages by ten points in 1880. The following year, owners, wanting to generate more fan attendance through batting prowess, reversed the trend and boosted offense by ordering the pitching distance back from 45 to 50 feet. The action triggered a jump in runs scored and a fifteen-point upswing in batting averages.[21]

As the National League attempted to calibrate its rules and on-field productivity to bottom-line revenue and labor-cost realities, the lone threat to its hegemony for two years after the collapse of the Northwestern League in 1879 came from the Eastern Championship Association of 1881, a feeble six-team circuit, with three clubs in New York and one each in Brooklyn, Philadelphia, and Washington, that barely lasted a season. But William Hulbert's sudden death from a heart attack in April 1882 signaled the return of more turbulent times. Even before his passing, his favoritism to Chicago, his administration of the reserve and the moral crackdown, and his expulsion of franchises from not only Philadelphia and New York but also Cincinnati had left the National League vulnerable to outside challengers and player abandonment. Additionally, in St. Louis, following the Browns' desertion in 1877 in frustration over Hulbert's moral strictures, its NL successors had struggled both on and off the field. Louisville still smarted over being squeezed out in 1877 and over having had an 1881 game with Boston canceled because of its inadvertent hiring of an expelled NL player. Cincinnati, having been expelled in 1880 because of its insistence upon twenty-five-cent admissions and beer sales, still represented backers willing to do "anything to beat Boss Hulbert."

In each vulnerable market, viable challengers had begun to emerge. In St. Louis, the alliance entity known as the Reds had been its champion in 1877 but then affiliated with the International Association the next year. By 1879, a new Brown Stockings nine had been formed by amalgamating the old Browns and Reds. Providing a playing ground was the Sportsman's Park and Club Association, created at the end of 1880 and led by Alfred H. Spink and Christian Von der Ahe. Von der Ahe, a jovial German saloonkeeper and boardinghouse proprietor, owned the property adjacent to the park's Grand Avenue site. Spink, for his part, also urged the creation of a similar new Cincinnati Reds organization by O. P. Caylor, after efforts in the Queen City to form a new league with flexible admission rates had collapsed. In June 1881, backers in Cincinnati agreed upon the goal of either resecuring an NL franchise or heading a new association. The 1881 St. Louis and Cincinnati nines featured a challenge series, and other clubs in Dubuque, Chicago, Brooklyn, and Akron offered the basis for a league network. A crowd of 7,000 spectators at a Louisville-Akron match demonstrated its fan potential.

Parallel developments had transpired in the East. In New York, the Metropolitans had been created in 1880 and had spurned membership in other leagues in exchange for scheduling games with the National League as a member of its alliance. The Metropolitans played a 151-game season in 1881 (including 60 tilts with NL clubs, a respectable 18 of which it won), netting $30,000. Among several contenders in Philadelphia, the 1881 version of the Athletics had gone so far as to launch a major road trip to St. Louis, Louisville, and Cincinnati as a feasibility test of a new East-West circuit. Their manager, Horace B. Phillips, then instigated a meeting on October 10, 1881, in Pittsburgh to discuss a new league. Unfortunately, only one city's representatives showed up. A second try in Cincinnati on November 2 drew attendance from the host club, the Pittsburgh Alleghenies, and clubs in St. Louis, Louisville, and Brooklyn. The result was the creation of a new rival league, the American Association, with Pittsburgh's Harmer "Denny" McKnight its president.

With the new league dominated by four brewmasters—Von der Ahe, John Hauck, Harry Von der Horst, and John Park—and with the association vice-president an officer of the Kentucky Malting Company, NL partisans quickly ridiculed it as the "Beer and Whiskey Circuit." Along with the initial five clubs, the Philadelphia Athletics joined once they secured their own grounds. The New York Metropolitans understandably hesitated, given their many scheduled games with NL clubs and fear of retaliation, but eventually joined as well. Brooklyn soon fell out of the circuit and was replaced by a Baltimore entry of Von der Horst's. Clubs paid $65 for NL-style territorial rights, $50 in association dues, and $65-per-game guarantees to visiting teams except for games played on July 4 or state holidays, when teams split the gate receipts fifty-fifty. Franchises were subject to expulsion for nonfulfillment of schedules, defaulting on gate obligations or dues, using disqualified players or playing other squads that did, or disobeying association officials and rules. Despite its lower admissions fees and its countenancing of alcohol sales, the American Association asserted its upstanding character by barring pool selling and gambling on its grounds and refusing to accept NL players expelled for morals violations. On similar grounds, the association employed a permanent umpiring staff at higher pay than the National League—$140 a month plus $3 per diem for expenses—and attired them in police-style garb of blue caps and blue flannel coats.[22]

Among the differences between the new circuit and the National League—besides Sunday games, twenty-five-cent admissions, and beer—were the enticements to member clubs and players that association teams could play outside clubs and hold exhibitions on off-days and that released AA players could be signed immediately by another association club (with the player receiving two weeks' severance pay) rather than only after a waiting period. But in most respects the initial policies of the American Association indicated its leaders' preference for accommodation rather than conflict with the National League. Nonetheless, the simple existence of a new "major" league increased the number of well-paying opportunities for players and stepped up the pressure on NL payrolls, even if most AA teams were not direct NL market competitors. Paired with a combative NL attitude—reflecting Arthur Soden's position as acting league president—the "Troy-Wise incident" quickly soured interleague relations. In the 1881–82 off-season, infielders J. J. "Dasher" Troy and Sam Wise signed with association clubs, only to jump back to Detroit in the National League. Since both men had played briefly for Detroit in 1881, NL officials claimed that they had never ceased being that club's property, and they refused to return the players to the American Association. The new league at its 1882 spring meeting retaliated by reversing earlier policy and permitting admittance to the National League's expelled, suspended, or blacklisted players upon approval of their appeals by the association's board of directors. Cincinnati tried in a Boston court to have Wise enjoined from playing in the senior circuit, and then expelled him from the American Association when their effort failed. The Philadelphia Athletics did likewise to Troy.

In May the American Association extended hostilities by canceling interleague tilts effective as of the end of the 1882 schedule. McKnight also ordered cancellation of an 1882 postseason series planned between the two leagues' champions. Attempting to secure a larger player pool from NL raiding, and to use it as a lever on its own recalcitrant employees, the American Association even tried to form its own satellite alliance of clubs. It signed at least thirteen NL players and tried to ensure rosters for the next season by offering still more NL performers "optional agreements" with advances—a kind of "counter-reserve"—for 1883. Amid the new round of competitive bidding, players now sometimes signed with the American Association, collected their option bonuses, and then jumped back to the National League. Catcher Charlie Bennett of Detroit signed an "option" with Pittsburgh in August 1882 for a $100 bonus, pledging to sign an 1883 contract at $1,700 at season's end, only to return to Detroit. Pittsburgh sued but lost, with the court ruling that the American Association reserve was invalid because it inequitably bound Bennett to provide services to the club but did not bar the club from releasing him. The association hesitated to follow up on the implications of this legal reasoning in order to attack the National League's reserve clause, which was just as vulnerable on the "equitable obligation" standard, out of fear of full-scale NL raids on its teams. In the absence of that strategy, however, the American Association could only blacklist Bennett and other jumpers, without securing their services. The National League threatened any deserters to the new circuit with blacklisting, while reinstating ten previously banned players from 1881 in order to deny their availability to the association.[23]

Each league and each club found itself scrambling to reserve as many players as it could, while trying to close off their avenues of escape. Besides the "stick" of the blacklist, owners offered the "carrot" of bonuses and multiyear contract extensions at higher levels of pay. Accordingly, salary levels for both the present and the immediate future jumped sharply (see Appendix, Fig. 1). According to Spalding's 1889 public listing of selected players, the 1882 average salary, $1,375, leaped to $1,835 for 1883. Mike Kelly's pay bounced from $1,400 to $1,700. More remarkable still was the good fortune of star catcher William "Buck" Ewing, who had made but $10 a week as a teamster before entering baseball at a $1,000 salary in 1881. His pay soared from $1,200 in 1882 to $3,100 the following season. Such escalations prodded discussions of a pay scale among NL owners, but such a system could hardly be implemented during the trade war, risking as it would a flood of desertions to the American Association. Ewing's employer, the New York Giants—created to do battle with the American Association's new Metropolitans—claimed a $40,000 payroll and the label of baseball's "Gilt-Edged Team." Even Providence, a financially crippled NL franchise, found it necessary for competitive reasons to raise its salaries from $1,278.51 per man in 1882 to $1,446.66 in 1883. The interleague war was so pervasive that it forced a jump in NL umpiring pay, to $200 per month plus expenses, for the upcoming campaign.[24]

Although the National League as a whole was not yet ready to fold, its weaker clubs were. Other teams might desert as well if the war continued indefinitely. In order for its Philadelphia entry, the Phillies, to compete against its market rival, the National League had grudgingly exempted it from the fifty-cent admission standard. Notwithstanding this concession, the Phillies' attendance fell to under 1,000 per game in 1883. The Troy and Worcester franchises collapsed at the end of 1882, despite league bailouts that enabled each to finish its schedule. In contrast, the American Association seemed in healthier financial shape, with the Philadelphia Athletics' three owners claiming $200,000–300,000 and Von der Ahe's St. Louis club $70,000 (although both figures are probably exaggerated.) Key to the association's victories were its advantages in the major urban markets other than Chicago. The six AA cities contained populations half-again as large as the total of the National League's eight communities. The Cleveland *Leader* even claimed that five of the six AA franchises outdrew the National League's headliner club, Chicago.[25]

The replacement of Soden as NL president by A. G. Mills, a Spalding protégé, signaled the senior circuit's desire for peace talks. Helping the National League avoid a complete hat-in-hand posture was the reemergence of the Northwestern League in early 1883 and its petition for inclusion in the League Alliance. With the northwestern circuit extending the National League network's territorial reach, Mills had the necessary leverage to bargain on more equal terms with the American Association. He recommended formation of a three-man commission, with representation from the National League, Northwestern League, and American Association—he would represent the National League and head the commission—to renegotiate a new cartelization scheme for the industry in the form of an enlarged League Alliance, and organized a February 1883 "Harmony Conference" to that end. Mills urged that the three entities respect existing player contracts on all but eighteen disputed players, whose ownership would be determined by a joint arbitration panel. His new "National Agreement," or "Tripartite Pact," would also enlarge the reserve clause to cover eleven players per team—in effect, entire squads—across the member organizations. Recognizing the American Association's "major league" status, the National League would join it in guaranteeing a minimum player salary of $1,000 per year for those with continuous service and a $750 figure for players in the third league. To further entice the American Association into accepting his proposal, Mills warned AA representative Caylor of rumors of a possible Players Protective Association and of the "wreck of clubs" and "eleven-man rule" that continued war and accompanying player leverage would bring.[26]

On March 12, 1883, the American Association consented to the pact. Besides establishing the pattern of interleague recognition of clubs' reserve claims upon players, the new relationship provided for the purchase of non-NL/AA players from other National Agreement teams by the "major leagues" if the affected "minor league" club consented. Similarly, other kinds of player transfers, such as "assigning" a player to another club while retaining his ownership or reserve rights, could be transacted on the basis of "gentleman's agreements" between the affected owners. Because of the sensitivities shown to each club's operating rights, and the largely horizontal rather than vertical integration of interleague governance under the National Agreement, the pact proved better as a means of delineating claims to players among management "equals" than as a means of creating an efficient method for feeding playing talent up to the National League or American Association. Nonetheless, the accord constrained interleague player raiding and salary warfare. As a result, only two NL franchises, Detroit and Cleveland, lost money in 1883, while Buffalo broke even, and Chicago and Boston, at the top of the scale, made over $20,000 and $40,000 respectively.[27]

The National Agreement, although extending reserve rights to American Association clubs, did not require uniformity of playing rules. With an eye toward minimizing their future labor costs, therefore, profit-conscious NL owners adopted more changes designed to curb offense-generated salary pressures (see Appendix, Figs. 3 and 4). Following communications with American Association president McKnight after the 1883 season, Mills approved the legalization of overhand pitching in the National League, a move the circuit had inched toward by allowing sidearm deliveries the previous year. For its part, the American Association chose to maintain for another year the ban on overhand pitches. Along with reducing the number of pitches for a walk to six, the move to allow overhand pitching dropped NL batting averages in 1884 by .014, despite the elimination of one-bounce foul-catch outs. Strikeouts in the National League doubled. League clubs also expanded their rosters to allow for more pitchers (Detroit would carry four on its 1884 team), making it possible to replace a tired arm with a fresh one. At the same time, limiting pitchers' newfound statistical leverage, the errors category was expanded for them to include not just their fielding miscues but also walks, wild pitches, hit batters, and balks.[28]

Steps aimed at controlling expenses, such as the National Agreement and rules modifications, made sense in the short run to the battle-scarred National League. But they also risked further player dissatisfaction and fan boredom, which in turn would be likely to trigger a new round of trade wars with new sets of outside challengers. The fledgling cartel did not have long to wait for such an eventuality. A ten-team Eastern League emerged in 1884, although by season's end it shrank to but six. A greater threat was the announcement of the Union Association on September 12, 1883, in Pittsburgh. The mastermind of the new rival was Henry V. Lucas, a twenty-seven-year-old railroad millionaire whose older brother had been in charge of the St. Louis club expelled by the National League in 1877. Blocked from reentry to the National League by the fifty-cent admission policy, and from AA membership by Von der Ahe's Browns, Lucas also claimed to be motivated by his outrage at the "injustice" of the reserve clause. Although Lucas's mouthpiece, the St. Louis *Republican*, did urge the abolition of the reserve in 1883, the statements clearly were propaganda for disgruntled players' consumption. In marked contrast, the Union Association's secretary, William W. White, hinted to the NL/AA combination at the same time that if it accepted the new circuit at equal status, the Union Association itself would adopt the reserve clause.[29]

With claims of a $100,000 war chest, the Union Association announced plans to challenge its rivals directly in at least six cities—Baltimore, Boston, Philadelphia, Chicago, Cincinnati, and St. Louis. It also placed clubs in two other urban locations, Washington, D.C., and Altoona, Pennsylvania. Brewers Ellis Wainwright and Adolphus Busch backed Lucas's challenge to the American Association in St. Louis, while A. H. Henderson subsidized the Baltimore and Chicago entries. Pennsylvania Railroad executives sustained the Altoona club, and George Wright, whose Wright and Ditson Company had been shut out of the National League baseball-manufacturing market by Spalding, provided the new association's official ball and headed up the Bean Town franchise. In a rather ludicrous display of hypocrisy, the American Association retaliated by denouncing its new rival, the "Onion" league, as a haven for "lushers," "deadbeats," and "played-out bummers." Turning the other cheek only slightly, the Union Association announced that while it did not seek to raid NL/AA teams of players under current contract, it refused to recognize the reserve clause and intended to secure any unsigned-but-reserved talent for the 1884 season.[30]

Even if the National League and American Association had wanted to accommodate the new league, they could not have done so without destroying the National Agreement, for it barred the admission of new teams into existing NL/AA market territories. The American Association therefore announced that it would expel any member club that even played another entity found guilty of violating agreement turf. The National League did likewise, with one notable exception—allowing the new Eastern League to have one of its clubs, the Baltimore Monumentals, in AA territory as the cost of absorbing it into the cartel. In retaliation, the Union Association managed to sign about thirty National Agreement players, banned its clubs from games with agreement teams, charged twenty-five-cent admissions, and tried to create its own "reserve teams" to stockpile cheap replacement labor. But the "preserves," as the association's opponents ridiculed them, soon "melted away" during the season. NL and AA clubs turned up the pressure by deliberately scheduling games for July 4 in UA cities as a direct attendance challenge. League officials even urged the wealthy Spalding to field a second franchise in Chicago in order to crowd out a UA contender, and the American Association expanded from eight to twelve teams to confront the adversary directly.[31]

The main weapon in the NL/AA arsenal, however, was the threat of player blacklisting to dry up UA talent acquisition. In December 1883, two months after the Union Association's founding, the American Association had indicated that it would adopt the National League's blacklisting policy against jumpers to the new rival. At the same time, it indicated that jumpers who returned to their former clubs before March would not be penalized. After the expiration of the grace period, NL president Mills ordered the alliance's Arbitration Commission, empowered to hear its disciplinary cases, to deny all National Agreement rights to any club that violated members' claims under the reserve clause. Even players from disbanded teams still had to wait for ten days before signing with any new club, giving ample time for collusive agreements to be reached in order to prevent costly intracartel bidding for the players' services and block outside offers. Clubs also now enforced reserve claims upon players they did not even intend to use—as Buffalo did in the case of Charles Foley—effectively denying such players' services to the maverick league—and the players' right to choose their employers.

Rising player costs, and the National Agreement's lack of explicit legitimation of direct player sales or trades within the same league, also led NL owners to seek ways around the normal waiver procedures. In the case of pitcher Tony Mullane, whom the St. Louis Browns wanted to trade to Toledo, tripartite chief executive Mills ruled that a qualified release preventing other clubs from bidding for Mullane was not legal under the National Agreement. The Browns, however, could circulate a letter stating their intentions and on that basis secure voluntary pledges from all other clubs not to negotiate with the player. Mullane's subsequent transfer to Toledo represented a clear loss of his employment options. Complicating the issue further was the fact that he remained under UA injunction for having jumped from the Browns to its St. Louis entry (for $600 more in salary than Von der Ahe had offered) only to jump back after receiving an advance. The success of UA attorneys in securing a restraining order barring Mullane from playing in St. Louis necessitated the American Association trade to Toledo, at the same $2,500 pay. Following another injunction against Mullane in a Cincinnati court (eventually reversed in the U.S. Circuit Court), NL and AA owners secured for their respective "claim-jumpers" fictitious nonbaseball jobs in order to explain their revised salaries while protecting them from legal retaliation—a throwback to the old days of under-the-table professionalism. In response, the Union Association abandoned all pretense of respecting National Agreement teams' current contracts and began signing "actives" as well as "reservists" for the 1885 season.

Feeling the financial strains and the competitive pressures of a pennant race, clubs rode their charges hard in search of "an honest day's work for an honest day's pay." In Chicago, captain Anson fined two players $50 each for dissipation, on the grounds that it had reduced their skill. His boss Spalding, who had taken over the White Stockings after the death of Hulbert, went so far as to charge that a third of the failing clubs in 1884 owed their fate to player drunkenness. But despite their disciplinary problems and rising payrolls, owners refused to take a step that promised to ease their problems with labor supply and payroll cost—opening their leagues to blacks. Fear of player and spectator reaction, not concern over their employees' job security, guided their actions. Besides their own racial prejudices, officials were afraid that the spectacle of black ballplayers would drive fans to a rival circuit in droves, with the players either leading or following. White ballplayers, besides harboring their own racial biases, additionally saw the potential newcomers as job-threatening "scabs"; they might well have deserted in huge numbers any clubs that shattered the color line, particularly at a time when other teams beckoned. Black catcher Moses Fleetwood Walker, the Oberlin-educated son of a minister and physician, who was a semipro player in Cleveland, did sign on with the Toledo organization of the American Association in 1884, as did his brother Weldy, an outfielder. But the National League's biggest gate attraction, Chicago, refused to take the field against the Toledo team and its black performers on July 20. White Stockings captain Anson insultingly referred to them as "chocolate-covered coons." With Toledo's own newest acquisition, the Irishman Tony Mullane, similarly griping about the Walkers' presence on the team, the two were released.[32]

For white players, the war with the Union Association did force open additional avenues of higher-paying employment and career advancement that the reserve and the National Agreement otherwise had blocked. Some thirty UA players who had not previously played in the big leagues managed to stay on after the war with NL or AA teams, having proven their abilities. But the biggest impact was on salaries (see Appendix, Fig. 1). The war brought NL executives, and to only a slightly lesser extent their AA partners, the worst of baseball worlds: a game with less offense due to earlier rules tinkering and with "diluted" talent that turned off fans and lowered gate revenues, accompanied by unstable player loyalties and soaring salary costs. Again NL owners discussed imposition of a salary scale, only to recognize once more its impossibility in the midst of interleague competition for talent. Star players wangled pay advances and two-to-three-year contract guarantees at huge increases. Following the disciplinary suspension of pitcher Charlie Sweeney by Providence in July, teammate and fellow hurler Charles "Old Hoss" Radbourne, who had been offered $2,000 to jump to the Union Association, instead negotiated a promise of free agency after the 1884 season. In addition, Radbourne said that if his club would pay him Sweeney's salary in addition to his own for the days he filled in for his ex-teammate, he would pitch *every* game for the rest of the season. Al-

Moses Fleetwood Walker, catcher on Toledo's American Association club in 1883. The first African American to reach the big leagues, Walker was one of only a few of his race permitted briefly to penetrate that level of professional baseball in the 1880s.

though he did not manage to do that, Radbourne did win an incredible sixty games in carrying Providence to the National League flag. Sweeney, in turn, jumped to the Union Association's St. Louis Maroons.[33]

NL and AA payrolls alike inflated to what owners considered dangerous levels. Von der Ahe's payroll in 1884, driven upward by direct UA raiding, soared to a $3,850-per-player average. Spalding's later salary list indicated a $165 average jump from 1883 to 1884, when the average was $2,000, and a $310 increase for 1885. The National League's Cleveland franchise collapsed at the end of the 1884 season, despite Mills's secretly lining up other club executives to pay it a 50 percent share of road gate revenues instead of the customary 30 percent and securing players from the Northwestern League's defunct Grand Rapids team. Buffalo and even champion Providence almost shared Cleveland's fate. As early as August, Providence's owner urged Mills to consolidate the league's clubs by "freezing out" the smaller markets and including only teams in big cities. The American Association, which had added Brooklyn, Washington, Toledo, and Indianapolis franchises to battle the Union Association, found three of the new clubs financially destitute. In order to recoup, the American Association now agreed to a postseason five-game series between its champion and the National League winner, a move it had rejected a year earlier.[34]

The Northwestern League, given its inferior markets and resources, had been left even more crippled. Despite Mills's defeat of a scheme by some NL owners to remove the Northwestern League from the protection of the National Agreement and then help themselves to its players, all but two of its clubs folded anyway. Demonstrating the every-man-for-himself attitude commonly adopted by leagues and individual owners when faced with a battle for survival, the Northwestern League's own secretary, Samuel G. Morton, it was discovered, had funneled players to the Union Association through an employment brokerage agency. The hand of Albert Spalding could be seen clearly in the machinations, for Morton was employed as a clerk in his Chicago business office. Spalding apparently had determined that he would capitalize upon the war's opportunities to enrich himself further as a covert player agent, meanwhile weakening a Northwestern League that he saw as a greater direct rival to his Chicago franchise than the fading Union Association.

By the end of the 1884 season, the Union Association was indeed dying. From the start, the St. Louis club had been the only association franchise that possessed the necessary backing, and that fact soon had translated into extreme competitive imbalance on the field. The champion Maroons, with a 91-16 record, finished twenty-one games ahead of their nearest rival. The association as a whole dropped between $100,000 and $250,000, and even Lucas admitted to losing $17,000. The Altoona franchise had withdrawn barely six weeks into the season, replaced by a Kansas City club. The Chicago entry, driven out by Spalding, moved to Pittsburgh in August and St. Paul in September. The Philadelphia Keystones disbanded in August; their place was taken by Wilmington from the Eastern League, which was in turn replaced by Milwaukee a month later. Only five of eight original UA franchises made it through the season to the league's December meeting, while thirteen clubs altogether had claimed circuit membership at one time or another.

Desperate to save his own franchise even at the expense of the league, Lucas sought National Agreement recognition for his Maroons. In order to comply with agreement territorial rights, he offered Cleveland owners a $2,500 bid, with $500 up front, to purchase their market claim. Despite Lucas's belief that his purchase offer included rights to Cleveland's players, Brooklyn gobbled them up for itself, causing him to refuse payment on the balance owed the Cleveland ownership. Doubling the UA magnate's frustrations, Cleveland then sued for the remainder and won. Lucas did see his ownership application approved by the National League, however, on January 10, 1885. Five days later, with only Milwaukee and Kansas City delegates in attendance, the Union Association folded.[35]

The National League baseball cartel, through a combination of "strategic surrenders" and marketplace victories, had survived the early rounds of trade war, salary escalation, and player jumping. In the process it had succeeded in extending its territorial reach, its market share, and its workplace control over its on-field employees' conduct, productivity, and compensation. Now that "peace" had returned, financial retrenchment and contract crackdowns upon the player force would surely follow once again. The unanswered questions, however, remained how the players would respond to the inevitable economic siege to come and how effective whatever response they made would be. Would another outlaw circuit ride to their temporary rescue, or would they finally be able to forge a collective counterweight of their own?

FOUR

RETRENCHMENT AND REVOLT, 1885-1890

The Union Association war left the National League–American Association cartel drained, divided, and desperate to regain economic control over its sport and its players. The struggle had revealed and intensified a continuing every-man-for-himself rivalry between the two leagues and their owners that carried over into "peacetime." Actually, the clubs were in better shape than they realized. Although two crippled NL franchises, Buffalo and Providence, failed to last past the 1885 season, the deletion of these weak links arguably made the senior circuit stronger. The cartel's dominance of the populous northeastern quarter of the nation also remained essentially unchallenged. The Southern League—an unstable aggregation of clubs in the Carolinas, Alabama,

Georgia, Tennessee, and Louisiana—threatened neither the markets nor the salary structure of the National League or American Association, nor did two four-team western circuits, the California League and the California State League, both with three franchises in San Francisco alone. The Eastern League, never a serious danger anyway, had shrunk to but six clubs in upstate New York. Expansion into Canada in 1886, and readoption of the title International League, did not change its status.

Nevertheless, NL/AA owners lamented the burdens of their offices, and desperately sought, as did other "captains of industry," ways to increase the stability, predictability, and profitability of their individual franchises and the sport in general. At the same time they maintained a wary eye on real or potential competitors, whether within their clubs' stockholders, their league, or the industry. In Boston, Arthur Soden headed a three-man executive team that voted itself $2,500 salaries but refused seventeen other major stockholders the courtesy of a financial report. As the largest investors, they mandated that directors' voting strength be based upon the number of shares held, rather than on a one-man, one-vote basis. With club boards of directors often mere window dressing, Soden and other "owners" of baseball franchises independently hired and fired field managers as well as players. According to *Sporting Life*'s Francis Richter, by 1886 only one "gentleman-sponsor" remained as the guiding hand of an NL club; all the other clubs were operated by tight-fisted entrepreneurs preoccupied with the bottom line.

In the aftermath of the Union Association war, club owners' actions in the 1880s reflected, borrowing the description of historian Robert Wiebe for the larger economic setting, a "search for order" in the baseball industry. What the operators of the National League and the American Association desperately wanted was a stable market monopoly free of outside challengers who would create pressures on attendance and labor costs. But given the continuing growth in the number and population of urban markets, trade wars were unlikely to end anytime soon. Such struggles escalated salaries and undermined clubs' abilities even to hold on to their talent, much less to control it. While trade war raged, owners could not enforce their controls without driving players into enemy camps and alienating fans. These costly realities of wartime, in turn, placed an even greater premium upon imposing a still more restrictive regime upon labor as soon as peace, however temporarily, was restored. The result was a roller coaster ride of relaxation and retrenchment in labor rights and wages that reflected the boom-and-bust nature of both the baseball industry and the national economy in the Gilded Age.[1]

A pattern of erratic growth, cutthroat competition for markets and labor, and volatility in wages and job security was all too commonplace throughout American business. But as a high-skill, labor-intensive entertainment industry, baseball could not resort to one of the favorite strategies of the era's industrialists to hold down costs and erode the collective solidarity and potential clout of its workers. In many other industries, management-directed investments in new plants, equipment, and production processes reduced the premium upon skilled labor and permitted the flooding of the labor market with less skilled and more ethnically and racially heterogeneous immigrant and rural-migrant workers. But baseball's drama of athleticism could not be performed by machines, and any measures to water down the skill levels required of professional ballplayers would dilute the product itself and threaten to drive away its paying spectators. No wonder, then, that viewed from the owners' perspectives, the marketplace pressures were enormous and their tools to control them inadequate. Even the most powerful among them, Albert Spalding, echoed the self-pitying laments of Carnegie and Rockefeller when he complained of the "man-killing experiences" of his position and "a pace that kills."[2]

Few if any of the owners of the National League and American Association, however, were inclined to sacrifice individual advantages in order to lessen the collective competitive pressures upon themselves. As one example, with the two leagues having avoided overlapping franchise rights at the end of the Union Association war in all markets save Philadelphia and New York, neither now wanted to relax such territorial barriers upon the other. The American Association's Von der Ahe, having just defeated his adversary in the St. Louis market, insisted upon compensation from Henry Lucas before allowing his admission into the National League. National League owners, however, pressed for such acceptance and claimed that the American Association itself had violated National Agreement rules. The American Association's Brooklyn club had circumvented the ten-day wait for open competition on released players by hiding the talent of the defunct Cleveland team from other potential suitors and then signing them en masse for 1885. Von der Ahe eventually yielded to NL pressure to admit Lucas into the cartel, but only after Spalding promised to permit a new AA club in Chicago if business "emergency" required it (a pledge the National League did not fulfill).

Albert Spalding, longtime Chicago White Stockings executive and dominant financial presence in NL management for a quarter of a century

An even bigger issue of contention between the victorious leagues, however, was the disposition of players who had jumped to the Union Association and subsequently been blacklisted by the National League and the American Association. Lucas, wishing to stock his team and still pay tribute to his "lost cause," urged the lifting of all such expulsions. Outside unionists agreed, claiming that the blacklistees were but "workingmen kept out of employment by a body of capitalists." Over AA grumbling, the National League in April 1885 removed nine players from the ineligible list, substituting $500–1,000 fines as punishments. Association resentment deepened when John B. Day, major owner in both the AA and NL franchises in New York, shuffled two stars from the Metropolitans to the Giants. Needing to maintain a club in that major market, the American Association fined, but could not expel, its disobedient child. With clubs in both leagues, emboldened by Brooklyn's action, ignoring the ten-day period and seeking covertly to beat out rivals in gaining the services of released "war veterans," NL and AA officials sought to restore some order by hammering out a new National Agreement at a joint meeting in Saratoga, New York, in August. Under its proposed terms, only clubs in the same circuit as a player's former team could contact him in the first ten days after his release. After that period, any signatory club could approach him. In turn, in order to hamper talent raiding that could compromise the integrity of pennant races, no club in 1886 would be permitted to make an in-season offer to a player for the following year until October 20. As a capstone of reasserted faith in each other's intentions, the two leagues also agreed to restore postseason championship competition, and the American Association restored the standing of its blacklisted players.[3]

The National League and American Association did not release their new pact to the public until October 1885, in order to allow each league time to set up its own procedures for player releases and club approaches under the ten-day rule. The American Association opted for a system in which the player could indicate which new team he wanted to join. If he did not choose one, the league secretary would assign him to the club that submitted a written desire for his services. If more than one team wished to secure him, the league representatives from the uninvolved clubs would assign him by their vote, and if the player then refused to report to his assigned club, he would be blacklisted. The National League's plan was quite similar, except that if more than one club expressed interest in the released man, the league secretary rather than club representatives assigned him to one of the bidders by lot.

That the new provisions did not eliminate tangled and contentious competition for player services was illustrated by the strange case of infielder Sam Barkley of the St. Louis Browns. With Barkley wanting to be traded, and both Baltimore and Pittsburgh AA teams interested in him, he verbally committed to Pittsburgh only to sign a personal services agreement with Baltimore. But when the latter's purchase money did not reach Browns owner Von der Ahe promptly enough, "der Boss" (as he was dubbed by players and the press) accepted a counterbid from Pittsburgh and released Barkley to them. Responding to the predictable appeal from the franchise scorned, the American Association board of directors fined Barkley $100 and suspended him for the 1886 season but allowed his new club to retain his rights. The league president, Denny McKnight of Pittsburgh, thought even that penalty too severe but was overruled 5-2 by his fellow owners, with St. Louis wisely abstaining. Barkley then sued to overturn his fine and suspension, which forced the American Association to "adjust" its ruling by raising his fine to $500 (which the Pittsburgh club paid) but lifting his suspension and awarding a substitute player to Baltimore. On the heels of the controversy, owners ousted McKnight as AA president in favor of Wheeler Wikoff of Columbus, only to have the Pittsburgh owner move his franchise into the National League after the 1886 season.[4]

When they turned to address their labor problem, owners resorted to means they had initiated in the past decade to control worker mobility and cost, including expansion of the reserve clause, blacklisting to deter player jumping and interclub bidding, and direct efforts at salary restraint. Under the new National Agreement, NL and AA clubs expanded the reserve clause to cover twelve players per team instead of eleven. Even if a player held out during his reserve year rather than sign a new contract, the club maintained that the binding clause merely "rolled over" in perpetual fashion. Thomas "Pat" Deasley, who had signed an 1884 contract during the Union Association war on condition he would not be reserved for 1885, found that his St. Louis employer exercised the contract's power anyway. Other AA clubs cooperated in the double-dealing, refusing to extend or entertain offers for his services. More commonplace, however, were attempts by owners in 1885–86 to renege on salary commitments and unilaterally seek cuts, efforts hampered by their prior willingness to extend multiyear deals during the war to ward off roster raids (see Appendix, Fig. 1). At the same Saratoga meeting that adopted the new National Agreement, owners proposed salary limits of $2,000 per player, and these were ratified in October.

Under the new salary cap for individual performers, owners pledged to deny bonuses over and above regular pay except for necessary travel expenses. *Sporting Life* defended the fairness of the move by asserting that only one out of every six NL/AA players would be affected by the limit and insisted that the restraining effect on future salaries would protect the viability of smaller-market clubs and player jobs. The magazine added that if the players did not like it, they were free to seek "other lines of work." It was, in fact, future cost containment rather than immediate slashing that the owners realistically sought. For the sake of current team harmony and immediate pennant chances, they proved hesitant to apply the cap and the prohibition on incentive bonuses to their veteran stars. Mike Kelly, for example, purportedly received a $3,000 bonus above the salary cap merely for posing for his picture. According to baseball authority Harold Seymour, the official Cincinnati payroll in the mid-1880s ranged from $500 to $2,000 per player, averaging $1,620. But a *Sporting News* report in 1886 claimed that Von der Ahe's St. Louis roster included three outfielders at $1,800 each, four infielders at $2,000 apiece, and two pitchers and two catchers who were each getting $2,200. First baseman and field captain Charles Comiskey also received the latter sum, plus an extra $500. Using Spalding's selective, retrospective lists, the salary average, which jumped an average of $310 per player in 1885, rose a more modest $170 to $2,480 in 1886 and declined the following season.[5]

Clubs usually preferred not to unload their stars if their presence paid dividends in championships and higher gate receipts. But if the expected return did not follow, owners could and did sell them off, or worse. Given widespread winking at official salary caps, it was such sales that most reminded veteran stars of their chattel-like status, particularly since they were not assured of receiving any of the money their sales generated for their former owners. During the 1885 race, Buffalo, unsuccessfully trying to stay solvent, sold its "Big Four"—Dan Brouthers, Deacon White, Jack Rowe, and Hardie Richardson—to Detroit and its ambitious new owner, Frederick Kimball Stearns, for $7,000. Not content with that transaction alone, Stearns spent a total of $25,000 on Indianapolis and Buffalo players in an effort to buy Detroit a winner. When NL secretary Nicholas Young barred the "Big Four" from Detroit's use for the rest of the 1885 season, they merely re-signed with their new team for 1886, successfully arguing that they constituted released players who could commit to any club they chose after a ten-day hiatus. Franchises that already anticipated foreclosure, such as Providence in 1885, found it in their interest not to declare dissolution until after selling their entire rosters to the highest bidder—in the Grays' instance, nearby Boston.[6]

Even in the case of successful owners, personal pique could trigger player auctions. Frustrated at the loss of his White Stockings to Von der Ahe's Browns in the 1886 postseason series, Spalding blamed the defeat on the intemperance of his stars, especially Mike Kelly, despite his extension of a $350 "abstinence" bonus. Weary as well of the daily grind of club affairs, he denied his team train fare back to the Windy City and then sold Kelly to Boston for the incredible sum of $10,000. Kelly at least did not suffer from the sale, receiving an increase in direct playing salary to $5,000 and his new team's captaincy. Far worse was the treatment extended to Browns player Harry Overbeck. After having sacrificed his eligibility in the Northwestern League by jumping from its Peoria club to St. Louis in the American Association, he was released by Von der Ahe after only a few games, leaving him clubless and salaryless. Overbeck did succeed in claiming $400 in salary from the Browns, but only after taking Von der Ahe to court. With club owners demonstrating no particular loyalty to their employees, even in the absence of the level of interclub bidding that had characterized the early 1880s, only two long-term veterans in the National League in 1887 possessed continuous records of service with a single club.[7]

An underexploited method of wage control available to the owners was the improvement and expansion of methods of acquiring and training new talent. Efforts in this direction would entail additional costs, of course, but, if successful, could expand the pool of skilled players and thereby reduce their average cost. However, many clubs' limited resources, the immediate rush to recoup past losses, and owners' short-term outlook combined to make new player procurement an area of lost opportunities. The Chicago White Stockings, given Spalding's ample funds and his earlier forays into the player agent business, not surprisingly led the way in planting agent-scouts in other communities. Spalding's edge also helped explain his willingness to auction off veterans after 1886. Nonetheless, the *Sporting News*'s urgings to other NL and AA clubs to employ "judges" to assess "minor league" talent fell upon deaf ears, as did the suggestion that franchises establish baseball training schools. Instead, clubs continued haphazardly to secure young players from area semipro teams or lesser professional nines in the Northeast and Midwest, from sandlots and tryouts, or from a growing number of college teams, based often upon word of mouth from self-proclaimed "touts" to the nearest field manager.[8]

In such recruitment, the established lines of ethnic and racial acceptance and prohibition changed little. The owners' recalcitrance illustrated the other half of the player value equation—the need for the player force to present an appealing visual product to a "respectable" white spectatorship. Management did not wish to risk additional player unrest on existing team rosters, or alienate middle-class fans, by opening the gates of participation further. That superb additional talent existed in one particular source was demonstrated by the rising numbers of African American ballplayers on segregated nines or sprinkled on obscure semipro and professional clubs. In 1885, a group of Long Island waiter/ballplayers formed the Cuban Giants, an independent club consisting entirely of American-born blacks but named so as not to invite dramatic attention and white retaliation. Other black clubs, including the Orions in Philadelphia and the St. Louis Black Stockings, predated the Long Island team. By 1886, black teams in New Orleans and five other cities created the Southern League of Colored Baseballists, only to fold soon afterward. Unable to offer wages remotely comparable to those in the National League or American Association, or to maintain a fixed schedule of games, the Cuban Giants' pay scale ranged from $12 a week for outfielders to $15 for infielders and $18 for each member of the battery. Following their creation, the Giants performed against other black teams in New York, such as the Gothams, as well as white college and semipro clubs and even NL nines. Cooperstown-born Bud Fowler (whose birth name was John Jackson) penetrated white professional baseball eight times with seven different franchises, and *Sporting Life* in 1885 admitted that only his race kept him from a major league career. Fleet Walker, having been driven out of the American Association in 1884, signed on briefly with Waterbury in the Eastern League in 1886, and another African American player, left-handed pitcher George Stovey, dominated that circuit in the late 1880s with Jersey City.[9]

Rather than permit racial diversity within their playing force, however, owners instead attempted to upgrade its image and, they assumed, its "responsibleness" through a more conscious recruitment of "college boys" as players. They found, however, that while such workers might present a more gentlemanly image to the public, their greater education and higher socioeconomic status often made them actually less tolerant of, and more openly militant against, denials of their basic employment freedoms. Management preoccupation with control over their charges and with spectator response to the product they offered also led to renewed vigilance in the policing of player conduct after the Union Association's demise. What management could not enforce during a trade war, for fear of driving labor into the enemy camp, could be pressed in its aftermath. Both trends related directly to the quality of play on the field and the perceived relationship between that play and the ethnocultural composition of the player force. Writers decried rising on-field violence and lack of sportsmanship, including the deliberate cutting, switching, or icing down of balls, faking of injuries, and spiking or tripping of runners. Most notorious were Von der Ahe's St. Louis Browns, a collection of "plug uglies" that included third baseman, coach, and champion heckler Arlie Latham. Latham, who had been sued by his second wife for divorce on grounds of assault, desertion, infidelity, and perversion, "jockeyed" enemy catchers nearly as sadistically, forcing the National League and American Association to adopt fixed coaching lines by 1887.

Consistent with the patterns of the past, few players were actually foreign-born save for a handful from Canada. But the influx of players of German and especially Irish descent, with their reputedly less "temperate" lifestyles, continued in the second half of the 1880s at a rate only slightly lower than that of the previous ten years (see Appendix, Fig. 2). Using Lee Allen's data as a rough guide, of 65 identifiable entrants into the majors from 1885 through 1890, men of Irish extraction made up 36 percent of the pool, while 31 percent were non-Irish British Isles descendants, and 24 percent claimed Germanic heritage. A modest introduction of French (7 percent) and Swedish (2 percent) players brought about a slight drop in the other groups' shares, but did not fundamentally alter the ethnic character and identity of the player force. Clubs accordingly mandated more vigorous spring training in sweaty climes such as Hot Springs, Arkansas, not merely to hone skills, but to "boil out" an off-season of intemperance and lechery and reestablish a regimen of discipline before the season's start. Owners cracked down on off-field conduct, fined players for losing equipment, and attributed their performance lapses to pregame lushery, whether provable or not. Following a nighttime escapade that management blamed for five errors the next day, John "Moose" Farrell, for example, received a $200 fine.[10]

As in so many aspects of baseball labor control in the 1880s, the Chicago White Stockings led the way in moral crackdowns upon players. In 1886 Spalding urged National League clubs en masse to hire a detective agency to shadow players and submit weekly reports to the league secretary. As for his own team, he ordered a "bone-dry" oath administered on the premises of his sporting goods store by field manager Cap Anson to all his players. As noted earlier, the sales of star Mike Kelly and teammate Jim McCormick resulted directly from the owner's conviction that their and other players' failure to uphold NL prestige in losing to the American Association Browns stemmed from their dissipation. Spalding retained his own private detective to trail White Stockings players both at home and on the road and threatened miscreants with fines of $100 per incident and nightly bed checks. When his exertions led to the catching of seven violators, the sheepish players suggested their own punishments of $25 fines per person, enough to pay the investigator's $175 retainer to the club. Unfortunately, Spalding could not always count upon even the self-disciplined behavior of his immediate disciplinary arm, Anson. Fined on several past occasions for arguing with umpires and for other forms of unruly behavior, the Chicago captain found himself levied $110 for an especially egregious on-field lapse in 1886.[11]

The responsibilities of umpires, and their controversial profile in the eyes of players and spectators alike, grew in accordance with management efforts to control player conduct. Arbiters found players increasingly contemptuous of them as "moral persecutors," as tools of management authority, as incompetents, and as "crooked cops." The level of corruption among umpires is impossible to measure with any accuracy, but it is probably fair to attribute many of their on-field lapses not to corruption but to the owners' constant shifting of playing rules, with its attendant confusion, and to the unrealistic demand that a single umpire accurately call an entire game. The National League took a three-umpire system under advisement in 1885 and experimented with it in the postseason series with the American Association champion that year, but owners refused to retain it, again probably for reasons of cost. By 1887, umpire Benjamin F. Young drew up a proposed code of ethics for his profession and a ten-point plan to elevate his colleagues' status within and outside the sport. But Young tragically died in a railroad accident en route to a game, and his recommendations seemingly expired with him. With the one-umpire-per-contest standard retained until the 1890s, overburdened arbiters also had to contend with paying their own expenses above a small per diem travel fare and purchasing and maintaining their own uniforms.

The owners' preoccupation in mid-decade with restoring profitability through a retrenchment in labor policies also extended to frequent changes in the player's "work rules" that manipulated his performance measures and therefore his salary expectations (see Appendix, Figs. 3 and 4). Owners solicited input from on-field participants, spectators, and sportswriters, but they zealously retained final decision-making power over rules changes. As for equipment controls, Spalding's dominance of the industry guaranteed the unchallenged retention of the dead ball. Club management encouraged, and writers parroted, spectator appreciation for players who exhibited self-effacing "teamwork" rather than a preoccupation with "record batting." Nonetheless, team owners did not reward such player statistical sacrifices at salary time. Hampered in their control of individual offensive production figures by playing grounds with unusual and sometimes tiny dimensions—often determined by the cost and availability of inner-city real estate lots—NL owners adopted a rule that a ball hit over a fence fewer than 210 feet from home plate constituted a double rather than a home run. Legalizing flat bats in 1885 encouraged placement over power, and pitchers received new incentives in the form of statistics that counted as assists their strikeouts as well as their fielding throws to the bases. Fearful that retention of the ban on overhand pitching would create performance and salary disparities with the National League and hand it a cost reduction advantage, the American Association lifted its prohibition only a year after the National League had done so. Wishing to ensure future uniformity of playing and scoring rules, and thereby foreclose an avenue by which their uneasy partnership could degenerate into a destructive salary war, the two leagues created a joint rules committee in November 1886. Three owners from each circuit constituted the panel, which then drafted a common code. Continuing on as a playing rules committee, the group, following consultation with three selected team captains from each league (but no players), could adopt changes by majority vote during each off-season.[12]

That the owners gained immediate financial benefit from their assertion of wide-ranging controls upon their players' livelihoods and incomes is incontrovertible. Despite 1885 being a weak season for many clubs because of the legacy of debts from the Union Association war and salary obligations, crowds occasionally rose to 10,000 and more. The National League's Philadelphia Phillies, who had drawn barely 100,000 in 1884, doubled profits to $13,000 in increasing attendance to over 150,000 in 1885, and they attracted still another 25,000 fans beyond that the next season. The top three NL franchises—Chicago, Boston, and New York—probably earned a cumulative profit of $100,000 in 1886, a good year for all the clubs. Regular-season ticket sales were supplemented by a broadening array of additional revenue sources. The 1885 interleague championship series netted the two participating clubs only $1,000 total, but by the next year Von der Ahe's Browns alone garnered $13,000. Keeping nearly $7,000 for himself, der Boss then allocated $580 each to his victorious players. In the American Association, of course, the major supplementary source of income was alcohol sales, which Von der Ahe attempted to maximize by hiring nonunion bartenders and waiters. Outside vendors of other concessions—from peanuts, sandwiches, and pies to soda water and gum—bid for and paid fees to clubs for exclusive rights. Cincinnati charged a $1,000 rights fee for its scorecard concession. Telegraph companies provided yet another source of income for clubs, paying fees and offering free service to franchises in exchange for the right to transmit game information to saloons and pool halls in the days before radio. Western Union, for example, paid Cincinnati $100 for its contract and threw in free telegraph service for the club. Only two years removed from the greatest threats to their security to date, NL clubs now could afford some "insurance" in the form of a common sinking fund, to which each club contributed $5,000 in $1,000 installments.[13]

But if the NL/AA cartel benefited from its renewed regimen of control, the player bore the burden of the industry's search for order. The fear of lost employment due to sickness or injury was the harsh reality behind such improvements as chest protectors for catchers, sliding pads underneath uniforms, and the wider use of masks and fingered—though usually still not padded—gloves. Playing rules barred in-game substitutions except when "serious" impairment occurred, with the opposing team empowered to determine whether impairment was serious. A near-riot ensued in 1885 during a game between the Chicago and Philadelphia NL clubs when the White Stockings refused permission for the opposing team to replace a catcher who had suffered a broken finger. The newly legalized overhand delivery brought increased abuse of pitchers' arms and heightened the risk of serious, permanent injury, a situation further aggravated by the fact that most teams still carried but two pitchers on their roster. Management was not, however, very sympathetic to pitchers' plight. In response to complaints, former pitcher Spalding accused one of his unhappy hurlers of being a "little sniveler."[14]

The rapid proliferation of management abuses pushed players together in search of relief. Ironically, the owners' own unwillingness to expand the racial base of professional ballplaying, partly out of fear of provoking white employee unrest, helped preserve a greater homogeneity and solidarity within the player fraternity. Aiding player unity as well was the failure of owners to invest in systems of youth training so as to more rapidly generate skilled players from other, non–Western European backgrounds. Despite the frictions that existed between ballplayers of English, Irish, and German heritage, the player ranks were far more unified than those of many other industries with a more diverse ethnic distribution of workers. In other fields, industrial employers, enabled by mechanization, already had begun to absorb into their work forces untrained first-generation immigrants from Southern and Eastern Europe as well as native-born migrants. Ballplayers were also much more alike in their universal claim to high skill levels, in contrast to other work forces sharply divided between ranks of skilled craftsmen, machine tenders, and manual laborers. The playing fraternity, in contrast, shared a collective pride in its unique abilities and an accompanying expectation of greater rights and compensation as elite artisans.

As early as 1880, in the retrenchment that had followed the demise of the International Association, the New York *Mercury* had urged the National League's players to "rise up in their manhood and rebel." Five years later, a Philadelphia sportswriter, William H. Voltz, tried but failed to establish a protective association with a benefit fund for sick and needy players. The key figure in the creation of baseball's first serious player union was a veteran on the New York Giants, John Montgomery "Monte" Ward. Born in Bellefonte, Pennsylvania, in 1860, Ward attended Pennsylvania State University as a teen, only to leave for a baseball pitching career in 1875. By 1879, hurling for the Providence Grays, he led the National League in wins and winning percentage with a 44-18 mark. Compiling a 158-102 record over seven seasons, he was even credited by some with the idea of the raised pitching mound to gain extra leverage against hitters. After the 1882 season Ward was sold to New York, where arm trouble forced him to make the transition from pitcher to shortstop. He flourished at this position too, amassing 111 stolen bases in 1887 and 2,123 career hits. Although writers commented upon the "Irishness" of his appearance, Ward was actually descended from English and Scottish ancestors who had come to the Keystone State in the 1850s.[15]

In many ways Ward exemplified the owners' professed desire for players of intellect, grace, and refinement. He spoke five languages and earned bachelor's degrees in law and political science from Columbia College in 1885 and 1886. But in club management's eyes he was also literally a "clubhouse lawyer," with an aristocratic bearing and a rebellious habit of reporting late to spring training. As early as February 14, 1885, he had written the New York *Clipper* criticizing the reserve clause, questioning its legality with keener insight than the typical player and concluding that not legal logic, but only the "intimidating effect" of the blacklist, held it up. Other players also viewed abuses of the reserve clause with anger, remembering how Boston had kept outfielder Charley

John Montgomery Ward, leader of the Brotherhood of Professional Base Ball Players of the late 1880s

Jones out of action for two years rather than hand over $378 of back pay. Friends and teammates had been forced to stage a benefit game to help him make ends meet until he finally resumed his career with Cincinnati. Capitalizing on player frustration, Ward and eight teammates, including Buck Ewing and Tim Keefe, formed a local of the new Brotherhood of Professional Base Ball Players in New York on October 22, 1885. Within a year, the association privately claimed 107 members but still had not publicly announced its existence out of fear of owner retaliation. But since chapters were established in every NL city and there were 30 or more members in the American Association, the secret could not be kept for long. With owners well aware of the brotherhood's existence by the end of the 1886 season, the players' union gave the official story of its creation to *Sporting Life*'s sympathetic editor, Francis Richter.[16]

Surprisingly, the owners' initial response to the brotherhood proved moderate. Among the reasons may have been the optimism generated by 1886 profits, the semiretirement of the ever-vigilant Spalding, and the belief that the new union could be killed, or at least co-opted, with kindness. Although NL president Nick Young refused immediate recognition, owners indicated a willingness to meet with Ward and some of his partners. A players' committee, including Ward, Ned Hanlon, and Dan Brouthers, with Arthur Irwin (credited with having introduced the padded fielder's glove) as an alternate, convened with management; they requested inclusion of complete and accurate salary figures in contracts, as well as guarantees against salary cuts for reserved players. The owners balked, as expected, since putting complete pay figures in writing would have openly revealed their own violations of the 1885 limit agreement and facilitated players' comparisons of their relative compensation.

On other issues, however, the two sides cooperated in a number of tradeoffs. At the players' urging, to underscore the importance of open covenants, the reserve clause became a formal part of written contracts. The players also received the concession that as formal parties to such contracts, they were entitled to ten days' notice before being reserved by a club. Rosters were increased, raising the number of major league jobs, as was the number of reserved players per club, to fourteen. In exchange for greater recognition in management councils, the brotherhood pledged to assist in the moral policing of its members in matters of gambling, drinking, and dishonesty. Ward would later endorse a graduated fine system for dissipation, escalating with each offense from $25 to $100 to expulsion. Perhaps overenthusiastically hailing Ward's exchange of player cooperation for owner respect, the *Sporting News* proclaimed him "the St. George of baseball, for he has slain the dragon of oppression."[17]

Ward's views, however, did not always reflect the sentiments or the priorities of all big league ballplayers. From his perspective as a veteran, he focused attention primarily upon continuing abuses of reserved players and demands that star players receive a share of their purchase prices when sold from one owner to another. Illustrating the brotherhood's greater concern with the issue of labor freedom of movement—of more immediate interest to highly rated veterans—than with base-level salaries, Ward authored an article in the August 1887 issue of *Lippincott's* entitled "Is the Ballplayer a Chattel?," which compared the reserve clause to antebellum fugitive slave laws. Ward's perspective also embodied an attitude not uncommon among the Knights of Labor, the Farmers' Alliance, and other labor aggregations of the era, in that he held a romantic, somewhat nostalgic, view of players as members of a producer class of yeomen and artisans whose control over their livelihoods had been seized by nonproductive, capital-manipulating moguls. Let the players reclaim their rights as proud, independent workingmen, he believed, and the economic rewards would inevitably flow to those who earned them through their honest toil.[18]

Like that of the Knights of Labor, the nostalgic "reform unionism" of the brotherhood stemmed at least in part from its higher proportion of "traditional" workers from "old" immigrant, Western European backgrounds. Accordingly, its "respectable" membership sought the restoration of each individual's economic rights and functional control over his work life and geographic mobility—the fulfillment of a "free labor" ideology—rather than a role as a collective bargaining instrument for incremental material gains within a management-administered wage-labor system. Following the brotherhood's principles, Ward did manage to secure isolated victories for particular players. He persuaded Washington owner John Gaffney, who previously had fined a player for missing a game because of his wedding, to give $100 in restitution to Cliff Carroll for having stopped a check while trying to impose a new contract at lower pay.

Ward's own belief in the free labor solidarity of ballplayers extended to blacks such as pitcher George Stovey, for whom he tried to arrange a contract with the New York Giants, but many of his colleagues objected, seeing blacks as inferior and as threats to their job security. Chicago and

Cap Anson refused to play a Newark exhibition against an International League team that included Stovey and Fleet Walker. Of an estimated ten African American players on integrated teams in 1887, seven performed in the International League. But even there, Buffalo teammates refused to have their picture taken with Frank Grant, a second baseman so skilled scribes dubbed him the "Black Dunlop" in comparison to NL star Fred Dunlop. Rather than risk integration of their leagues, the National League and American Association in 1887 extended separate sanction to the League of Colored Base Ball Clubs, with teams in New York, Philadelphia, Boston, Cincinnati, and other cities. But the Jim Crow organization folded within a month, and in mid-season the International League began phasing out black players by barring new African American entrants. By the start of 1888, only three blacks remained in the circuit.

Confident of their controls over player movement through the enlarged reserve, and buoyed by the profits of 1886, owners opted to relax restraints upon offense in order to boost attendance (see Appendix, Figs. 3 and 4). A "strike zone" replaced the system of batter requests for pitch locations; but walks now counted statistically as hits, the number of balls for a walk was reduced from seven to five, and strikes for an out were raised to four. The National League and American Association also prohibited pitchers from running up to gather momentum (as they could in cricket), and a hit batsman, so long as he had not deliberately let the pitch strike him, now received first base. Especially because of the "walk-as-hit" change, batting averages soared. Of thirteen players who batted .400 during the 1880s, eleven accomplished the feat in 1887, including Boston's James "Tip" O'Neill, whose average was .492. Batting averages jumped twenty-five points overall in the NL/AA cartel, .18 in the National League, and .30 in the American Association. Runs per game leaped by .89, and NL pennant winner Detroit averaged a .343 batting figure. To ease the statistical pain upon pitchers and catchers, owners had removed the rule charging errors to hurlers for walks, wild pitches, hit batters, and balks and to catchers for passed balls. But that also meant higher earned run averages, which climbed .79 that season.[19]

After but a single season, however, owners concluded that they had relaxed the reins too much. Even before the 1887 campaign, Detroit's Stearns, who had accumulated a very expensive payroll and had sold but 600 season tickets, complained about the National League's decision to institute a $125 gate guarantee to road teams instead of a percentage split. Despite winning the pennant, the Detroit franchise lost money.

Renewed difficulties for NL and AA clubs sharing the same markets caused the National League to lift the fifty-cent admission requirement in those markets, and Pittsburgh and Washington offered special discount fees admitting three fans for $1.00. Operating expenses continued to climb. For Cincinnati, one road trip alone cost nearly $1,200 in such charges as railroad and local transportation, hotels, and meals. More ominous still was the escalating pressure upon salaries. While the "cheapest" Southern League franchise, New Orleans, paid out $1,740 a month in team salaries, or about $1,000 per player over the course of the season, the American Association's Von der Ahe lamented that his circuit's top three pitchers already demanded $9,000 for the next season. Frustrated at his team's "world series" defeat by Detroit (10-5, in a series expanded to generate more money), the Browns boss kept the entire $12,000 left over after $24,000 in expenses and refused to give any of it as shares to his ballplayers. In the off-season, Von der Ahe sold three lesser players and then unloaded star pitchers Bob Caruthers and Dave Foutz to Brooklyn for $13,500. When the spring of 1888 began with holdouts and the refusal of his nine to play an exhibition against the Cuban Giants, the owner blamed greed and sheer cursedness rather than "honest prejudice" for their acts.[20]

The salary storm unleashed by the owners' rules relaxations hit with full fury by 1888 (see Appendix, Fig. 1). Adding to the wage climb were the huge increases extended to veterans publicly identified with the Brotherhood of Professional Base Ball Players. The pattern demonstrated either the owners' fears of the union or their hopes of co-opting its leaders through financial generosity. Whatever the motivation, Ward's pay rose $1,000 (to $4,000), and that of his teammate and brotherhood secretary Tim Keefe went up by the same amount. Buck Ewing's salary climbed another $1,000, up to $4,500, and Ned Hanlon's went up $700 to $2,800. Fred Dunlop, another member of the high-priced and well-unionized Giants, received a $2,500 increase to $7,000. Using Spalding's salary lists, after a decline in average pay of $135 per man from 1886 to 1887, the figure jumped by 7 percent, or $160, for 1888. Even umpires' salaries climbed, with top arbiter John H. Gaffney, who introduced the practice of moving out behind the pitcher when a runner reached base, drawing $2,500 plus expenses. Adding to the concern over salaries was the emergence of professional leagues in the Midwest and Northeast as market and talent competitors. The Western Association, an eight-team circuit assembled from the ashes of the old Northwestern League, included two franchises in NL/AA cities. In the Northeast, the International League's club shifts produced an eight-team network including operations in Toledo, Detroit, and Buffalo for 1889.[21]

Faced with the specter of rising costs and reduced revenues, the National League and American Association again manipulated gate prices, reimposed restraints on offense, and attempted to sell costly players or exploit their reserved status to make and save money. Having revoked all special concessions rates prior to the 1888 season, the National League adopted a modified gate percentage plan that mandated the installation of turnstiles and granted visiting clubs a minimum guarantee of $150 and one-fourth of the standard fifty-cent charge. The American Association also tried the National League's fifty-cent admission rate, which proved a disaster for many of its clubs. By the end of July, the American Association reversed itself in a desperate effort to boost attendance, and some NL teams, led by the Phillies, were also pleading for a return to quarter ball. Partly, the decline in spectatorship was the owners' own doing, the result of repealing pro-offense rules changes in hopes of reestablishing salary discipline when it came time for 1889 contract discussions. In 1888 the NL/AA cartel not only eliminated the statistical counting of walks as base hits, but, more significantly, they also returned to three-strike outs. The NL/AA composite batting average fell by thirty-two points, the ERA by 1.22 runs, and runs by 1.6 per game. Chicago, unloading more expensive contracts, sold pitcher John Clarkson to Boston for $10,000. Pittsburgh, having acquired Jim McCormick from Boston at the end of 1886, claimed him as a reserved player not only in 1887 but 1888 as well in retaliation for his holdout for higher pay.[22]

Underscoring baseball management's concern over labor costs, schemes for a cartelwide wage scale received ever more serious consideration, in spite of the constraints they implied upon individual owners. Even before the crunch in 1888, *Sporting Life*'s Richter had proposed a "Millennium Plan" the previous December to provide market and labor stability in the baseball industry. Under his scheme, all major league clubs would be members of a confederation that distributed shared revenues according to leaguewide scales. Minor league clubs would hold reservation rights upon their players, but the majors could draft a limited number of them each year. A joint arbitration commission would administer the structure. At the NL/AA level, the entire league rather than individual clubs would hold reserve rights except for one player per club (presumably the captain). The rest would be distributed according to an annual lottery. Veterans would be graded on the basis of position, skill, teamwork, and moral conduct, and salary scales would be based upon those classifications. Top pitchers and catchers would earn a $2,500 maximum, infielders $2,200, and outfielders $2,000. Players on pennant-winning nines would receive an additional 20 percent bonus, and other first-division clubs would receive prorated lesser amounts. Unpicked players in each year's lottery would fall into a separate category, forming teams that would play exhibitions (serving as talent tryouts) against regular clubs and be paid out of gate receipts from these games.[23]

NL and AA owners rejected the Richter plan, with its pooled profits and laborers, as too socialistic. But some new form of salary limits was clearly on the way. The Southern League already had inaugurated maximums of $2,000 a month on its clubs' 1888 payrolls, with plans to lower this to $1,200 and then $800 over the next two years. Albert Spalding, whose reappearance as an active participant in NL business after the 1888 season constituted another sign of forthcoming management militancy, offered his own blueprint to league president Nick Young. Spalding proposed a salary classification system that encompassed not only the National League and American Association but lesser leagues as well. Leagues would be classified from A (the top circuits) to D, with A-team wages limited to $200 per player per month or a $2,000-per-season player maximum. D-level performers could not earn more than $600 a year or $60 a month. As expected from a big league owner, he offered lower franchises reserve rights in relation to their peers, but teams higher on the classification scale could grab players from below by providing ten days' notice and a $25 payment.[24]

During the 1888–89 off-season, the National League adopted a slightly different, and less comprehensive, plan for salary classification put forward by Indianapolis's John T. Brush. It classified players and established salary maximums in each category, from A to E, on the basis of skill assessments and "habits, earnestness, and special qualifications" as determined by the owners. A "class A" player could receive no more than $2,500, a B performer $2,250, and so on in $250 increments down to the E category's $1,500 limit. The immediate targets of the Brush Classification Plan, as it became known, were not the twenty or so stars making more than the stated maximums. Some of them were under multiyear deals, and clubs hopeful of a pennant were unlikely to embitter their main warhorses and gate attractions through precipitous cuts aimed at them. Instead, the plan effectively threatened future opportunities for higher salaries for younger, aspiring stars. As such it threatened player solidarity by driving a wedge between the two groups of players—at least until attrition removed the last of the pre-classification veterans—in the form of a de facto two-tier wage scale.

Underscoring the suspicions of Ward's brotherhood toward the owners' intentions was the fact that the Brush plan had been adopted while Ward and many other union leaders had been diverted overseas on a postseason all-star tour. Sponsored by the clever Spalding, the tour had taken the all-stars around the world to Honolulu, Australia, Egypt, and Great Britain, culminating in an April banquet at Delmonico's in New York. Ward, having heard rumors of the scheme, left the group several weeks early to return to the States, citing pressing personal business. Reporters found this a believable explanation, since he had become estranged from his wife of a year, Helen Dauvray, a New York actress and the sister-in-law of Ward's teammate Tim Keefe. Of special concern to Ward was the fact that the classification scheme appeared to directly violate assurances he thought he had received a year earlier that reserved veterans without new contracts would not have their salaries cut. All attempts by the brotherhood leader to obtain a preseason meeting with Spalding were, however, curtly rebuffed.[25]

Other signals of an impending labor-management showdown included additional rules changes by the owners to further restrict batting averages (see Appendix, Figs. 3 and 4). They included lowering the number of balls for a walk to four, declaring the deliberate fouling off of pitches an out, counting a sacrifice as an at bat, and, most importantly, allowing substitutions at any time during the game. The latter led to increased use of replacement, or "relief," pitchers without first having to station them elsewhere on the diamond. In what may have been a direct attempt at "union-busting" within one team, the Giants also tried to sell Ward to the Washington NL club, with Nick Young himself offering the brotherhood player $6,000 of the sale price if he did not contest the deal. Ward refused, forcing New York to keep him. The union membership rejected issuing an immediate strike call on May 19, but formed a grievance committee and continued to seek a meeting with owners. After a brotherhood petition to president Young urging him to repeal classification and halt additional player sales, the National League formed its own three-member labor panel. Spalding, its instigator, met with Ward on June 25 but refused any serious negotiating until the league's end-of-season October meetings.

Player grievances continued to accumulate. The AA leadership openly encouraged player sales by struggling franchises. Spalding continued to deny White Stockings shortstop Ed Williamson, who had broken his ankle during the world tour and had it misset by a London physician, any of his 1889 pay except for $157 for his passage home. When St. Louis's William "Yank" Robinson appeared at a game in dirty pants, Von der Ahe fined him on the spot as well as ordered him to change. Robinson sent a boy across the street to clean the pants, only to see the boy along with the pants barred from readmission to the grounds. When Robinson then unleashed a stream of profanity, his owner publicly "dressed him down" and suspended him. With his teammates threatening not to make their road trip to Kansas City in retaliation, upon the pleading of manager Comiskey, the owner eventually reinstated Robinson. In Louisville, owner John Davidson fined six players after a loss to Baltimore, threatening another levy if they lost the next afternoon. In response, the team staged a brief two-day strike. A subsequent investigation showed that the struggling owner had concealed other bottom-line reasons besides competitive fire for issuing $7,435 in fines, and some of the money eventually was refunded.

By July 4, rhetoric on both sides had become more militant. Brotherhood secretary Keefe hinted at broader collective action for 1890, declaring, "The League will not classify as many as they think." Boston's Arthur Soden retorted by threatening to hire strikebreakers. The union rejected another proposal for a strike of lucrative Independence Day games, this time in support of players Jack Rowe and Deacon White. The two Buffalo natives and past performers for its NL team had been moved, along with the entire franchise, to Detroit by new owner Stearns in 1885. Both subsequently had sought to invest in and play on the Buffalo team in the International League, only to be sold by Stearns to Pittsburgh rather than receive the remainder of their 1888 salaries. The two refused to report, and Stearns insisted that they would play for Pittsburgh or no one. A defiant White maintained, "No one can sell my carcass unless I get at least half." At Ward's urging, the two holdouts finally reported to Pittsburgh at mid-season, with White receiving a $5,000 salary, prorated for the remainder of the schedule, and $1,250 of his original purchase price. The brotherhood president also advised them, however, not to sign a new contract for 1890 but instead to treat 1889 as their reserve year, making them free agents available for employment elsewhere next spring.[26]

Players' salaries, especially those of veterans, did not immediately tumble in 1889 (see Appendix, Fig. 1). Like the salary limits and disciplinary crackdowns of 1885, the economic effects of the Brush plan required another year to be fully felt. The New York Giants had a $46,000 payroll, or a $3,060 player average, and the largest payroll, Boston's, totaled almost $50,000, a $3,320-per-player sum. Acquiring that roster, however, had cost the Bean Town franchise $73,000 in purchase costs. Spalding's list of players suggested a $165 average increase in player salaries from the previous campaign. At the same time, batting averages dropped another .24 and runs per game another 1.17. Nonetheless, club profits in 1889 surprisingly improved upon those of the season before. The Giants, NL champions, netted $45,000 in profits and drew 201,662 fans for 63 home games, while AA winner St. Louis averaged over 5,000 spectators per contest. The two teams divided a postseason series purse of $16,362. Even the lowly Phillies, whose attendance had plummeted 100,000 from 1887 to 1888, registered a jump of 130,000 to 281,000 in 1889.[27]

As the pennant races heated up, the motives behind Keefe's cryptic comments and Ward's advice to Deacon White manifested themselves. On Bastille Day, July 14, the brotherhood president revealed to other union representatives his plans for a new league to begin the next season. The main early financial benefactor of the enterprise was Cleveland traction magnate Albert L. Johnson, brother of the later-famous reform mayor Tom Johnson. Pittsburgh player representative Ned Hanlon conferred with Johnson during a Cleveland road trip, and other brotherhood officers followed suit when their clubs visited the city. Preoccupied with maintaining secrecy, the businessman placed a sentry at the entrance corridor of his meeting place, the Hollenden Hotel, and paid off corner policemen to ensure their silence and further deter intruders. Johnson and the brotherhood covertly began securing player contracts with the new league for the coming year. In order to accurately estimate potential attendance, Cleveland second baseman Cub Stricker spied on the local NL turnstile count. Johnson visited other cities, including Boston, New York, and Philadelphia, to line up additional players and backers, and Tim Keefe made plans for his own sporting goods company that would supply the new entry's official baseball.

The past two decades of urban growth gave a rival league a fighting chance to either supplant or force coexistence with the NL/AA cartel. The number of American cities with over 100,000 residents had doubled to twenty-eight since 1870. As for Johnson, his professed motivations merged outrage at player mistreatment and the reserve clause with the lucrative possibilities of the enterprise for his transit business. With so much recruitment activity under way, it was only a short time until the brotherhood's plans leaked to the press. In September, *Sporting Life* printed the story with a confirmation by Johnson's brother. NL owners professed not to be worried, but their actions and subsequent words told a different story. Before the 1890 season, the league "traded" its weakest franchises, Indianapolis and Washington, to the American Association for two stronger clubs, Brooklyn and Cincinnati. Spokesmen launched a protracted propaganda campaign against the motives and abilities of the brotherhood. Spalding called it an "oath-bound secret organization of strikers," and in a letter to A. G. Mills, he insisted that the players had no legitimate basis for grievance against NL owners, whom he described as "conservative businessmen." Spalding maintained that the established circuit might be better off without such "sore heads and speculators," and he intimated that except for a handful of "malcontents," the vast majority of players had been misled by outside agitators and Wall Street types who were using them to break into baseball ownership. Ironically, although it was mere hyperbole on his part, Spalding's last charge would ultimately prove at least partially accurate.[28]

While his rhetoric escalated, Spalding performed a public charade of reasonableness by inviting the brotherhood's grievance committee to talks with NL owners. But the invitation came far too late. Ward replied that in response to earlier NL intransigence, the union's panel had disbanded and that the brotherhood as a whole now intended to address the basic issues in its own fashion. With both sides quietly attempting to stockpile talent for the coming season, in early October Ward completed the formality of notifying his NL owner, Day, that he would not play for the Giants in 1890. Other union members similarly declined new contracts from their former clubs. In retaliation, Spalding threatened injunctions against those who, though lacking new NL contracts, refused to be bound by the reserve clause. Despite the threats, a group of thirty to forty brotherhood members gathered in New York City on November 4, 1889. The next day, they declared the existence of the Players' National League of Base Ball Clubs. An enterprising turnstile manufacturer even telegrammed the gathering to offer his product to the new circuit in place of Spalding's services.

The Players' League, like the Populist movement of the same era, projected itself as a democratic alliance of toilers and honest entrepreneurs, dedicated to tearing down the accumulated barriers of ownership and power between labor and capital. It called for seven clubs in cities with NL competition (Boston, New York, Brooklyn, Philadelphia, Pittsburgh, Cleveland, and Chicago), plus the Buffalo franchise in which players Rowe and White had invested. An eight-member board, consisting of four players and four nonplayer "contributors," would run each club and select its officers. Above the club level, a "senate" of sixteen men, two per club and equally divided between players and backers, held interclub power and elected league officers. Officers consisted of a president, a vice-president, and an outside secretary-treasurer without vested interest in any club at a $4,000 salary. At its next meeting, on December 16, 1889, the Players' League senate chose New York real estate executive and tobacconist Colonel Edwin A. McAlpin as president, Chicago contractor John Addison as vice-president, and former sportswriter Frank H. Brunell as secretary-treasurer, and adopted a draft constitution.

In the "manifesto" accompanying its constitution, the Players' League offered its own Declaration of Independence and listed past NL offenses as justification for rebellion. Employing workingman's rhetoric typical of the day, the delegates indicted the old league for having stood only for "dollars and cents" instead of "integrity and fair dealings," and for treating its workers "as though they were sheep." But despite Ward's hopes that the new circuit would have teams share equally from a pooled set of profits and losses—a scheme similar to Knights of Labor and Farmers' Alliance producer cooperatives—at backers' insistence a more competitive capitalistic structure was adopted. Individual clubs agreed to split game receipts fifty-fifty, and the home team retained all its concessions profits. Each club would deposit its share of the gate in its own rather than a league fund, and each would have the responsibility of meeting its own expenses according to the mandated priority of operating expenses first, player salaries second. As reassurance to the players, backers accepted a requirement that individual clubs guarantee payment in full of salary obligations, backed up by a league insurance fund of $40,000. The league's money men also agreed to contribute $2,500 per club to a $20,000 pennant-race prize fund, with the champion receiving a $7,000 share. If, after all the previous outlays, a club generated additional profits, the first $10,000 could be claimed exclusively by the team's backers, the next $10,000 (if any) to the players, and any additional earnings split equally between the two.[29]

The Players' League enticed NL veterans not only by guaranteeing payment of salaries but also by abolishing the reserve. But in order to achieve similar ends, the new circuit offered three-year contracts at 1889 salary levels or, in the case of players for whom the National League had used the Brush Classification Plan to cut wages in that year, at 1888 amounts. No player could be released by his club until the season ended, and then only by a majority vote of his franchise's board, half of whom would be teammates. Players could augment their "board-room" clout further by investing directly in the clubs, since such actions were not barred. In order to convey an image of responsible self-regulation along with their greater rights, the Players' League retained penalties against dissipation and other disciplinary lapses, but it did abandon the blacklist. Nonetheless, the National League's three-man "war committee" of Spalding, Day, and John I. Rogers of Philadelphia portrayed their own circuit as the true, traditional defender of baseball integrity and their opponents as having "no moral foundation." Playing up the fact that professional ballplayers drew bigger salaries than Ameri-can workers in general (see Appendix, Fig. 1), promanagement writers depicted Players' League player-delegates as spoiled and greedy, wear-ing fur-lined overcoats, silk hats, patent leather shoes, and scarves with $5,000 brilliants, carrying gold-headed canes and smoking expensive ci-gars. One editorial asserted that players who now purported to be their own masters would find fans less tolerant of their "little sprees, esca-pades . . . and drunkenness on the ballfield." Hoping to rekindle reader memories of the Haymarket affair, venerable Henry Chadwick, editor of the National League's *Spalding Guide*, labeled the brotherhood's man-ifesto a "revolutionary pronunciamento" of a minority third who had used "terrorism" to drag along the rest. The English-born scribe cited as evidence of the union's sinister designs its choice of Guy Fawkes Day (when in 1604 Catholic dissidents attempted to blow up the House of Lords) to announce the existence of the rebel circuit. Not above "waving the bloody shirt" either, Chadwick dubbed Ward the "mastermind" of "secessionists," while a Cincinnati paper sympathetic to the National League chided the union head, calling him "John 'Much-Advertised' Ward" of overblown "oratorical flights."[30]

While press adversaries of the Players' League attacked it with dispar-aging descriptions resembling those employed by conservative critics of other labor movements, the new circuit also had its defenders. The St. Louis–based *Sporting News* needled Spalding and "Awful Gall" Mills and blamed the showdown on the National League's own "mean, niggardly, close-fisted acts" and "high-handed manner." *Sporting Life*'s Francis Richter voiced similar sentiments. Other trade unionists, including Ma-jor Samuel L. Leffingwell, voiced their support and urged the brother-hood to affiliate with either the American Federation of Labor or the Knights of Labor. The union refused, largely out of fear of losing its sepa-rate identity by being subsumed within a craft union of theatrical workers. The brotherhood's pronouncements amply displayed the fact that its members saw themselves, however well paid, as members of the producing class. Ward declared, "That we receive larger salaries and that our hours of work are shorter leaves us none the less workingmen." For him, the central issues were worker control and freedom of choice, not money alone. "I would rather work for $10 a week and keep my personality, i.e. have some volition in the conduct of my own affairs than be made a monkey of or simply an animated being by such methods of government as used by the [National] League, for $100 a week."[31]

In order to reinforce a responsible image, the Players' League indicated that it would not engage in double contracting by signing jumpers with existing active pacts. Nonetheless, it did well in securing players' loyalties. Upon polling 50 players in the Midwest, Ward insisted that all but Indianapolis "spy" and "informer" Jack "Judas" Glasscock backed the brotherhood "like rocks." Actually, owner Brush succeeded in getting back not only Glasscock but two-thirds of the rest of his infield. But by the end of 1889, the union had signed up 71 NL players, along with 16 from the American Association and 4 from other leagues. In the spring the total rose to 188, and PL secretary Brunell claimed that the National League had resecured contracts from only about "20 deserters" and additional unknowns. Given the conflicting claims of both sides and the shifting numbers over time, an accurate count is probably impossible. But according to one estimate, by the start of the season the National League had retained only 38 of its players from the year before. With only 4 "real" players at its disposal, Pittsburgh's squad drew catcalls as a "crowd of stiffs." In contrast, of 124 men who appeared in ten games or more in the Players' League, 81 were former NL veterans, while 28 came from the American Association and 15 from other circuits. Ironically, the leapers included such later management legends of tightfistedness as Charles Comiskey, who joined the Chicago Players' League club as player-manager, and Connie Mack, who not only left his Washington AA club but invested $500 in his new franchise.[32]

Among star players, virtually the only one who did not jump to the Players' League was Cap Anson, who was more "management" anyway in view of his captaincy and his stockholdings in the White Stockings. The National League tried to counterattack jumping by offering its own three-year deals, repealing the classification plan, and expressing a willingness to give players more say in their prospective sales. The owners also now allowed fined or penalized players the right to appeal their sentences. In individual cases, the National League went to extraordi-

The Boston Players' League team of 1890. In the center of the second row is player-manager Mike "King" Kelly, the most famous player of Irish extraction of his era.

nary lengths to try to lure back defecting stars. Spalding offered Mike Kelly, who had been named as player-manager of the Boston Players' League team, $10,000 to jump back, but Kelly refused. Almost enticed back was Buck Ewing, New York PL team player-manager, who reportedly accepted an offer from A. G. Mills only to renege when other desertions did not follow. An embarrassed Ewing then concocted a tale in which he denied ever accepting the bribe, claimed to have acted as a brotherhood spy in stringing Mills along, and purportedly briefed Al Johnson on the clandestine meetings that Cap Anson had arranged. Unconvinced brotherhood members ostracized Ewing on and off the field for much of the season. Of course, when efforts to retain or regain players failed, owners had to sign new players to fill their depleted rosters. Among these new players was a fireballing right-handed pitcher brought into the big leagues when Cleveland purchased him from the Tri-State League's Canton club for the 1890 season and named Denton True "Cy" (for "Cyclone") Young.[33]

From a financial standpoint, the American Association was more vulnerable than the National League, given its greater number of overextended franchises. Hoping to exploit this weakness, Ward initially offered AA owners neutrality and focused player recruitment upon NL rosters, in hopes of prying the American Association away from its National Agreement support of the senior circuit. The Players' League even offered a counteralliance with comparable territorial protections. Once the American Association rejected its offer, however, the brotherhood belatedly raided AA teams. For its part, the National League sought to duplicate its previous strategy against the 1884 Union Association by maintaining the cartel and by scheduling games in the same cities and on the same dates as the Players' League, thus holding down its gate receipts and raising bidding costs for grounds. NL chieftains assumed that even though their clubs also would suffer, their deeper pockets would ensure their survival, though perhaps not that of the partner AA. For their collective fortunes, NL clubs agreed to raise the visiting team's gate share from 25 percent to 40 percent.

The National League also sought revenge in court, demanding injunctions to block jumpers and to uphold the reserve clause. Appropriately, the league's law firm, Evarts, Choate & Beman, earlier had refused to represent an Irish bakery woman on the grounds that whether she worked ten hours a day or more was a matter exclusively between her and her employer, and not a matter for public regulation. Unfortunately for the National League, in most instances courts upheld players' rights to move and in so doing undermined the intimidation of the blacklist. The Giants sought injunctions against Ward and Ewing and were denied both requests. New York State Supreme Court judge J. Morgan Joseph O'Brien ruled in January that the club's contract obligations to Ward had been indefinite and lacking sufficient fairness and mutuality to be binding (since under the reserve clause, Ward was bound indefinitely to the Giants, but they were obligated only to provide ten days' notice before unilaterally releasing him). In Ewing's case, federal judge William P. Wallace upheld the definiteness of the contract but also found it insufficiently mutual in obligation. In March, Philadelphia sued George Hallinan and lost on similar grounds. When Kansas City's John Pickett jumped from the American Association to the Players' League, a local judge did apply the entertainment law precedent of *Lumley v. Wagner* (1852). It stated that the law could not compel an individual to perform specific acts under a personal services contract but could be used to bar him from providing the same services for another employer if his services were truly special, unique, or extraordinary. Pickett, however, effectively avoided the ruling's injunctive impact by playing for a Philadelphia PL club outside the court's jurisdiction.[34]

In the effort to win the propaganda battle, both sides inflated their own attendance claims and disparaged the other's. But according to the *Reach Guide* of 1891, the Players' League drew 980,887 fans to the National League's 813,678. Probably the combined total fell short of figures compiled by the National League alone in the preceding year, and one of the vulnerable clubs, the Phillies, dropped in attendance by almost half, to under 150,000 spectators. The National League's estimated payroll costs for 1890, in turn, reached $311,964, including $70,500 in "buyback" bonuses to jumpers. Even though the Players' League outdrew the National League, its games broke even in less than one out of six contests. To meet the financial emergency, the brotherhood's clubs assessed themselves an additional $2,500 apiece for leaguewide use. By season's end, the Players' League lost an estimated $340,000, and NL ledgers fell in the red by anywhere from $250,000 to $500,000. Pittsburgh, with its weak roster and 23-114 record, did much to drag down attendance figures for other clubs.[35]

New York, stripped by brotherhood desertions of its many stars, sought and received a talent infusion from John Brush, who sold stars Glasscock, Amos Rusie, and Jesse Burkett to the Giants. Nonetheless, owner Day pleaded for $80,000 from the National League in July, threatening to sell out to the Players' League if he did not get it. Under the pressure of Day's "blackmail," various owners bailed him out by buying parcels of club stock. Spalding purchased $25,000 worth and distributed it to his partners, including Anson. Boston's Soden bought an equal amount, and Brush canceled the same value of notes owed him on his player sales. Despite the National League's claims of greater moral probity, F. A. Abel, a professional gambler, acquired $6,250 worth of Giants stock, as did former player and sporting goods businessman Al Reach. By the time all the transactions were concluded, Day retained but a $20,000 share in his club, but the National League had prevented one of its most visible franchises from falling into enemy hands. The same could not be said of the Cincinnati club, whose owner sold it to a Players' League syndicate for $40,000.

Supporters of the old cartel understandably entertained growing doubts about its survival, and indeed the survival of the game itself. One such scribe contributed a rhyme on the issue of "who killed baseball," leaving little doubt about his own opinion:

Who killed baseball? "I" said John Ward: "of my own accord, I
   killed baseball."
Who saw it die? "We," said the slaves; "from our own made
   graves, we saw it die."
Who'll make its shroud? "I" said Buck Ewing, "I'll do it well, I'll do
   the sewing, I'll make the shroud."
Who'll dig the grave? "I," said Brunell, "I'll do it well, I'll dig the
   grave."
Who'll be the parson? "I," said Cub Stricker, "I'll let her flicker, I'll
   be the parson."
Who'll carry the link? "I," said Jay Faatz "I watched the gates, I'll
   carry the link."
Who'll be chief mourner? "I," said Tim Keefe, "I'm filled with
   grief, I'll be chief mourner."
Who'll sing a psalm? "I," said Comiskey; "though it's rather risky,
   I'll sing a psalm."
Who'll toll the bell? "I," said "King" Kelly; "I'll toll it like ——, I'll
   toll the bell."
And now all the cranks have forgotten the game
And the ex-slave perceives that D. Mud is his name.[36]

Reports of the imminent demise of the National League, however,
proved greatly exaggerated. Instead of the National League, it was the
Players' League that expired, and in no small measure at the hands of its
own contributors. In October, Columbus AA director Allen W. Thurman
pleaded with NL owners for peace negotiations and the consolidation of
the three major circuits into two eight-team leagues. Giving the presentation a conspiratorial flavor was the fact that three Players' League
backers—Johnson, realtor Wendell Goodwin of Brooklyn, and stockbro-
ker Edward Talcott of New York, were huddled but a block away at the
time. When the three obtained a meeting with Spalding and Day, they
foolishly threw away any advantage they might have had by revealing
specifics about the sorry financial state of their own circuit's franchises.
A reheartened National League formed a negotiating committee of Spalding, Day, and Charles Byrne of Brooklyn—a panel whose composition,
as with that of the Players' League delegation, underscored the cen-
trality of New York–area territorial compromise to a settlement. The
American Association selected its own three-man group, including Billie
Barnie of Baltimore, Von der Ahe, and Thurman. At an October 9 joint
session, the three panels agreed to impose a two-week truce on raids of

contracted players. During the hiatus, rumors of secret player deals and separate territorial bargaining between competing Pittsburgh and New York ownership groups ran rampant.

Players' League team backers not party to the secret discussions grew more and more uneasy. The Wagner brothers, Philadelphia butchers and PL team stockholders, telegraphed president McAlpin to protest the rumored New York coup. A similarly worried Ward, fearing that player and leaguewide interests could be betrayed by a handful of self-seeking backers, convened a brotherhood meeting on October 20. It appointed a three-member player panel of Hanlon, shortstop Arthur Irwin of Boston, and Ward and dispatched them for inclusion within an expanded twelve-person interleague negotiation that would give the Players' League equal representation with the NL/AA cartel. The action, however, proved too little and too late. NL and AA representatives refused to seat the player delegates, and even two of the three Players' League backers, Goodwin and Talcott, concurred in this decision. Johnson made a largely symbolic argument for the inclusion of Ward's group, but was voted down. Spalding, for his part, accused Ward of bad faith in even doubting the intentions of men who had "lost $300,000 pressing their cause" and insisted that matters be settled "between the moneyed men of both organizations on a purely business basis." After Johnson left the meeting along with the repulsed players, the conferees completed their business.[37]

The National League and American Association had defeated the Players' League by driving a wedge between its backers and its performers. Spalding and Thurman cemented the triumph by traveling to other "enemy" cities and promising their investors generous peace terms. Talcott, contradicting his earlier pledge to other PL contributors not to strike a separate, premature deal, merged his franchise with the Giants. When a bitter Ward blasted the action as that of a "weakener," Talcott retorted that he and others had sacrificed $3,000 a month only to receive "high-priced ballplaying" and deserved some greater return. Sensing the end, Ward did not even attend the brotherhood's November annual meeting in Pittsburgh, dispatching Judge Edward Bacon of Brooklyn as his proxy instead. The Pittsburgh PL club merged with the old Alleghenies and then disappeared in favor of a new organization that included former Players' League investors on its board. Chicago's Addison sold his franchise to Spalding at year's end, eventually garnering $18,000, which he prorated to stockholders at 60 percent of value. In contrast, his players, despite the league's earlier promises, received cash settlements of less than 10 percent of the amounts owed them, while six player-stock-holders received compensation at only 50 percent of par. Addison himself fared far better, receiving $1,500 in Giants stock from Talcott and McAlpin and complimentary season game passes from Spalding. In Brooklyn, a new NL entity integrated three former PL backers as its majority stockholders, while others secured an additional $40,000 of ownership interest.

Excluded remnants of the Players' League contributors appointed a new committee to resume negotiations, but the victorious cartel no longer had reason to be interested. In Philadelphia, where the American Association had expelled its renegade Athletics, Spalding and Thurman proposed replacing the team with the Players' League entry. AA executives wanted to drop their Toledo, Rochester, and Syracuse clubs in favor of other PL substitutes, and to have the National League open up Boston for them in the form of the PL remnant. The National League also repeated earlier vague possibilities of a second cartel team in Chicago, suggesting the PL franchise as its basis. But owners of existing clubs that would be hurt by such maneuvering, particularly Boston's Soden, resisted strenuously. The end result was that the three struggling AA clubs were bought out of the league for $24,000, and Soden granted permission for a second Bean Town franchise under onerous conditions. The new club, the former PL entity with AA affiliation, would have to charge fifty-cent admissions, return all former NL players, and not use the word "Boston" in its name. In turn, the American Association admitted the Washington PL team into its ranks and awarded its new Philadelphia franchise, under the old name of the Athletics, to the Wagners. The Buffalo PL club, lacking a major league counterpart with which to merge, folded, and what remained of the Brooklyn operation "fused" with the local NL club. Perhaps as his penalty for standing by the players at the last minute, the one Players' League magnate left completely out in the cold was Johnson, whose talks in pursuit of Cincinnati or Cleveland ownership shares proved fruitless.[38]

Why had the Players' League lost? Participants and observers alike offered varied postmortems. A bitter Ward blamed the outcome on the "stupidity, avarice, and treachery" of key financial backers. One of the benefactors, J. Earl Wagner, deflected blame by citing the Ewing incident as the point at which the Players' League's credibility had been forfeited. He also pointed to the New York club backers' betrayal of their colleagues as leaving him and others with no alternative. Secretary Brunell concurred, blaming the "treacherous eagerness" of the New York and Brooklyn investors to get "out of the wet." The *Sporting News* ascribed the result to faulty leadership and financial mistakes, and the Pittsburgh *Dispatch* blamed the circuit's utopian structure. Certainly the effort suffered from inadequate capitalization and an excessive faith in contributors' willingness to subsume individual interests for the sake of all. In retrospect, the brotherhood's PL experiment had been doomed from the instant it had been forced to rely upon outside resources and management expertise to sustain it. The league's capitalist benefactors had never shared the ideals of the players, but had viewed the circuit as their own opportunity to break into the baseball ownership cartel, thereby providing the National League and American Association with the wedge to break the partnership of convenience apart. At the end of their venture, Ward and a small company of friends could only raise glasses to their noble failure at the "wake" they held in Engel's Saloon in New York.[39] The funeral they commemorated, however, was not merely that of a league but also that of an effective labor brotherhood that could hope to stand up to the baseball industry. It would be twenty years before another generation of ballplayers managed to launch an effort of comparable ambition and purpose.

FIVE

MONOPOLY BALL, 1891-1899

Having crushed the Players' League, the National League wasted no time in heralding the restoration of order within baseball's labor relations. The owners' official mouthpiece, the *Spalding Guide*, even claimed that the players secretly welcomed their defeat, quipping:

> Backward, turn backward, O Time in thy rush,
> Make me a slave again, well dressed and flush!
> Bondage come back from the echoless shore,
> And bring me my shackles I formerly wore.[1]

In actuality, the Players' League debacle left the professional player force demoralized and collectively powerless. Once more, the sport's on-field professional performers found themselves almost wholly dependent upon the continued expansion of the baseball market to spawn a new round of trade wars before they could have any hopes of regaining some leverage in their dealings with their bosses.

At first glance, even that potential source of hope for baseball's laborers seemed to have vanished in the wake of the Players' League defeat. NL magnates Mills, Spalding, and Byrne drafted a new National Agreement in advance of the 1891 season and were joined as partners in the accord by the American Association and the Western Association—the descendant of the old Northwestern League. The new pact granted interleague arbitrative control to a National Board consisting of three owner representatives, one from each circuit. The board claimed the power to review player contracts, hear player grievances and complaints of contract violations, assign umpires, and rule on player-management, interclub, and interleague disputes without appeal. With the reserve clause reestablished, clubs also reasserted their power to sell players without their explicit consent or compensation. Owners empowered the National Board to release a reserved man if his club fell more than fifteen days in arrears in paying his salary or failed to make a contract offer by March 15 of each year.

The "peace" pact lasted but two weeks. Grievances had been building between the victorious NL and AA owners over the rights to former participants in the defunct Players' League. The NL had been raided more severely of playing talent, and the senior circuit was determined to grab the best "refugees" before the National Board could begin operations. That way, the new interleague panel would be left only with reassigning the "leavings." For its part, the American Association was equally bent on securing its share of brotherhood veterans, for it had emerged from the war in far worse financial shape. NL clubs began contracting and reserving as many as twenty-seven players per team, despite the new National Agreement's requirement of considerably lower reserve levels. Spalding's Chicago club, for example, attempted to reserve twenty-three men. With interleague mistrust and covert player-bidding rising, assignment rulings by the National Board on two PL veterans shattered the cartel. Second baseman Louis Bierbauer and outfielder Harry Stovey had performed for the AA Philadelphia Athletics in 1889 but jumped respectively to Brooklyn and Boston clubs in the Players' League. When the Players' League collapsed, the new Philadelphia owners, the Wagners, failed to bring Bierbauer and Stovey back under contract. Instead, Bierbauer signed with NL Pittsburgh and its owner

J. Palmer O'Neill. (Palmer became known as "Pirate" Palmer for his raid on Bierbauer, and the nickname stuck with his club.) As for Stovey, the Wagners had intended to sell him to the new Boston AA club, but the player rejected their contract offer and signed instead with Soden's NL entry.

To the shock of AA owners, the National Board, with their own president as its chairman, sided in both cases with the National League. Thurman even personally voted with the majority. In revenge, AA owners called a special meeting, presided over by the circuit's vice-president rather than Thurman, and replaced him as league president with Cincinnati's Louis Kramer. More importantly, the American Association abrogated its obligations under the National Agreement and "seceded" from the cartel. Lacking an official position in any particular circuit, Thurman nonetheless technically remained chairman of the National Board. Showing good sense, he resigned his chairmanship a month later. Since the American Association had withdrawn from the National Agreement, a second NL member, president Nick Young, assumed his place.

Both sides of the dual-league cartel prepared for the second trade war in two years, a war that promised to destroy one or the other "major" league. The American Association invited PL refugee Al Johnson to establish a Cincinnati franchise and offered him a seat on the circuit's board of directors. The National League counterattacked by questioning its rival's motives in breaking away, claiming that player ownership disagreements had been a smokescreen for the real issue—the American Association's determination to move into the National League's Cincinnati territory in violation of National Agreement market protections. Spalding, hauling out old rhetoric from the Players' League war, called the American Association's action "the work of a few irresponsible professional managers with anarchistic tendencies." In order to close off the Queen City to the American Association, NL owners bought "insurance" to the point of excess. NL owners urged John Brush, holder of the league's territorial claim on the city, to reach an accommodation with Johnson. When he failed, the others bought off Johnson for $30,000. Ironically, even in Johnson's own makeshift franchise a group of NL owners already held a majority of stock, suggesting that the American Association's window of opportunity in Cincinnati could have been closed without paying him. Following Johnson's "betrayal," Von der Ahe led efforts to erect another AA franchise, with Mike Kelly its on-field captain, and took Johnson to court to block his "sale" of territorial rights.

After a decade of litigation, Johnson's death in 1901 led to a division of moneys among the various parties.[2]

The last thing either league needed so soon after the conflict with the players' union, of course, was another trade war. To provide for its "war fund," the National League imposed a 10 percent tax upon its clubs' gate receipts. Intent on denying revenues to its adversary, the National League also canceled all of its spring exhibition games with AA clubs and refused to sanction a postseason interleague championship series. The other circuit retaliated by voting to extend its regular season an additional week. The American Association in particular could not afford any dropoff in revenues, for three of its franchises—Columbus, Louisville, and Cincinnati—were weak, and the league's clubs still owed substantial obligations from the buyout of its defunct Toledo, Syracuse, and Rochester teams at the end of the Players' League war. Hoping to shore up its weak links, the circuit divided gate receipts equally between home and visiting clubs in 1891 and pooled leaguewide the earnings from holiday tilts. With the Players' League demise a fresh example, the American Association also tried to prevent selective betrayal, or "dinky-dink," by individual owners by requiring each club to hand over a major-ity of its stock for literal "safekeeping" by the league president. In Au-gust, the American Association permitted its Boston entry to charge a lower twenty-five-cent admission in order to stay afloat.

As in all previous trade wars, however, the primary battles were fought over playing talent. The warring majors raided each other, and both plundered the minors. When the American Association's Balti-more club tried to prevent Clarence "Cupid" Childs from jumping to the Cleveland NL team, the senior circuit claimed that its rival had forfeited all reserve claims by abandoning the National Agreement and the Na-tional Board. A local court agreed. Columbus similarly failed to retain Charles Reilly, who jumped to Pittsburgh. Mark "Fido" Baldwin followed the same path and then served as an agent enticing others to the Pirates. When AA magnate Von der Ahe filed charges against him, Baldwin countersued for harassment and four years later won a $2,500 jury ver-dict. NL owners, recognizing the legal vulnerability of the reserve clause as demonstrated in court during the brotherhood war, offered alterna-tive pacts to players that nonetheless would lock in their services beyond a single year. Players could opt for a seven-month seasonal contract with specific renewal clauses for one or more seasons, or they could choose calendar-year, multiyear pacts with pay in monthly or twice-monthly installments. Through such measures the National League "won" the bidding war, as such AA stars as Pete Browning, Dave Foutz, Bob Caruthers, and Arlie Latham jumped to the senior circuit. Along with Dan Brouthers, Mike Kelly was one of the few to spring in the other direction, going to Boston only to be "loaned" during the season to the desperate Cincinnati franchise.[3]

In both leagues combined, only four or five teams broke even or made a profit. In Cincinnati, both clubs dropped money. With the losses threatening to "snatch defeat from the jaws of victory" for both circuits only a year after their triumph over the Players' League, rumors of peace talks surfaced by August. Von der Ahe sold his claim to Cincinnati territory to NL rival Brush for $12,000; then he consolidated his team with the Western Association's Milwaukee club and finished the AA season with it. Each circuit designated three-man "peace commissions." Hopes for a treaty at month's end were shattered, however, by the news that Mike Kelly had jumped back from the American Association to Boston in the National League for a contract offer that included European trips for himself and his wife. John Brush also succeeded in enticing Charles Comiskey back to his Cincinnati NL club. As the season wound down, the National League gave permission for clubs in competing territories to offer twenty-five-cent admissions. In anticipation of a second year of war, the league also assigned its weaker teams specific AA players to raid in the off-season. The scheme presumably would not only hurt the enemy but also ensure that NL clubs would not bid against each other and drive player pay still higher.

The American Association did its best to fight back against the NL onslaught. The circuit recruited backers for a new Chicago entry for 1892 with $50,000 of capital stock, offering the new club the inducement of keeping all of its home receipts except those from holiday contests. In the attempt to halt the flow of deserters to the National League, the American Association's owners even tried a public campaign to convince players that they, in contrast to rival owners, respected players' rights. Spokesmen claimed that their circuit, unlike the National League, treated players as "gentlemen," not "slaves or brutes." But players' memories of the American Association's collusion against the Players' League told a different story. In any event, in a period of renewed bidding the performers usually did not make their choice on the basis of noble rhetoric; they based it on who made the best offer, which—given the sounder financial position of its owners—usually meant the National League. As present and future salary commitments soared for both leagues, however, the Cleveland *Leader* bemoaned the pay costs as a "business absurdity." When pennant races proved unable to mitigate the fiscal disaster, peace discussions were renewed. NL owners leaked through the press their scheme to collapse the two circuits into a single twelve-team entity, folding the weakest AA clubs. New peace commissions formed in November 1891, and Von der Ahe, the American Association's strongest financial force, became the object of special NL courtship. As the price of his cooperation, der Boss, who conceded that the "weak-as-dishwater" Boston and Milwaukee clubs should be scrapped, demanded assurances that Sunday baseball and liquor sales would be allowed within the National League.[4]

On December 15, 1891, owners on both sides reached a peace agreement in Indianapolis. Four AA clubs—Baltimore, Washington, St. Louis, and Louisville—survived within a new circuit called the National League and American Association of Professional Base Ball Clubs, with a ten-year, "ironclad" pact. The twelve "survivors" bought out the dissolved franchises in Boston, Philadelphia, Columbus, Milwaukee, and Chicago for a total of $131,000, paid out of a 10 percent deduction from 1892 gate receipts. Sunday ball was permitted where consistent with state and local ordinances—as was the case in Cincinnati, St. Louis, Chicago, and Louisville. Fifty cents became the standard admission charge, but with leeway allowed for other rates for special seating areas. In order to recoup profits and maintain fan interest in all the markets of an expanded league without divisions, the 1892 season was split in two, with each half's winners meeting in a postseason series. Of special importance to the new major league monopoly, however, was the restoration of limits on player mobility and value. The peace pact called for the restoration of a fourteen-player reserve per team and club roster limits of fifteen. The existing player claims of surviving clubs would be honored by fellow owners. A two-person ownership panel distributed the remaining players from disbanded franchises.

Following the end of the one-year "reprieve" granted baseball labor by the NL-AA war, the shrinkage of the majors into a single-league monopoly provided the surviving owners with the opportunity to impose—and maintain—unprecedented controls upon player supply and demand, and therefore player compensation. The collapse of the Players' League and the American Association within two years meant that only 180 roster spots now existed for perhaps as many as double that number of major leaguers. Now, the victorious National League could use the surplus of big leaguers to dismiss the most troublesome veterans and to intimidate the rest into having second thoughts about the possibility of renewed collective mobilization. Any acceleration in labor turnover, in turn, would only multiply the difficulties of building and sustaining a union in an industry already marked by the brevity of its workers' job tenure. Creating an even greater imbalance in labor supply and demand and a ready pool of cheap entry-level replacement players for the National League was the new National Agreement announced on March 1, 1892. In it the National League offered cooperating minor league clubs and leagues security from player-bidding by their rivals and in-season raids on their reserves by NL teams, in exchange for the right to draft minor league players at artificially low prices between seasons. At the end of each minor league season, the NL clubs could draft players at fixed prices determined by the classification of the club's league as either "A" or "B." Each NL team could select a Class A player for $1,000 and a B-league performer for $500, with the money paid to their former owners. Class A teams similarly could draft players from B rosters, and selections had to occur between October 1 and February 1 each offseason. Minor leagues considered lower than B level in the eyes of the National League and nonsignatories to the National Agreement, in contrast, possessed no reservation rights at all that the National League would respect.[5]

Given the lack of outside competition, the National League did not simply content itself with the formal controls on player services provided in the National Agreement. Anxious to recoup the losses of 1890–91, the owners stretched even those controls to extreme levels. Although each club was supposed to abide by a fourteen-man reserve limit, owners ignored it and expanded the number of players under contract exclusivity. Within a few years, all clubs actually had at least sixteen players under reserve, with Cincinnati having as many as thirty-three. At the same time, they reduced the number of players on their active rosters (and therefore drawing major league pay) to thirteen per team by mid-season of 1892. The result was that the number of big league jobs not only had been pared from 180 to 156, but clubs were preventing the free movement of many more players, and slashing their salaries, by locking them up under reserve. Increasingly owners put such talent in "cold storage" on minor league teams, where they could remain sharp, receive only minor league wages, and yet not be counted against the minors' own reserves. The practice represented an abuse of minor league clubs as well as individual players, for the major league owner could recall these reserved players during the season without paying the off-season compensation that would be owed for drafting a minor league reservist, and the shuffling of such talent created havoc for the minors' rosters and pennant races. The major league owner, having recalled his property, was under no obligation to send the player back to the same team if he no longer wanted the player's services.[6]

Even when a major league player retired, his former club now could attempt to restrict his future opportunities with another team as a manager or coach by keeping him on reserve. When Monte Ward retired as an active ballplayer in 1894, the Giants retained their claim on him, fearing that the former brotherhood head might "unretire" without their receiving any compensation. Ward, who challenged the Giants' claim, eventually won his case before an NL arbitration panel two years later, but only because his former "master," Edward Talcott, failed to show up to present management's case at the hearing because of illness. A more frequent source of abuse was the situation in which an owner controlled both a major league and a minor league franchise. The prime example of such an owner was Brush, whose contemporaneous ownership of the Western Association's Indianapolis team along with the NL franchise in Cincinnati helped explain his ability to control so many players on reserve. Brush would send down major leaguers to thrash competitors of his minor league club and then when Indy established a comfortable lead in its circuit, bring them back up. He also used his Cincinnati franchise to "launder" players procured from Indy's own rivals for its benefit. In order to try to discourage individual owners in the minors from facilitating such schemes, the Western Association ordered the leaguewide division of draft fees paid any of its clubs by the National League.[7]

The capture of signatory minor leagues as a cheap labor pool and a repository for reserved players enabled the National League to plan upon an extended period of low salaries. For the present, since they faced no outside competition, they could disregard prior verbal assurances and even signed contracts they had extended to players while the trade wars still raged. Before the 1892 season, led by Brooklyn and Philadelphia, the NL owners slashed player salaries by as much as 50 percent in some cases, and then they cut them further at midyear (see Appendix, Fig. 1). Louisville reduced the pay of half of its players, and Boston cut the salaries of all, despite faring better in revenue because of on-field success. St. Louis teammates took $200–500 cuts. Cincinnati's Tony Mullane found his pay slashed $700 to $3,500. When he retaliated by holding out for the second half of the season, the club, undeterred, offered him but $2,100 for 1893. Brooklyn pitcher Thomas

Lovett, a year-long holdout in 1892, sacrificed $3,000 only to be cut in pay the next year. Teammate George Haddock, a thirty-four-game winner in 1891, experienced a similar fate.[8]

As bad as these instances of precipitous cutting were, other players suffered even worse fates. When Baltimore's Charles Buffinton, a ten-year veteran, held out at mid-season, no club ever hired him again. High-priced player-managers were a particular target for cost-conscious ownership, and vulnerable not only for their performance but for that of their teammates as well. Pittsburgh's Thomas Burns, signed to a three-year deal at $4,500 a year, found himself fired after only two months and had to go to court to retrieve even $1,500 in settlement. Even when players "won," they ended up losers, as the case of John Pickett illustrates. A court denied Baltimore's right to release Pickett at mid-season, since his particular contract mysteriously had lacked the standard stipulation that ten days' notice were required before release. A jury awarded him $1,285.72, but afterward NL owners all refused to hire him. The major league monopoly had determined not only to cut pay in defiance of its own prior pledges, and to ignore multiyear contracts, but even to freeze out of the game those who tried to challenge its power outside its own internal governance structure.[9]

With other multiyear pacts from 1890 or 1891 scheduled to expire before the 1893 season, Boston owner Soden predicted additional cuts of 20–30 percent. NL president Young foresaw the same reductions and "a howl from the players, but it will not avail them anything." Following the end of the 1892 season, in October the owners effected a leaguewide cut through the expedient of "releasing" all of their ballplayers rather than paying them their last two weeks of pay to November 1. Having made all their former charges free agents, the owners ensured their retention nonetheless by colluding not to bid on any of each other's releasees. Three teams—Boston, Cleveland, and Chicago—received exemptions from the mass release, the first two because they needed their rosters intact for the championship series and Chicago because of contract complications (its player contracts typically ran for twelve months and did not expire until February 1). Boston exacted alternative economies, forcing its championship players to split a mere $1,000 bonus fifteen ways and to utilize the cheapest horsecar transportation to and from series games to save Soden money. In New York, Giants owner Day released Shorty Fuller, Mike Tiernan, and Amos Rusie, who had refused mid-season cuts, at year's end. Day already lagged three months behind in paying team salaries, or a $1,000 average arrears per player, and he forced the rest to accept 25 percent of par with promissory notes for the remainder. The more "generous" John Rogers of Philadelphia allowed his players to earn back their two weeks of lost pay at year's end by playing additional exhibitions.[10]

The full meaning of Soden's and Young's earlier salary warnings became clear by March of 1893. With a new season about to dawn, the owners announced a new maximum salary of $2,400 a player and set a target for team payrolls of $30,000. With player-managers typically receiving $500–600 more than other performers because of their additional responsibilities, for many clubs it meant "formal" salaries closer to $1,800 a man (although some stars continued to receive under-the-table extras). Typical of the new salary regime were the reported figures for the Philadelphia Phillies:

		Salary	
Player	1889	1892	1893
Clements	$2,450	$3,000	$1,800
Delahanty	1,750	2,100	1,800
Hallman	1,400	3,500	1,800
Thompson	2,500	3,000	1,800
Allen	–	3,000	1,800
Hamilton	–	3,400	1,800
Cross	–	3,250	1,800
Keefe	–	3,500	1,800
Weyhing	–	3,250	1,800

Players could do practically nothing about such arbitrary reductions, having no rival leagues to which to flee. In the words of Giants infielder Denny Richardson: "Baseball is a big monopoly. Players can't kick with only one major league. They must accept their reductions or retire." By the 1893 season, the $3,000 salary, commonplace at the beginning of the decade, had virtually disappeared, and even the $2,500 income had grown far scarcer (see Appendix, Fig. 1).[11]

Lacking any collective leverage, those individuals who chose to fight it out in 1893 found their struggles futile. Ad Gumbert held out in opposition to Chicago's cutting his salary from $2,700 to $1,800 and sued the club for the wages lost during his protest. Traded to Pittsburgh in June, at least he received a prorated version of a $2,400 salary from his new team. But his suit for back pay was not even decided until 1898, and when it was, he lost. Bill Joyce, a $2,800 ballplayer for Brooklyn in 1892, found himself traded to Washington and offered but $1,800. After sitting out the season in protest, he found reemployment only at a still-lower wage in 1894. Not only did the market monopoly and the reserve clause prevent players from testing their real value in an open labor marketplace, but the National League even ignored its own earlier assurances not to lower a man's wage from the previous year during his reserve season.[12]

In 1894 some players tried to recreate a circuit resembling the old Players' League in order to exert a degree of leverage. The proposed new "American Association" would feature twenty-five-cent admissions and the Keefe baseball and would feature a schedule that avoided direct competition with the National League. Like earlier challengers, the new circuit would respect existing, active NL player contracts, but not the reserve clause. Although the idea won sympathy from segments of the baseball press, most notably the *Sporting News* and the New York *Clipper,* the National League quickly crushed it by threatening any jumper with permanent blacklisting. Few active players were willing to take the chance, given the ease with which the shrunken NL cartel could replace them. Prominent in the failed effort were three former National Leaguers, Billie Barnie, Fred Pfeffer (who had been a brotherhood activist), and Al Buckenberger. In November, the National League suspended all three and indicated that they would be permanently blacklisted if they did not recant by December 31. When Buckenberger did, the National League rewarded him by making him St. Louis's manager for 1895. Barnie's repentance and restoration took longer, but following a stint as an Eastern League manager, he became Brooklyn's field leader in 1897. The more militant Pfeffer assumed coaching duties at Princeton University, while publicly campaigning for his reinstatement via a petition effort that secured 10,000 signatures. When Louisville defied the league by offering him a contract at $2,000, the other owners permitted his return in exchange for his signature on a "loyalty oath" and payment of a $500 fine, which friends collected for him. In the aftermath of the challengers' abortive effort, the National League adopted a resolution stating that in future any club officer, manager, or player would face lifetime banishment for attempting to organize a rival league.[13]

As part of the process of payroll slashing and profit restoration by the NL monopoly, clubs trimmed veterans from their rosters, and job security eroded. As early as 1892, according to one account, the typical NL club's average age was but twenty-five, with only two players over thirty.

By 1893, only 54 of 128 brotherhood men from 1890 remained in the majors, alongside 52 of 121 NL veterans of the same year. At the same time, given the shrunken number of major league teams and jobs after 1890–91, many talented prospects remained bottled up in lower-paying leagues or abandoned baseball entirely, although a small share of retired veterans moved on to coaching, managerial, umpiring, or front-office duties at the major league level. An 1895 estimate concluded that one of every five minor league recruits managed to dislodge a veteran player. Pitcher Amos Rusie held out again in 1896, demanding the restoration of $200 in deducted pay after winning twenty-four games for a ninth-place Giants team. With the legal aid of John Ward and the threat of a lawsuit, he prevailed, receiving a $3,000 salary in 1897. But most veterans could not take the risk of holding out and being replaced by a $600 rookie.[14]

While individual players occasionally won Pyrrhic victories, the general market situation for their services continued to decline. By 1898, an average NL club paid out about $40,000 in payroll on eighteen players, or an average of $2,200, with managers receiving $4,000 but enjoying less and less job security (see Appendix, Fig. 1). The stalemate in wages—still lower a decade later than they had been in the late 1880s—led the entire Baltimore Orioles squad, three-time champions during the decade, to threaten a teamwide strike. In response, many of its players were sold to pennant-hungry Brooklyn for the 1899 campaign. That club—one of the highest paid of the era—retained manager Ned Hanlon for $10,000 but paid its top four stars only $2,400 each. The other eleven members of the Trolley Dodgers (nicknamed after a series of local transit mishaps) received far less; in fact seven of them earned under $1,500 that year. On the Boston Beaneaters of the same year, two performers received slightly more than $2,400, eight others earned exactly $2,400, and the rest of the team enjoyed salaries far below that level.

Management economies imposed upon players extended to postseason play throughout the decade. With a $500 Temple Cup (named in honor of a Pittsburgh businessman) offered each year from 1894 to 1897 to the winner of a postseason series between the top two finishers, owners collected additional revenues but shared little of it with their hirelings. The players' share was divided 65/35 between winners and losers to stir more ardent efforts, and in 1894 the winners garnered $800 each and the losers $450. But in subsequent years the winners' shares fell to $600, then to $200, and only slightly rebounded to $310 in 1897. By

1899, according to one account, the average major leaguer made $2,000, a standstill since the 1880s (see Appendix, Fig. 1). Although artificially lower than his due in a free and competitive labor marketplace, the major leaguer's compensation remained, however, far higher than that of the player stored away in the white minor leagues, which by decade's end were thirteen in number and employed 1,200–1,500 performers per season. There, the average annual salary reached but $571. And on the best black teams, whose talent was systematically excluded from both the majors and the white minors, the lack of access to a broader employment market in "organized baseball" meant but a $466 average yearly figure for the brightest stars.[15]

Because of the efficiency of the owners' labor controls and the new labor surplus, within two years of the National League's victory over the American Association the surviving league was able to inject more offense into the game via new rules changes, and thereby boost gate receipts, without triggering the usual magnitude of salary inflation (see Appendix, Figs. 3 and 4). Anxious to make up for the lean years of 1890–92, in 1893 the National League lengthened the pitching distance from fifty feet to sixty feet, six inches. Desperate pitchers tried to compensate by building up the pitching mounds. The overall statistical results were astonishing, as batting averages jumped 35 points, ERAs rose by 1.38 runs, and runs allowed increased by 1.45 per game. In 1894 Boston center fielder Hugh Duffy compiled a .438 average. Leaguewide, the ERA, which stood at 3.28 runs a game in 1892, reached 5.32 in 1894. Believing that the fans wanted not simply more hitting but lustier clouts, owners then abolished the flat bat and made a foul bunt with two strikes an out. At the same time, not wanting to overdramatize individual notoriety at the expense of team success, they rejected a proposal by Chicago owner and Spalding front man James Hart that individual numbers be attached to uniforms.[16]

The owners' subsequent actions after 1895 suggested that, having raised offensive production to new heights, they desired to stabilize the numbers at that level. This was hardly surprising, since 1894 had been the decade's first really profitable season for them. Also on the owners' minds was the national economic depression, already two years old but as yet not seriously harming baseball attendance and revenues. Nonetheless, caution was the watchword, with owners refusing to risk offense changes in either direction that might trigger a delayed attendance decline or increase the upward pressure on future salaries. Reflecting the desire to lock in a stable new order on the field as well as in the labor marketplace, the National League passed laws regulating hitting and fielding equipment. Bats were limited to a 2¾-inch diameter, while the size and weight of gloves, except for catchers and first basemen, were held to not more than 14 inches in circumference and ten ounces. In 1896, a new pro-offense rule authorized umpires to keep a dozen balls on hand to facilitate replacement of those that became badly soiled or defaced during play but was counterbalanced by another lifting the requirement that pitchers hold the ball in front of their bodies before throwing. The repeal of the 1887 regulation meant that hurlers could more easily incorporate deceptive motions in their deliveries as they tried to overcome the immediate handicap of the longer pitching distance.[17]

Sportswriters expended considerable ink pondering the occupational health effects of the new pitching distance upon hurlers. In expectation of more cases of arm strain and injury, teams carried additional hurlers on their rosters by going from a two-pitcher norm at the beginning of the decade to four or five per team by 1896, probably the major contributor to a gradual decline in batting average after mid-decade. By the 1896 season, the twelve NL clubs contained fifty-one pitchers. The beleaguered moundsmen developed compensating pitches to replace lost velocity, including the "inshoot," "drop," "jump ball," and change-of-pace. But managers still expected complete games, and it remained fairly common for pitchers to throw 400 innings and win 25 or 30 games in a season. In mid-decade, the owners even considered, but did not adopt, rules permitting a late-inning designated hitter on the grounds that a weary pitcher's last at bat constituted a sure out. By game's end, they noted, he was usually only "fit for the ambulance." Pitchers, like players generally at the time, were not overpowering physical specimens at any rate, averaging about 5'10" and 170 pounds.[18]

In most other respects, the health and safety of players improved, offering a modest bright spot in an otherwise dismal decade of repression for baseball labor. The National League required all its clubs to provide visitors a club house, with a stove if necessary. Long- and short-distance travel for players became safer and more comfortable, as it did for Americans generally, and railroads, transit companies, and hotels bid against each other to provide improved accommodations for major league clubs at discount rates. Facilities for the minors, of course, lagged far behind. But at the NL level, some clubs retained professional trainers by mid-decade, and Brooklyn even hired a team physician. Treatment involved a blend of "modern" techniques, such as "Roentgen rays," warm-up exercises, and physical therapy with hot water, on the one hand, and superstitions and home remedies, on the other. It says something for the improved health prospects of players that the 1895 Cincinnati Reds, out of all the teams in major league history whose entire roster had died by 1990, claimed the highest average age of mortality, at 69½ years.[19]

Despite prevailing attitudes toward labor on the part of management in the baseball industry, some owners could be generous when it came to prominent and valuable stars. Infielder John McGraw, for example, received $1,200 in back pay from his Baltimore club one season despite missing action with typhoid illness. But for the journeyman, such charity was rare. Alcoholism and destitution remained serious afflictions, and baseball, like other industries of the day, still provided no pension system. Individual acts of volunteerism remained the lone sporadic responses to premature player death or disability. When Mike Kelly died, owners did offer $1,400 to his widow. When Hub Collins died, fellow players staged a benefit game and contributed to a $3,000 fund. But the nonstars who suffered unexpected medical hardships simply disappeared "beneath the cracks" if, as was likely in the economic retrenchment of the 1890s, they had failed to set aside earnings for the future. Similar fates awaited those who, through lack of education or work skills, found themselves unprepared for life after baseball.

The success of the NL baseball cartel of the 1890s in establishing a dictatorial regime over its workers' mobility and compensation, and in establishing the minors as a cheap labor replacement pool, meant that its owners felt no economic pressure to broaden the ethnic and racial bases of the player force. As in other aspects of their rule, once having seized dominance they sought a stable, profitable equilibrium, in this instance an ethnocultural and socioeconomic profile for the player force that encouraged the ethnic middle-class's growing spectatorship while maintaining a Wasplike respectability in the players' image and conduct expected by Victorian fans. Successful sons of the "old" Irish and German immigration of previous decades living in northeastern urban neighborhoods showered adoration upon their baseball heroes. In 1891, Mike Kelly's worshipful admirers gave him a horse and carriage. Midwestern teams catered deliberately to German fans, with the St. Louis club, for example, providing advertisements in German-language newspapers. In New York, where a baseball-hungry populace, 77 percent foreign-born, wanted to attend Sunday games, the Giants evaded laws against Sunday ticket sales by selling "programs" and accepting spectator "contributions" instead. The Polo Grounds featured a particular section of bleachers dubbed "Burkeville" because of the boisterous Irish fans who filled it at Giants home games.

Notwithstanding the growing courtship of ethnic spectators, the composition of the player force actually turned slightly more, rather than less, Waspish in the 1890s (see Appendix, Fig. 2). Earlier accounts have claimed the 1890s as the peak era of Irish on-field participation, but subsequent evidence suggests that the assertion may be somewhat deceiving. According to Lee Allen's data, the Irish share of the player ancestry pool among entrants into the big leagues dropped from 36 percent for the 1885–90 period to 22 percent for the years 1891–99. The British Isles' "non-Irish" contribution, in contrast, climbed from about 31 percent to approximately two-fifths of the total, and the German proportion rose from 24 percent to about 30 percent. Within the latter number were a handful of Jewish players: eleven members of that faith had reached the majors by 1900, and four attained managerial positions. French and Scandinavians followed at 4 percent and 1.5 percent respectively. Italians, the only non–Western European group identified, rounded out the total with 1.5 percent. What probably accounts for the perception of on-field "Irishness" in the 1890s is the fact that the descendants of Erin, having penetrated the major league player force in its "immigration" of the late 1870s and 1880s, now constituted a larger segment of the game's most visible veteran stars and managers than before. In addition, outside observers in the press and middle-class public still tended to equate on-field roughhousing—with which the game in the 1890s was replete—with the Irish influence, whether the association was consistently true or not.[20]

Notable for their gains as a share of the "British" group of ballplayers were Scots and Scotch-Irish entrants, a trend reflecting the increasingly dense "feeder" system of town, mill, and industrial semipro teams in the smaller manufacturing centers and villages of the interior Northeast that now supplemented the traditional metropolitan sources of players. Such semipro teams, numbering in the thousands, provided entry-level opportunities into the profession at typical sums of $5 a game or $15 a week. Reflecting the broadening small-town and urban talent roots in the northeastern quarter, but slower progress elsewhere, a study of 168 NL players of 1897 contained only 3 performers from as far south as Virginia and only 7 (all from California or Oregon) from the West. In contrast, 34 hailed from Pennsylvania, 31 from Massachusetts, 20 from Ohio, 19 from New York, and 11 from Missouri. Paralleling this talent distribution, the National League had no teams outside the Northeast and Midwest, and of the thirteen minor leagues in existence by 1899, only three operated outside the same regions—one in the South, one in Texas, and one on the West Coast. The other noteworthy "demographic trend" within the player force, reflecting the growth of baseball programs in higher education as well as the owners' continued preoccupation with the gentlemanliness of their charges, was the growing recruitment of college players. The physical reality and the cultural symbolism of the trend found fictional expression in the Frank Merriwell stories, begun in 1896, and similar creations.[21]

Of no great surprise—given the racial intolerance and increasingly formalized segregation of the era and the owners' other repositories of cheap labor—was the continued, and vigilantly policed, exclusion of African Americans from both the National League and the white minors. In baseball, as in the larger society, Jim Crow became even more rigid in the 1890s. Although fifty-five blacks managed to penetrate some twenty different white leagues between 1883 and 1898, none reached the majors in the 1890s. With the collapse of talent demand after the brotherhood war, from 1891 to 1898 only four white minor league clubs employed a total of three different African American players, despite the growing number of black youth, church, occupational, and company clubs that served as training grounds. As a result, the very best talent on black nines continued to earn, on average, more than $100 less per year than a mediocre minor leaguer, and far less still than an NL journeyman. Even those suspected of being part black, such as Lou Nava in the 1880s and George Treadway in the 1890s, found themselves hounded by white players and fans alike. White leagues went so far in enforcing Jim Crow as to drastically curtail the number of exhibition games played against black clubs. Ironically, it may well have been easier to smuggle a woman onto a white minor league roster than to get a black man on one. Ed Barrow managed to introduce Lizzie Stroud into the Atlantic League under the fictional last name of Arlington. But with Barrow interested in her services only as a sideshow attraction, she soon disappeared from the circuit.[22]

In the constricted baseball labor environment of the 1890s, the National League's player surplus and consequent job insecurity bred internal division and on-field frictions in the playing ranks. Whatever the immediate trigger—natural combativeness, veteran players holding on against younger challengers, the financial incentives of postseason pay for underpaid performers, on-field ethnic tensions, or something else—

ballplaying had become increasingly rough and rowdy. Owners hesitated to crack down completely, assuming, much like hockey executives today, that to do so might cost rather than gain fans. In 1896, Cleveland players, protesting a decision to suspend play in a game with Louisville, caused a riot that led to their arrests and $50–100 fines in a local court. Before the 1898 season, owner John Brush authored and announced a twenty-one-point "Purification Plan" intended to rid the game of "obscene, indecent, or vulgar language" by players in front of the "refined and cultured class" of spectators. Umpires were ordered to report such incidents to an NL Board of Discipline with the power to fine or suspend offending players. But when a former Giant, James "Ducky" Holmes, publicly insulted New York owner Andrew Freedman before a game with Baltimore in July by calling him a "sheeney" and the executive demanded that the umpire remove Holmes from the park, the arbiter refused on grounds that he had not personally heard the slur. Freedman, a Jewish realtor-politico and ally of Tammany boss Richard Croker, pulled his team off the field, forfeited the game, and refunded the fans' money. The disciplinary board fined Freedman and suspended Holmes for the remainder of the season, but fellow owners Soden, Brush, and Frank Robison of Cleveland, whose dislike of the Giants owner occasionally smacked of anti-Semitism, thought the penalty on the player "illegal." *Sporting Life* concurred, insisting that the "trifling offense" of "insulting the Hebrew race" had produced a "perversion of justice." Reacting to the pressure, the board reversed itself and reinstated Holmes after only ten days. In many other cases, too, the same moguls who cried for gentlemanly on-field conduct secretly paid their employees' fines when they transgressed in the cause of team victory.[23]

The owners' pursuit of victories, pennants, and profits, combined with their sensitivities over maintaining a proper balance between player aggressiveness and decorum, placed increasing burdens upon their on-field supervisors, the managers. In order to support their field bosses' authority over the players, owners awarded managers higher pay than their charges. But with such higher compensation also came greater front-office expectations of success, greater occupational and psychological separation from the players, and fragile job security. Manager insecurity was hardly eased by the immediate presence of a number of veterans "retired" in the major league downsizing after 1891. Owners insisted that their on-site overseers vigilantly stand watch over players' "physical condition and moral habits." Frank Selee, who guided Boston to three pennants in 1891–93, became the first manager to lead his team in street clothes from the bench and visibly symbolized the gradual separation of manager from player in attire, age (as the number of players over the age of thirty shrank), and income. Other, less successful managers found their efforts rudely rewarded with firings. The venerable Harry Wright, having been hired by Philadelphia for $2,000 in 1892, got the axe at the end of 1893. At age forty-six, longtime Chicago skipper Cap Anson received his pink slip in 1898. Anson grew so furious that in revenge he tried to buy out his former team, which pundits now called the "Cubs" because of its youth. Only two managers retained posts for the entire decade. But the era's champion of managerial musical chairs was New York's Freedman, who hired and fired sixteen different managers in his eight-year reign from 1895 to 1902, a record that even the mercurial George Steinbrenner of the modern era could not outdo.

The mixed signals sent in regard to on-field player conduct, and the dubious conduct of the game's employers themselves, made matters difficult for those baseball workers dubbed "the men in blue." Harry Wright's appointment as chief of umpires in mid-decade sent a signal of intended integrity, but his position in fact was largely symbolic. It did little for the arbiters' image of integrity that NL president Nick Young admitted that he occasionally assigned umpires to work particular games on the basis of their past "popularity" with local fans. Most umpires, even more than players, still came from Wasp backgrounds, although some Irish veterans such as Tim Keefe did make their way into the profession. Keefe, however, resigned in 1895, calling the abuse he and others suffered "absolutely disagreeable." He continued, "It is the fashion now for every player to froth at the mouth and emit shrieks of anguish whenever a decision is given which is adverse to the interests of the club." The Orioles' John McGraw claimed that "artful kicking" to keep umpires aware of his presence gained his club as many as fifty extra runs a season. For their abuse, arbiters even by the late 1890s earned only $1,500 for seven months of employment, less than they had gotten at the start of the decade.[24]

In the short run, the NL cartel was able to regain its profitability up to the middle of the 1890s by means of its strategy of restoring the reserve, holding the minors hostage, limiting individual salaries while imposing wage scales, and boosting offense. In 1892 visiting NL clubs received 50 percent of the base admission rate, which with different prices charged for different seating, actually meant a 40 percent visitor take. Although the levy on teams had been raised from 10 percent to 12.5 percent to 16 percent to finance the 1891 buyout of AA teams, the National League still had to issue promissory notes at the end of 1892, and eleven of twelve teams probably lost money that season. For the next campaign, the Phillies had to revert to quarter ball, and they arranged more favorable gate-sharing terms with the four former AA teams now in the National League. Owners also switched from a percentage scheme for splitting the gate to a scheme based on payment of a flat sum. These steps, combined with the league's economies against labor, enabled it to pay off the rest of the merger debt and compile a $25,000 surplus, although only four individual teams made $15,000 or more in 1893. The following season proved the best since 1889, with all but one club in the black. Included in the reasons for this financial success—apart from savings in labor costs—was the owners' increasingly creative use of stadium rentals for other amusements, already so widespread that the National League found it necessary to require that such added activities not delay games by more than half an hour. 1894 profits ranged from $5,000 to $40,000, with the Giants, who averaged 2,500 fans a game, and league champion Baltimore at the top. With Sunday and holiday games now drawing 5,000–10,000 spectators, 1895 proved to be an even better year.[25]

The owners' "magic," however, quickly disappeared after 1895. As one example, the Philadelphia Phillies' attendance, which had reached nearly 475,000 fans in 1895, fell to 265,000 by 1898. That same season, the club grossed but $49,000, their second-worst year of the decade (the worst being 1891). Only half of the NL teams made profits in 1898, and in 1899 major league attendance as a whole fell by half a million fans. Baseball historians have given various reasons for the sharp decline, and the answer surely lies in some combination of those reasons. One factor was the belated impact upon attendance of the severe business depression of the 1890s, which hit baseball late but persisted several years longer than in the general economy. A second cause was the confusion and lack of conformity in scheduling lucrative Sunday tilts. In cities such as Cleveland, local laws still prevented baseball on the Sabbath, while eastern and western clubs in the circuit attempted to coordinate schedules while fighting with each other to secure more such dates for themselves. The lack of a successful New York team after 1895 also hurt, given the importance of fan attendance in that huge market to both the Giants and its visiting opponents. The sad decline of the Giants on the field in the late 1890s paralleled the reign of the erratic Andrew Freedman as their owner, which can hardly be a coincidence.

Even in the absence of salary pressures, other operating expenses connected with the upkeep, transportation, lodging, and workplace facilities of the teams had continued to rise. Existing wooden structures had to be modernized, or, when they burned down (as they frequently did), they had to be repaired or replaced. In 1894 alone, grandstands in Philadelphia, Baltimore, and Boston all burned, and St. Louis experienced six fires in ten years. Insurance for these risks, as well as windstorm damage and lawsuit liability, added more costs. Travel expenses bit deeply into every club's pocketbook, with the average team traveling nearly 10,000 miles by 1895 (a 113,637-mile total for the league) and $1,500–2,000 road trips not unheard of. By 1898, a typical club's expenditures featured a $40,000 player payroll, $4,000 for the manager, $18,000 in administrative costs to the league, $17,500 for grounds upkeep, $13,000 or more for travel, and $1,000 for insurance. Another account in 1899 estimated the total operating costs of a "cheap" club at $45,000, those of an average one at $66,500, and an "elite" franchise's at nearly $100,000.[26]

A crucial final difficulty for the National League was its lack of competitive balance, a problem that, according to the champions of the reserve clause within management, could not occur. Nonetheless it did, and in a single circuit without divisions it meant that attendance plummeted in most cities as early as the summer. For the entire decade, Louisville and St. Louis usually stayed at or near the bottom. Cleveland, however, set a new low for ineptitude in 1899 with a 20-134 record, predictably resulting in an average attendance of less than 200 a game. Only three teams won regular-season pennants in the period—Boston (1891–93, 1898), Baltimore (1894–97), and Brooklyn (1899). Some writers, most notably baseball historian Charles Alexander, have criticized the owners for not adopting geographically based divisions better suited both to sustaining fan interest and to reducing transportation costs. The solution seems so obvious that one has to wonder why the National League failed to turn to the expedient. The likely reason stemmed once more from the owners' mistrust of each other and the perceived dangers of coalescing into rival camps, thereby triggering a trade war and labor turmoil from within. A "Rogers faction" already opposed a "Brush faction" within the ownership community, and nearly all the other owners detested Freedman for one reason or another. If the National League adopted regional divisions, it could encourage additional separatist tendencies, culminating in a complete split and a war that would destroy the owners' hard-won labor controls in an orgy of parasitic talent-raiding.[27]

It was such an understanding of the fragility of owner unity, the lessons of other leagues' failures from internal fragmentation, and the need to shore up ailing franchises that led NL franchise ownerships to become even more interlocked. This response, however, created its own problems in compromising the integrity of pennant races and encouraging public suspicion that outcomes were manipulated or fixed, often through the suspicious bartering of player services. As early as 1891, Chicago's Jim Hart accused the Giants of holding out three stars in a season-ending series with Boston so that the latter would win the pennant. As motivation, he cited Giants owner Day's financial obligations from the 1890 brotherhood war to Boston owner Soden, who had purchased stock to shore up the ailing New York franchise. Hart's case would have been more persuasive if Chicago itself had not been the possessor of even more Giants stock than Boston from the same bailout. Nonetheless, Soden showed a similar largesse toward New York two years later in "loaning" his contracted employee, Mike Kelly, to the Giants. Interlocking stock connections also "greased the wheels" of Monte Ward's transfer from the Dodgers to the Giants the same season.

As owners' profits declined after mid-decade in spite of their maintenance of vigilant controls on their labor, the consolidation of club finances increased, as did the number of suspiciously unbalanced trades, sales, and "releases" of players. Von der Ahe, embroiled in depression-ravaged real estate investments as well as personal scandal in the form of adultery and divorce proceedings, tried to sell his club. However, over his opposition it passed into court-ordered receivership with the National League's blessing. Von der Ahe then attempted to regain the St. Louis club presidency. But after a series of shuffles, Frank Robison claimed it in 1899; then, like a corporate raider, he stripped his Cleveland club of its player assets to restock his new property. Brooklyn's success in 1899 came about because of a similar set of circumstances. Two Baltimore investors, manager Ned Hanlon and club vice-president Harry Von der Horst, went in together to buy a half-interest in the Dodgers, while Brooklyn operators Frederick Abell and Charles Ebbets did the same with the Orioles. Hanlon then moved over from Baltimore to become Brooklyn's field manager and brought with him most of its player talent, save John McGraw, including batting wizard "Wee" Willie Keeler. Hanlon's new team won the pennant, while Baltimore sagged to fourth. Before the 1900 season, Pittsburgh's Barney Dreyfuss emulated Hanlon by buying Louisville in order to strip it of its players, including the talented Honus Wagner.[28]

Fans in adversely affected cities understandably resented such personnel machinations, and the National League's growing financial problems, shaky hold on key markets, and abusive labor relations presented a golden opportunity for a new challenger who promised a "squarer" deal for fans and ballplayers alike. The man who would exploit the opportunity was Byron Bancroft "Ban" Johnson. Born in 1864, Johnson attended Marietta and Oberlin colleges in Ohio and played college baseball. Hired as a sportswriter for the Cincinnati *Commercial Gazette*, he struck up a strong friendship with Charles Comiskey, who was the Reds' manager at the time, and became a sharp critic of John Brush. As one who covered the Players' League war, Johnson carefully noted the losing circuit's errors, including its parceling out of gate receipts and its imbalanced travel schedules. At Comiskey's urging and with Brush's reluctant acceptance, he assumed the presidency of the Western League, an eight-team circuit with clubs in Indianapolis, Kansas City, Milwaukee, Minneapolis, Toledo, Grand Rapids, Sioux City, and Detroit by 1894. A party to the National Agreement, the league operated as a Class A circuit and already had begun to acquire more than its share of grievances against the labor policies of NL owners such as Brush. As an example of NL manipulations, the senior circuit after the 1896 season plundered Western League champion Minneapolis, whose owners had just completed costly ballpark improvements and then found their club crippled competitively and financially for the next season.[29]

In 1899, the Western League began to make threatening noises at the National League by indicating its intention to place franchises in the Chicago, St. Louis, and Cleveland markets. Remembering the Players' League outcome, to protect his circuit from internal betrayal Johnson required his clubs to hand over 51 percent of their stock for his direct safekeeping. NL owners did not immediately heed the threat, however, as they were distracted by similar moves by disgruntled former members of their own fraternity—Von der Ahe and Anson—who were talking about the creation of a new American Association. In October, Johnson publicly announced that his circuit was changing its name to the American League and following through with its expansion plans. More concerned about a prospective AA team in the Windy City led by the revenge-minded Anson, Hart allowed the Western League to locate a team in Chicago in exchange for a fee and continued player-drafting rights, while promising to respect its own in-season player reservation rights.

Although publicly appearing conciliatory at first, the National League circled the wagons by jettisoning its weakest franchises and increasing

Ban Johnson, founder and longtime president of the American League and member of baseball's National Commission

even further its level of ownership consolidation, while keeping the defunct clubs' players as the league's contract hostages. At the December 1899 meeting, NL owners received committee recommendations to buy out the Louisville, Cleveland, Washington, and Baltimore clubs for $110,000. The sixty or more players left without teams were to be auctioned off as property to the eight surviving franchises. Some of the buyout price would be raised by selling territorial rights to minor league bidders, while $50,000 would be garnered through another levy, of 5 percent for two years, on gate receipts. By auctioning the stranded players, the National League also could prevent them from being available to the Western League or any other potential rival. In similar fashion, the four "condemned" franchises still retained technical exclusivity of territorial rights until the completion of the buyout in two years, thereby denying them to any non-NL suitor. As an indication of the degree of ownership intermingling, by the beginning of 1900 Cincinnati's Brush held some Giants shares, while Boston's Soden was New York's largest minority stockholder. Abell claimed 40 percent of both Baltimore and Brooklyn, as did Von der Horst, and smaller portions of New York. Hanlon and Ebbets each owned 10 percent of the Dodgers and Orioles. Robison claimed both the St. Louis and Cleveland clubs, and Spalding held both Chicago and New York shares.[30]

Internal owner bickering, however, continued to plague the National League when it could least afford it. Much of it was triggered by the temperamental Freedman, who called for an even more centralized "syndicate" ownership of all league clubs and a similar pooling and central allocation of all member clubs' playing talent. Given his team's dismal performance in recent years, it came as no surprise that Freedman wanted such a reshuffling of player talent and that the new system would give New York special drafting privileges. Failing league acceptance of that scheme, the mercurial owner demanded the retraction of his 1898 $1,000 fine, the firing of league president Nick Young, and special rights of first choice of the four defunct teams' released players. Irritated, but aware of the need for a common front and the importance of a league presence in the New York territory, fellow magnates agreed to return Freedman's $1,000, plus 6 percent interest, provide him first crack at Washington's roster and an equal shot at the rosters of the other three clubs, and rescind an earlier ban on Sunday exhibition games by the Giants in Weehawken. Unsatisfied, Freedman refused to pay his 5 percent to the buyout fund and demanded territorial rights to Brooklyn because of New York City's annexation of it and other boroughs in 1899.

As Francis Richter accurately stated, by 1900 the moguls of the National League monopoly had made their circuit ripe for picking because of their "gross individual and collective mismanagement, their fierce factional fights, their cynical disregard of decency and honor, their open spoilation of each other, their deliberate alienation of press and public, their flagrant disloyalty to friends and supporters, and"—last but certainly not least—"their tyrannical treatment of their players."[31] Ban Johnson and his group of rival owners now prepared to exploit all of these weaknesses in a war that threatened to destroy the National League's short-lived baseball labor monopoly. In doing so, they were handing the players a new opportunity to reclaim a significant measure of the marketplace leverage that the National League's major league monopoly had denied them for nearly a decade.

SIX

BASEBALL PROGRESSIVISM AND THE PLAYER, 1900-1909

The dawn of a new century inaugurated in America a reform impulse from the cities and states, carried by insurgents pledged to unseat a corrupt Old Guard and restore clean, efficient government. Within a year, through the historical accident of an assassination, "progressivism" claimed one of its own in the White House. In similar fashion, Ban Johnson in 1900 was prepared to challenge baseball's entrenched powers, purportedly in the name of honesty and efficiency. His American League possessed solid financial backing, and he had cultivated an image of moral probity for his circuit by refusing to tolerate the "usual" level of on-field rowdiness and by giving his umpires unprecedented backing. The placement of his Chicago franchise had even been accepted grudgingly by the National League, although owner Comiskey's new White Stockings were prohibited from using the name of the city in their logo. Prospects of success and major league status for the Windy City team (and others in the American League) made even the White Stockings' malodorous South Side home near the stockyards tolerable.

While a new trade war loomed, a new players' organization also prepared to exploit the war and play the two major leagues off against each other for its members' benefit. Throughout the United States, the severe depression of the 1890s, with its wage cuts, bankruptcies, layoffs, and business consolidations, had triggered a general surge of labor countermobilization in the industrial economy, led by Samuel Gompers's moderate American Federation of Labor. Similarly, on the baseball front, at New York's Sturtevant House on June 10, 1900, three delegates from each National League entry formed the Protective Association of Professional Baseball Players, with a $5.00 initiation fee and dues of $2.00 a month. The representatives selected Pittsburgh catcher Charley "Chief" Zimmer as the new union's president, with Cubs pitcher Clark Griffith vice-president, Hughie Jennings secretary, and Bill Clarke treasurer. Also in attendance was a representative of the AFL, Dan Harris, who extended the "moral support" of his organization. The new baseball union did resemble AFL craft affiliates in its abandonment of the nostalgic, utopian aim of restoring a lost "workplace democracy." With its members aware of how the high hopes of the Brotherhood of Professional Base Ball Players had been dashed a decade earlier, the Protective Association instead planned to use the leverage offered it by the forthcoming trade war to push for pragmatic gains in job security and benefits. Illustrating their caution, the delegates declined immediate affiliation with the AFL out of fear of owner retaliation and sought to promote an image of nonconfrontation by forswearing the use of a strike as a weapon. Although the organizers intended their handiwork to remain secret until season's end to avoid management reprisals, the names of Protective Association members leaked within a matter of weeks. The group's moderate stance, however, drew praise from the mainstream baseball press, including *Sporting Life.*

Approximately a hundred players, including some new members from the American and Eastern leagues, attended a second meeting at which they approved a constitution drafted by Buffalo attorney and former Louisville player Harry Leonard Taylor. The Protective Association's platform called for an end to "farming," selling, or trading players without their prior consent or compensation, a ban on unfair and unilateral pay cuts and fines, and replacement of a reserve clause of indefinite duration with a more limited alternative. Taylor, chosen by the players as their legal counsel, requested and received authority to examine and exercise prior restraint over all members' new contracts before signing. Once more, player representatives attempted to project a cooperative spirit toward owners by offering to use their influence with other team members to help restrain on-field rowdyism.[1]

When Taylor requested a meeting with NL owners in the fall of 1900, however, the owners replied with vituperation. Part of the reason for their condemnation was a list of formal demands that Taylor had submitted to them in writing. They included far-reaching changes in the uniform contract that would give the right to break a contract with ten days' notice on grounds of noncompliance to players as well as owners. The word "assign" would effectively be stricken from the management vocabulary under another provision that called for a ban on player transactions without consent. The list further included a demand for the salary lid to be lifted from $2,400 to $3,000 per player. The Protective Association also wanted clubs to pay for its members' uniform costs and doctor fees for in-service injuries, and it urged creation of a new arbitration panel, consisting of an owner, a player, and a third party acceptable to both, to hear player grievances.

NL owners wasted no time in blasting both the proposals and the legitimacy of their presenters. Philadelphia's Rogers claimed that baseball had no room for a labor federation, since it was a "sport," not an industry. Boston's Soden bluntly stated, "I do not believe in labor organizations or unions." Throwing down the gauntlet to the Protective Association, he added defiantly, "When a player ceases to be useful to me I will release him." In contrast, the more temperate response of Soden's business partner, James Billings, drew for him the nickname "Benign Billings." The New York Giants' John Day threatened to raze his park rather than agree to meet a "secret organization of ballplayers." Press leaks from management characterized association vice-president Griffith, who had won twenty games a season for six years only to draw a $2,500 salary by 1900, as a "free silver politico-pitcher." While in Boston for a late-season series with Chicago, Griffith actually followed Soden into a saloon demanding to know if he had received the union's written demands. When the owner insisted that he had not, the Cubs hurler pulled the very document out of the magnate's pocket to prove him a liar. Nonetheless, NL president Nick Young curtly informed Griffith of

Harry Leonard Taylor, legal counsel to the Protective Association of Professional Baseball Players in 1900

Catcher Charles "Chief" Zimmer, president of the Protective Association

the owners' continued rigidity, stating "They aren't going to give you a thing."[2]

Despite the owners' characterizations of the Protective Association, it was a far less "radical" challenger to organized baseball than the brotherhood of a decade earlier had been. The brotherhood had resembled the Populists or the Knights of Labor in its advocacy of workers' reclaiming of the control of ownership itself—of the means of production—and the restoration of free labor economic democracy. To accomplish that aim they had gone so far as to create their own separate, rival league, only to see it collapse with the betrayal of their financial backers. In contrast, the Protective Association embodied the more restricted horizons of the "new" trade unionism in its self-proclaimed emphasis upon pragmatic negotiation, designed to promote incremental bread-and-butter gains rather than open defiance of management prerogatives. The danger with such narrowed horizons, however, lay in the fact that the National League's new management rival, Ban Johnson's American League, might lure association members to its side in the trade war with generous individual promises or even group concessions on job tenure and benefits, only to abandon recognition of the union and prior pledges to it when it proved no longer "useful." Ironically, given the nonconfrontational posture of the Protective Association, only if its membership remained undivided, resisting co-optation by either side, and thereby capable in management's eyes of collective defiance through a strike or formation of a new players' circuit, could the union ensure that its wartime gains would last into peacetime.

For his part, Johnson, a student of the Players' League war, privately planned to drive a wedge between the Protective Association and the National League that would facilitate widespread player jumping to his circuit. With only three NL clubs showing a profit in 1900, the American League announced in September its intention of claiming major league rights and status for the coming campaign. Already prepared for head-to-head market showdowns with the senior circuit in Boston (where the Indianapolis club had relocated), Philadelphia, and Chicago, the American League abandoned its "protected" position under the National Agreement and refused to pay the National League the "protection fee" required of minor leagues. Johnson indicated a willingness to discuss the American League's moves with NL owners, but he refused any solution short of access to major league markets and major league status and exemption from having his circuit's players drafted. Griffith, who after a 14-13 season with the Cubs had jumped to the White Stockings, served as the main recruiting agent for the challenger league within the Protective Association. Charles Somers, a Cleveland millionaire and main stockholder in that city's AL franchise, also bankrolled Comiskey's move into Chicago and shored up the Boston and Philadelphia clubs. Connie Mack assumed field management and partial ownership of the Athletics, and, ironically, Ben Shibe, sporting goods partner of NL investor Al Reach, also bought into Philadelphia's American League team. Johnson also succeeded in luring John McGraw away from his involvement in plans for a revitalized American Association, convincing him to manage the American League's Baltimore club. In retaliation, the National League refused to receive Johnson at its annual meeting, sent friendly signals to the new American Association, and granted the former AL territories of Kansas City and Minneapolis to a new Western League to close off avenues of escape for the challenger.

The one crucial path of opportunity that NL owners failed to seal off tightly enough, however, was the courtship of its players by Johnson and his agents. The senior circuit's magnates finally did invite a four-member Protective Association delegation, consisting of Taylor, Zimmer, Jennings, and Griffith, to their December meeting. But the National League's designated reception committee of Soden, Brush, and Rogers—its composition alone a sign of intransigence—immediately informed its counterpart that it had not been empowered to negotiate on any of the union's demands. Taylor retaliated by warning the owners of his power to prevent players from signing their 1901 contract offers. Faced with the National League's intransigence, Taylor left the meetings prematurely to attend to other legal business in Buffalo. While he was away, the pro–American League representatives within the union, especially Griffith, began to "play" by encouraging others to join them in the new circuit, with or without Taylor's blessing. Ban Johnson enticed some by indicating a willingness to recognize the Protective Association formally, prohibit farming without consent, and abandon a salary maximum. He also capitalized on Taylor's earlier instructions to members to hold off on signing new NL contracts and projected an "honorable" image for his circuit by announcing that the American League would not recognize the reserve but would honor active NL player contracts. Lured by Griffith, McGraw, and Mack, some players committed immediately to the new major league, while others tried to play off one league's offer against the other's while delaying the actual signing of new contracts.[3]

Too late, the National League responded. In February the owners agreed to sit down with Association members other than the "radical"

Clark Griffith, a vice-president of the Protective Association and covert recruiter for the American League

Taylor, who again stayed behind in Buffalo. The National League offered the union formal recognition, the elimination of farming and selling without player consent, retention of a player's salary level upon demotion to the minors, and a reserve limited to a more precise yearly "option to renew." The magnates, however, still refused to grant a balanced arbitration mechanism and demanded in return for their generosity Protective Association cooperation in suspending and blacklisting players who jumped to the American League. Zimmer wired Taylor, who had directed him not to sign any accords until he had scrutinized them, and received his consent. But even though Zimmer, as president, seemed to indicate his union's willingness to become a disciplinary arm of the National League, many in its membership already had voted otherwise with their feet. Under membership pressure by late February, which eventually forced Zimmer out in favor of Tom Daly, Protective Association representatives employed a loophole in the document which stated that jumpers would merely be suspended "pending final action" by the association. "Final action" quickly translated into immediate reinstatement.

Lured by the American League's promises of no salary cap and lucrative offers from individual teams, players jumped in droves to the challenger, and salaries soared (see Appendix, Fig. 1). Of 182 AL players in 1901, 111 had seen previous NL service. Even the National League's mouthpiece, the *Spalding Guide*, admitted that the rival circuit had gobbled up 74 NL actives. AL agents enjoyed particular success in luring away the brightest stars, among whom only Honus Wagner escaped their clutches. The Boston entry secured Cy Young from the NL team in St. Louis for $3,500 and Chick Stahl, Ted Lewis, and Jimmy Collins from its Bean Town NL rival. Collins became player-manager at a $4,000 salary. Rejecting late appeals from his former owner, Robison, Young retorted, "Your treatment of your players has been so inconsiderate that no self-respecting man would want to work for you if he could do anything else in the world." Comiskey's Chicago club, with Griffith its talent agent, snatched Fielder Jones from Brooklyn. Hugh Duffy crossed over to the American League as Milwaukee's player-manager. Mack's Athletics obtained pitchers Charles "Chick" Fraser and Bill Bernhard, but their prize catch was second baseman Napoleon Lajoie, who immediately became the circuit's brightest star. John McGraw, recruiting talent for his Baltimore club, nabbed Brooklyn pitcher Joe McGinnity. Never one to accept readily obstacles that stood in the way of winning, McGraw even contemplated smuggling the African American star Charles Grant onto the Orioles under the ruse that he was a full-blooded Cherokee Indian named "Charlie Tokóhoma" but then changed his mind and declined to sign him.[4]

In a desperate attempt to hold the line on future salary escalation without handing the American League obvious ammunition in the player-bidding war, the National League adopted offense-suppressing rules changes (see Appendix, Fig. 4). The owners approved a new five-sided home plate to improve umpires' vision of strikes and made a batter's first two foul balls strikes. The American League, for its part, went only halfway, adopting the former rule but not the latter. The result was that the new major league generated more offensive fireworks, which pushed up the postseason salary demands of its nonpitchers but also appealed to more fans. Lajoie, for example, compiled a .422 batting average in 1901—the highest AL figure of the twentieth century. Despite the American League's not having a franchise in the enormous New York–New Jersey metropolitan market, which according to the 1900 census contained over 4.6 million people, the National League's blunders helped its rival amass very respectable attendance figures. Even though the American League had to share its three largest markets with NL competitors, and none of those markets contained as many as a million people, the senior circuit outdrew the new league by only 1,920,031 to 1,683,584. In 1902, the American League would win the battle—and the war—2,206,457 to 1,683,012.[5]

Although the bidding war hurt the contesting major leagues, it punished the minors at least as much. Minor league clubs lost players to both leagues without the compensation of draft fees, and to prevent even more losses to jumping they found themselves boosting their own pay. Of the two "higher" circuits, the National League was the more hated by the minors, both because of its past abuses in relation to them and because the American League in grabbing up talent at least acknowledged openly that it was an "outlaw" league operating outside National Agreement provisions. NL owners, in contrast, gobbled up replacements without compensating their former clubs, yet they did not formally abrogate their obligations under the National Agreement until September 1901. When the National League did abrogate the agreement, Western League president Tom Hickey called upon other minor league leaders to attend a strategy meeting in Chicago on September 5. Six came, including Pat Powers of the Eastern League, Michael Sexton of the Three-I (Illinois, Indiana, Iowa) League, John Farrell of the New York State League, W. H. Lucas of the Pacific Northwest League, William Meyer of the Western Association, and Tim Murnane of the

New England League. The conferees also received statements of support from the Southern Association, the California League, the North Carolina League, and the Connecticut League.

Following two days of sessions, the gathering adjourned; it reconvened in New York on October 25, and on that date a new ten-year National Agreement between the minors was announced. The new pact restored the reserve, imposed salary limits upon minor league players, and created a management-controlled National Board of Arbitration to hear grievances and impose penalties upon violators. The minors now claimed their own federation, the National Association of Professional Baseball Leagues, and in a choice bit of irony, the association retained John Montgomery Ward's Wall Street law firm as its legal representative. The minors also asserted the right to draw up and maintain their own classification levels and their own rights, procedures, and prices for drafting players. The new National Association demanded that the National League respect its handiwork, and the National League drew more condemnation for "outlaw" behavior when it refused to do so. The *Sporting News* blasted the National League's unwillingness to honor the minors' separate National Agreement as "foolhardy" and an "asinine departure from the regular." But with the American League having forced its hand by depleting it of many of its players, the outmaneuvered senior circuit could no longer afford to respect the minors' reserve rights and restrain itself from wholesale raids on their talent.[6]

By December 1901, the National League's management lay in disarray. The owners cringed at the idea of retaining the bland Nick Young as president but could not agree upon a successor. In addition, a powerful faction sought full-fledged syndication of the circuit's franchises into a giant (or perhaps more accurately, Giant) holding company. At a secret conference held at Andrew Freedman's Red Bank, New Jersey, estate, Freedman, Brush, Soden, and Robison hammered out the scheme, which leaked to the public courtesy of the New York *Sun* on December 11. The proposed National Baseball Trust, with preferred stock paying a 7 percent dividend, would issue common stock to subordinate franchises featuring interlocking directorates. Freedman's New York Giants would hold 30 percent of the trust's total stock, over twice the proportion of any other club. The other Red Bank conspirators would each claim 12 percent, giving the bloc approximately two-thirds control. In contrast, syndication opponents Rogers, Hart, Dreyfuss, and Ebbets would receive 10 percent, 10 percent, 8 percent, and 6 percent respectively. Under the plan, the trust would be governed by a five-member board of regents chosen by the stockholders, with two among them selected as operating president and treasurer at $25,000 and $12,000 salaries. The board also would assume responsibility for assigning each club its field manager at a fixed $5,000 income and for licensing and assigning all players.

When all of the NL owners met (according to a later account in *Sporting Life*), opponents of the Red Bank faction, led by Pittsburgh's representative, called for the election of the retired Albert Spalding as the new NL president. The Freedman group opposed this, first demanding a vote on their proposal, which, if successful, would have made the issue moot. The next day, Spalding himself arrived to speak against the trust scheme—an irony given that he had been a past proponent of combination and player-rationing plans when they had benefited his Chicago club. On the fifth day of the meetings, following repeated deadlocks, the Red Bank faction withdrew, enabling the others to ram through Rogers's selection as chairman pro tem and Spalding's election as league president. In retaliation, the absentees obtained an injunction preventing Spalding's installation, creating a leadership impasse just when the embattled circuit could least afford it. Bowing to the inescapable, Spalding resigned in the spring, and a fragile three-person executive committee of Brush, Soden, and Hart presided over league affairs.[7]

Not only was the American League winning the war on the field, at the gate, and in the boardrooms, it was also scoring triumphs in the courts in legal skirmishes over rights to player contracts. In March 1901, the Phillies had first tried to block Nap Lajoie, along with Chick Fraser and Bill Bernhard, from jumping to the rival Athletics. Lajoie had gone to the American League team because the NL club had paid teammate Ed Delahanty a higher salary of $3,000 in 1900. The American League's Mack offered Lajoie $24,000 over three years, or $8,000 a year for 1901–03. Even though the National League's Rogers was prepared to outbid Mack, proposing a $25,000 figure for Lajoie over just two seasons, his unwillingness to pay the player $100 retroactively to equalize his 1900 salary with Delahanty's cost him the player. All the star second baseman did for his new club in 1901 was win the triple crown, leading the junior circuit in batting average, home runs, and runs batted in. In the meantime, the Common Pleas Court of Philadelphia ruled against the Phillies' injunction request on the grounds that their contract had lacked sufficient mutuality.

Five days into the 1902 season, the Pennsylvania Supreme Court reversed the earlier ruling on the basis of the *Lumley* principle, which upheld such injunction requests if the jumping player's talents were truly unique (hardly a debatable matter in Lajoie's case). The court also upheld the mutuality of the Phillies contract, since it had spelled out a definite reserve period of three years at a $2,400 annual salary and had even included specific language barring Lajoie's services for another club. Nonetheless, Ban Johnson neatly sidestepped the obstacle and in the process exercised the kind of personal muscle that no one in the National League's chaotic officialdom could match. Although Fraser jumped back to the Phillies, the AL president arranged for Lajoie and Bernhard to be transferred to the Cleveland club. Since the Pennsylvania injunction could only be enforced on its home soil, the two could play for their new team, home and road, except when it traveled to Philadelphia to meet the Athletics. On those occasions, the former Philadelphians remained at the beaches of Atlantic City on paid vacation. When the frustrated Phillies sought to extend the force of the injunction to Cleveland, a common pleas court located there threw out the request for lack of jurisdiction.[8]

Emboldened by its success, the American League continued to plunder NL rosters. After the 1901 season, Ban Johnson had dropped Milwaukee from the circuit, transferring the franchise and players to St. Louis. The move made economic sense, for St. Louis claimed the second largest market for legal Sunday baseball (after Chicago). Owner Robert Lee Hedges then raided his NL rival of players Jesse Burkett, Jack Harper, and Bobby Wallace. A St. Louis court subsequently denied an injunction request intended to force shortstop Wallace back to his former team. Similar efforts targeted at Harper also failed, and Judge John A. Talty, refusing to consider the Pennsylvania Supreme Court ruling against Lajoie as precedent, blasted the National League for violating Harper's Fourteenth Amendment rights to equal treatment and due process. In Baltimore, McGraw lured old teammate Joe Kelley away from Brooklyn, and Washington even landed the Phillies' Delahanty. In June 1902, Connie Mack secured the uproarious George "Rube" Waddell, a 1901 veteran of Pittsburgh and Chicago who had jumped in the off-season to the California League. Between bouts of intoxication, the pitcher managed to win twenty-three games for the Athletics in only half a season. By winning over prominent players with big paychecks, Johnson also had crippled the Protective Association. With association president Daly himself among those profiting by jumping (from Brooklyn to Chicago in 1902), the union's July meeting failed to draw any nonofficer members, and the organization effectively collapsed by the end of the season.

By midyear of 1902, the only threat to AL victory lay in the possibility of internal betrayal. It nearly occurred, owing to a falling-out between Ban Johnson and John McGraw. McGraw, whose Baltimore team already had earned notoriety for its on-field rowdiness, believed that Johnson was out to get him and his players. Johnson, in turn, viewed the feisty Irishman as an 1890s-style baseball "anarchist." Concluding that Johnson's plan to move the Baltimore franchise to New York at season's end was designed to freeze him out of its operation, and being under AL disciplinary suspension at the time, McGraw in July conspired with the National League's John Brush to obtain a majority of Baltimore franchise stock. After more maneuvers, the two sold the stock to the Giants' Freedman, and McGraw jumped to the Giants with four of his players. Two others leaped to Brush's Cincinnati club. "Little Mac" received a four-year managerial contract at $11,000 a year, which he justified, along with the jump, by claiming to have spent $7,000 of his own Baltimore wages as advances to players without reimbursement from the league. At season's end, Brush's purchase of the Giants from Freedman completed the transactions.

Once more, Johnson deftly sidestepped what could have proved a fatal blow. He reassembled a makeshift Baltimore squad to finish the year, drawing upon donated players from other AL teams. Minority stockholders of the old Baltimore regime now received recognition as the team's new ownership and were provided with financial infusions from other league owners. At the end of the year, Johnson went ahead with the franchise's relocation to New York for the 1903 season. One remaining concern was park facilities in the club's new market. In all prior instances, the American League had been able to secure playing sites either through purchase of former NL properties or by erecting new parks. In New York, however, Freedman's Tammany connections threatened literally to create roadblocks to the construction of a new stadium. Worried that the Giants would "arrange" to have the city cut a new street through any proposed building site, Johnson made the necessary financial arrangements to buy his new Highlanders adequate political "insurance."[9]

Having been outdrawn in 1902, and now facing a challenge from the American League in its largest market, the National League was left with no choice but face-saving surrender. In the negotiations, the Protective

Association played no role, having evaporated. In December, in a move signaling compromise, the National League tabbed the appropriately named Henry Clay "Harry" Pulliam, Pittsburgh's club secretary, as its new president. With only the obstinate Brush holding back his approval, Pulliam approached Johnson to seek peace. Committees from each circuit—Johnson, Comiskey, Somers, and Boston's Henry Killilea from the American League and Pulliam, Robison, Hart, and Cincinnati's August "Garry" Herrmann from the National League—talked treaty on January 9, 1903. Two days later, the parties reached agreement. The American League adopted the National League's playing rules, including the foul-ball strike, and each side agreed to honor the other's active player contracts and reserve lists. Players outside those categories would be pooled and "legally awarded" to clubs in one or the other circuit. Having economized on salaries and travel costs through a reduced regular season of 140 games, the new partnership returned to the 1890s norm of 154 games.

With franchise territorial rights the biggest point of contention, Johnson got to keep his New York club in exchange for disavowing similar intentions in Pittsburgh. The National League, in turn, relegated the American Association to a minor league for the protection of AL markets. Neither circuit henceforth could shift a franchise without the prior consent of a majority of clubs in each league, producing a sixteen-club cartel with team locations that would go unchanged for half a century. The American League and National League shared New York, Boston, Chicago, Philadelphia, and St. Louis; the National League claimed Brooklyn, Pittsburgh, and Cincinnati; and the American League held Washington, Cleveland, and Detroit. As for players who had jumped leagues shortly before the announcement of the peace pact, the new regime tended to honor their new allegiances. Batting star Willie Keeler and spitball ace Jack Chesbro were permitted to move to the American League's New York entry, and Sam Crawford went from NL Cincinnati to AL Detroit. The Phillies also agreed to lift their local injunctions against Lajoie and Bernhard.

Understandably furious at the turn of events was new Giants owner Brush, who saw the American League's moves to strengthen his market adversary upheld. In addition to their decisions in the Keeler and Chesbro cases, the two league presidents agreed that George Davis, a former Giant who had jumped to AL Chicago in 1902 only to seek return to New York, would have to remain with the junior circuit after sitting out a year. In this instance, the player had wanted to return to the Giants and play immediately so much that he had retained John Montgomery Ward as a legal representative. In a related tragedy, Ed Delahanty, who like Davis had been a Giant only to leap to an AL team (Detroit), left his club and boarded a train for New York when he learned that his former teammate intended to rejoin the Giants. On the way, a conductor ordered him off the train near Niagara Falls owing to his intoxication and disorderly behavior; Delahanty fell off the railroad bridge while trying to cross it on foot and drowned in the raging waters. While Brush was left frustrated, Ban Johnson enjoyed the fruits emanating from his circuit's victory in the form of favorable rulings. When he transferred the contract of Detroit's Norman "Kid" Elberfeld to the New York Highlanders, the New York Supreme Court refused to grant Brush's demand for an injunction blocking the move. Johnson similarly arranged the "trade" of AL hitting star Pat Dougherty from Boston to the Highlanders for a reserve utility infielder, Robert Unglaub, despite the patent inequality of the transaction.[10]

Under a new National Agreement drawn up by the two league presidents, a three-member National Commission consisting of them and a third management representative acceptable to both, serving as chairman, would govern "organized" professional baseball. Garry Herrmann, president of the Cincinnati NL club but also a longtime friend of Ban Johnson, received the nod as commission chairman. No player membership, or even advice, was solicited for the new industry governing panel. The National Association, the blanket organization of the minor leagues, also lacked direct representation on the body, but it at least carried official "litigant" standing as a "party of the third part." The National Commission now retained the authority to issue regulations and final rulings in cases involving interclub, interleague, and major league–minor league disputes and to serve as the final avenue of appeal for player grievances against either major league or minor league management. The National Commission also presided over the resumption of club reservation rights, the classification of minor leagues, and the drafting of players. With the limitation that the majors could take a maximum of two players from any one Class A minor league franchise, the commission sanctioned the division of the minors' circuits into four classifications, A through D. With each major league club able to draft an unlimited number of minor leaguers at the end of each season, draft prices were fixed at $750 for Class A talent, $500 for B, $300 for C, and $200 for D.[11]

The cheap draft prices offered to the minors at the end of the American League war reflected the restoration of the majors' monopsony

*August "Garry" Herrmann, Cincinnati Reds president and chairman of the
National Commission*

power and their desire to bring their long-term labor costs quickly back under control. As had become the norm, then, the return of industrial peace brought the usual rounds of salary retrenchment (see Appendix, Fig. 1). Ban Johnson soon abandoned much public pretense of concern for players, stating that they could not expect wartime salaries to prevail. Clark Griffith, once the Protective Association's vice-president, rationalized slashing the salaries of former union brothers by claiming that a real cut was "a reduction in salary already contracted for" but that a pay reduction for a player in his reserve year was not really a cut. Owners in the smaller markets, with onerous war debts to pay off, proved most desperate to reduce salaries. Connie Mack's 1903 payroll, for example, came to but $36,000, probably the lowest in the majors. With multiyear contracts delaying immediate reductions in some cases, by January 1905 a desperate Robison, employing National Commission chairman Herrmann as an intermediary to AL president Johnson, urged adoption of across-the-board pay cuts to bring the major league per-player average down to $2,400. Robison even had the nerve to describe his remedy as "not very excessive." To sweeten the pot for the top teams, he added the suggestion of a $10,000 first-place bonus purse and a $5,000 amount for second place. But the moneys would be raised through continuing a 5 percent assessment on clubs' operating receipts, meaning that the same clubs' available funds for regular salaries would be depleted to finance the bonuses. Nonetheless, the *Sporting News* endorsed Robison's scheme and even proposed more drastic pay cuts of ⅓ and a return to a $35,000-per-club payroll limit, despite team rosters that now numbered from twenty-one to twenty-five players.[12]

By 1906, salary-reduction trends had become more dramatic. Veteran Bobby Wallace of the St. Louis Browns claimed the highest salary at $6,500, but younger stars such as Chicago's Joe Tinker and New York's Hal Chase commanded but $1,500 and $2,500 respectively. The Cubs' Johnny Kling received $3,500 the next season but no raises for the two years after that. With an upsurge in holdouts in the spring of 1908—the Giants' Mike Donlin unsuccessfully demanded $6,000 and Boston's Jake Stahl $5,000—Braves owner George Dovey proposed fixed sale prices for players and a system in which the National Commission would centrally distribute all major league playing talent. Once more the *Sporting News* championed a similar economy plan, proposing a formal wage scale for entry-level major leaguers. For the first three years a player would be a "ward" of the National Commission, which, rather than a particular club, would hold his contract. A player entering the majors from a Class A league would receive a capped salary of not more than $1,800 his first season, with maximum increases of $300 each of the next two years. Class B promotees to the big leagues could make no more than $1,500 in their initial year, with subsequent $300 increases, and Class C rookies $1,200 and $300. Only after three years' tenure would players be able to enter individual negotiations with particular clubs for higher pay. In justifying its plan on the basis of cost savings, the newspaper noted that few playing careers lasted more than five years, thereby assuring overall wage savings to the industry.[13]

Although no formal collective action followed to enact the particular wage scale proposal, the owners of the two circuits made sure through private collusion that comparable results were achieved. One source estimated that 12 of the 16 clubs effectively followed the pattern in their own player dealings. The predictable result, like that of the Brush plan of two decades before, was a two-tier wage system in which a few veteran stars earned impressive salaries, and therefore elevated the overall average, while most players found their wages virtually unchanged from those of comparable performers of a decade earlier (see Appendix, Fig. 1). By 1909, Honus Wagner made $12,000, tops in the majors. Nap Lajoie earned $7,500, the Giants' star pitcher Christy Mathewson $6,000, and slugger Ed Walsh $5,000. A few high-payroll teams in larger markets also boosted the average, with the 1909 Chicago Cubs claiming a $90,000 outlay. But even with such upward "leveraging," the average player continued to earn under $2,500, while rookies drew from $1,500 to $2,000 and marginal reserves sometimes still made under $1,000.[14]

Once more a players' union had failed to meet the test of time, and the owners had succeeded in pitting veterans against entry-level players and stars against journeymen in tugs-of-war over pay and job security. Without representation or collective power, nonstar players found themselves in no position for individual heroics such as holdouts. Compared to what players could expect in the semipros and minors, even $1,000–1,500 a year was good money, and thousands of players stood waiting to take a major leaguer's place. Semipros might get $5 a game, or $10 on Sunday, or $100 a month. Minor leaguers at the low end could earn less than top semipros and at the top end as much as major league newcomers. But regional variations in minor league wages, like such variations in other industries of the day, meant that while a veteran minor leaguer in the Northeast might make $300–400 a month, or $1,500–2,000 a year, in the Southern Association the scale was $100 a month lower. A scout first discovered pitcher "Smokey Joe" Wood, a native of

Ness City, Kansas, hurling for a barnstorming "Bloomer Girls" team at $20 a week. Given the number of major league aspirants each season, a Christy Mathewson might opt to walk out (as he did in 1903) when ordered to pitch a season on two days' rest between starts, but few others in the majors could dare to do the same. Despite the shortness of playing careers, fans rarely felt much sympathy for players who made more money than they did for performing at a "game." By decade's end, the average steelworker earned but $700 a year, a cotton mill employee only $250, and the typical worker in manufacturing generally perhaps $650.[15]

Hanging on to a major league job was more necessary than ever from a financial standpoint for the player, yet more difficult to do because of the growth in minor leagues providing replacement talent. It was especially crucial because postcareer opportunities, unless one managed to store away present earnings for the future, remained scarce. Some could at least find work as coaches or umpires at some level of the expanding baseball organizational pyramid. At the major league level, however, the total number of coaching, managing, and umpiring jobs each season still stood at fewer than fifty. Owners provided no system of pensions, although occasionally for individual players some owners provided handouts and former teammates staged benefit exhibitions. John McGraw and Garry Herrmann each earned some notoriety for their beneficence to destitute former charges. But when Ezra Sutton died in poverty in 1907 and sportswriters suggested the establishment of a pension plan or an old-age home, a proposal by Ban Johnson for an indigent-relief fund financed out of World Series receipts received no formal action.

Besides the threat to a major leaguer's career posed by upwardly mobile aspirants, injury or illness constantly loomed as risks. With no guarantees of pay for the sick or injured, and no pay at all until the regular season began despite playing 30–40 spring training contests, players did what they could to stay healthy enough to remain in the lineup. Catcher Roger Bresnahan of the Giants pioneered in the use of shin guards in 1907, but his early use of a crude batting helmet did not catch on as quickly. Given the primitive state of antiseptics, spikings could produce life-threatening blood poisoning. Forced by money-conscious owners to double up in rooms on road trips, and given $3.00 a day in meal money, players often tried to save the money in order to supplement their incomes. Given prohibitions on wives accompanying their husbands, and the boredom of the road, alcoholism and social diseases created additional health hazards. Even if a player claimed no other maladies, the bulky uniform he wore on a hot afternoon could cause him to lose ten pounds in a day in the midst of a 154-game season. Team trainers were really only rubbers, with the most famous being John D. "Bonesetter" Reese. A Welsh steelworker who hailed from Youngstown, Ohio, Reese gained renown among the players for his manipulation and massage skills. By 1909, clubs such as Detroit carried accident insurance, but as protection against such off-field calamities as train wrecks rather than playing injuries.[16]

With the accessibility of cheaper minor league talent after 1903 enforcing a restored fiscal discipline upon major league payrolls, AL and NL management complained whenever minor league clubs and players demanded higher levels of compensation. A talent scout for Garry Herrmann lamented as early as 1904 that drafted players placed too high a premium upon their own value, as if they were the "prize cattle at the fair." The same agent targeted in particular minor leaguers from the West Coast leagues, who, as he put it, "get eight-months' work with a pretty stiff salary, which makes them a little independent about going East." The National Commission hesitated to approve higher draft prices, fearing that it would undermine salary discipline from below. As Ban Johnson explained it, "If you hand a disobedient child a stick of candy and pat him on the back, you cannot hope to make him amenable to discipline." Even at modestly rising prices, however, the minor league draft was a great bargain for the majors. In 1907 alone, the National and American leagues drafted 117 players at a cost of $131,475, or an average of about $1,125 per player.[17]

The poorer, small-market, or simply "cheaper" clubs, seeking to recoup the costs of draft prices, sometimes blatantly violated the implied promise of higher pay contained in promotion to the majors. In 1906, Connie Mack offered his new acquisition, Clarence Russell, an $1,800 starting salary that was less than his Class A pay. After a holdout by Russell, the tight-fisted Mack did raise the figure to $2,400. Less fortunate was James Wiggs, who abandoned baseball rather than take a pay cut for reporting to Brooklyn. Blacklisted by the National Commission, Wiggs eventually won reinstatement on his third try, but only after his most productive years had been lost. In its ruling, the commission grudgingly conceded that promotion to the majors should translate into a "reasonable" pay increase.

Besides the direct expedient of cutting salaries, major league owners in the aftermath of the American League war employed other old or refined methods of cutting labor costs. These included trades, sales, and punitive fines. In 1904, St. Louis's Robison circulated sale prices ranging from $1,350 to $3,000 on five different players, for a total of $9,900 asked on players who had earned barely over $3,000 in combined salaries in 1903. When Al Bridwell demanded a $300 raise from $2,100 to $2,400 in 1906, citing an outstanding rookie season and verbal promises from Cincinnati's Herrmann, he received instead a trade to the Boston Braves and a new round of salary haggling. Some owners reportedly traded malcontents for such items as a bird dog, a turkey, or access to a training site. Clubs would trade or sell disgruntled players to a cooperative fellow owner who would either perform the salary cutting directly or recoup the money by charging the player for his own transportation costs, new uniform, and new equipment. In one instance, Cincinnati traded Jack Harper to Chicago because the latter's player-manager, Frank Chance, had been beaned by him. Once Harper had changed teams, his new boss benched him and had his salary cut from $4,500 to $1,500. The National Commission refused his appeal, and after an unhappy period of inactivity Harper left the game.[18]

Another trick entailed threatening a player with a fine, trade, release, or suspension unless his performance picked up, then fining him $100 after it did on the grounds that the improvement retroactively proved his prior "slacking." Other management tactics included loaning or renting players to supposed rivals for brief periods, with fees collected from the borrower in exchange. In 1905, for example, Cincinnati loaned catcher Gabby Street to the Boston Braves for three games. But the fastest-expanding area of abuse of players' rights at the major league level stemmed from the National Commission's misguided attempt to create a "secondary market" for released players through a waiver system. At first applicable exclusively in the majors from 1903 to 1905, under the rule a team could ask for waivers on a player, which then permitted other teams in the same league to attempt to sign him.

Supporters claimed that the waiver rule made the "free-fall" of a major leaguer to the minors less likely. But the process remained fraught with abuse. Clubs were under no obligation to inform a player that he had been placed on waivers, or that he had been claimed by another club, or even that another club had shown interest—for such knowledge might facilitate more costly direct negotiations by players with other franchises. In addition, the National Commission imposed no limits on how many times a club could ask for and then revoke waivers on a player, converting him into a kind of human yo-yo. Clubs would test the waters to help determine a player's market value at periodic intervals and sometimes solicit collusive gentleman's agreements, instead of revoking waivers, to insure that the player actually "cleared." Then the owner could claim that his charge had been formally released from his old contract and could be re-signed at much lower pay. Brooklyn's Ebbets used the "waiver wire" to punish the recalcitrant Mike Mowrey and Ollie O'Mara, arranging with other clubs not to claim them and then slashing their salaries. Even the claiming of a waived player by another club did not necessarily mean the fulfillment of a fair process. Some owners offered themselves as middlemen who cut the claimee's salary and returned him to his old club for secret compensation or brokered the player to another club entirely.[19]

An entire category of abuses of players' rights to compensation and choice of employer grew out of the revised postwar relationship between the NL-AL cartel and the minor leagues. Under the 1903 National Agreement, the practice of "farming"—reassigning major league players to a friendly "subsidiary" club in the minors—implicitly had been prohibited through a ban on interlocking franchise ownerships. In its place the pact created an "optional assignment" procedure in which a major leaguer could be sold to a minor league club, with his former employer retaining the option to repurchase. Despite Ban Johnson's assurances that the "covering up" of major league talent on compliant minor league franchises would be rooted out, the process was flagrantly abused. Owners would demote players to a minor league club and save a month's salary without declaring a formal rate cut, since minor league seasons were a month shorter than the majors. The American League's Chicago White Sox maintained a cozy exclusive relationship with Milwaukee of the Western League and New Orleans of the Southern Association. The New York Giants held similar working arrangements with their own client clubs. Brooklyn's Ebbets, in order to avoid technically violating the option rule, "sold" and "repurchased" players repeatedly from the same minor league partner. One player subjected to similar "laundering" jumped to an outlaw minor league and then sought reinstatement by the National Commission on the basis that in his farming he had been the "victim of a conspiracy" to deny him his rights. After two rejections of his case, the commission finally concurred, deciding that he had been "punished enough."

Complicating matters was the fact that such major-minor collusion did not always originate from the top. B, C, and D league clubs would sell players to a higher minor league club in order to get a better price than the majors' listed draft fee. In order to avoid wider-scale plundering of his roster, a minor league owner also might sell his players exclusively to one particular major league franchise before the start of the draft period. The major league owner then would wait until the end of the draft period on March 1 and sell back most of the purchasees. Such arrangements could be in the major league club's interest also, for in exchange for such consideration it might gain the one player it truly coveted (the Giants obtained star pitcher Rube Marquard in such fashion from Indianapolis in 1908 for $11,000), receive use of a spring training facility, be promised first pick of the team's talent crop next year, secure cooperation from the minor in absorbing surplus demotees, or even garner a direct commission fee.

Under pressure from other owners with shallower pockets and less skill at manipulating the minors, and with denunciations of individual abuses offered by Johnson and Griffith, in 1905 the National Agreement parties widened the waiver rule to permit not just intraleague claims on waived major league players but also interleague ones within the same classification level. The waiver rule also was made available to parallel leagues in the high minors. Under the change, a high minor league club, or a major league franchise, at the same classification level as a team now waiving a player it had drafted or purchased the year before, could claim him even if he did not hail from the same circuit. By widening the range of possible bidders, the National Commission believed that even fewer high-level players would "fall through the cracks" of organized baseball. Two years later, the National Commission attempted to limit the frequency of "covering up" by allowing major league clubs to option a player to the minors only once a season. The next year, it stipulated a $300 minimum payment requirement upon any major league team seeking to repurchase its optioned players.[20]

Major league owners responded to the attempts to restrain their excesses by turning to yet another handy expedient—quietly increasing to astounding numbers the players they drafted and thus directly claimed as reserved men. By recognizing no effective limit, clubs thus placed dozens of players under major league contract in "cold storage" on minor league rosters. Obviously the wealthier clubs could better afford to buy up more talent and maintain such expanded payroll lists, and so the practice aggravated an already serious degree of on-field competitive imbalance. The typical range of winning percentages for the period were a gaping .385 to .615, compared to figures of .430 and .570 for later years. By 1909, Brooklyn held 61 players in reserve, Cleveland 60, and six others clubs over 50, while the less prosperous Washington franchise in the American League claimed "only" 29 and two other teams about 30. In order to compete, poorer clubs resorted to the stratagem of drafting a larger number of players than they intended to reserve and then discarding all but the best to the minors via sales. One club profited by $27,000 in one year in this way, but at the human toll of raising and then dashing many minor leaguers' hopes.[21]

In the first decade of the twentieth century, Ban Johnson, with his obvious zest for the exercise of power, dominated the baseball scene in much the same way that Theodore Roosevelt dominated national politics. The National Commission's role as final arbiter of baseball industry disputes over labor issues also evoked comparisons to Progressive Era labor conflict-resolution devices, such as Roosevelt's arbitration panel in the 1902 national coal strike and similar bodies sponsored by the National Civic Federation. Both examples reflected a new faith that creation of formal processes of mediation and resolution alone would result in a "square deal" for contending classes and the avoidance of strikes and labor violence, thus alleviating the rationale for union shops. But as with so many other examples from the period, creation of a new arbitration process for the baseball industry did not in itself ensure fair and just decisions for its workers. The baseball officers and owners to whom the National Commission reported were usually civic figures with political connections, but those in the host cities with whom they in turn shared financial interest and ideological outlook were Old Guard businessmen and corrupt machine politicians rather than reformers. The National Commission's own chairman, Garry Herrmann, for example, served as a loyal lieutenant of Cincinnati's "Boss" George B. Cox.[22]

Baseball labor could hardly be confident of a square deal from the National Commission when it was not even represented on the panel. Such an omission did not necessarily have to be fatal, however. Even though the minor leagues also lacked official membership on the commission, their formal recognition in the National Agreement and their practical leverage as potential generators of trade war and as the suppliers of entry-level talent for the big leagues meant that their interests could not be ignored as readily as those of the players. High minor leagues, in particular, could demand better treatment or threaten outlaw status and another destructive trade conflict. The National Commission at mid-decade took steps to pacify and incorporate back into organized baseball the outlaw Pacific Coast League and the American Association, allowing each to retain its jumpers from other circuits. In an effort to head off additional rebellions, the commission reduced the number of Class A players available for drafting from each club to one and raised their draft prices to $1,000 each. Similarly, when in 1905 the Tri-State League grabbed other circuits' players and became an outlaw, the commission threatened use of the blacklist but sought peace in the form of a new agreement in early 1907 that allowed it to keep its jumpers. By that year, the minors had grown from thirteen leagues at the start of the decade to thirty-four, with 14 million fans, approximately 250 clubs, and a pool of some 4,400 players, figures that demanded respect from the majors.

The California State League met with a sterner reaction from the lords of baseball, but that was owing largely to the National Commission's fear of antagonizing the Pacific Coast League into a second secession if it treated the rival California league leniently. When the California circuit, with its winter schedule, declared itself outside the National Agreement and its reserve obligations, the National Commission cooperated with the minors' recognized trade association, the National Association, in blacklisting any player who failed to honor his contract by not returning to his former club within thirty days. Blacklistees breaking active contracts were sentenced to five years' suspension, and reserve jumpers to three years. Players who complied, such as the renegade Hal Chase, still faced fines imposed by the two governing bodies. Players on teams that merely played a club from the California State League faced $100 fines for a first offense and blacklisting for a second. With former major leaguer and San Francisco native Bill Lange retained as a recruiting agent, other leagues raided the California State League's talent. Forced to give up the fight, the league found itself consigned in the aftermath to the smaller markets of central California, while the Pacific Coast League held the larger cities of the West Coast.

Amid continued grumbling by the high minors, talk of creating a new classification level with higher draft compensation, and demands for preferential treatment, the major leagues gave additional ground. In 1909, the top three Class A circuits—the Eastern League, the American Association, and the Pacific Coast League—received standing as a new, separate Class AA. The new classification meant that these three leagues received higher pay for draftees to the majors, while ensuring that those circuits still at A level would not have their draft fees cut. The solution represented rejection of an alternative that would have been harsher to some leagues—the demotion of the weaker Class A circuits to B standing if the 1910 population census justified it. By decade's end, the minors had grown to over forty leagues, making them through the National Association an even more populous, wealthy, and powerful constituency to be antagonized only at the National Commission's own risk.[23]

In contrast, the players, whether major leaguers or minor leaguers, no longer had any such collective leverage, organizational legitimacy, or protective cover as might have been provided by a union. The Protective Association had collapsed, and former leaders had been driven out of the game or co-opted into the ranks of management. The Eastern League retained the union's former legal counsel, Harry Taylor, as its president in 1905. After a relatively comfortable exile as manager of the same circuit's Baltimore club, Hughie Jennings was hired by Detroit as its field manager in 1907. The Supreme Court's 1908 *Loewe v. Lawler* decision, better known as the Danbury Hatters case, apparently put even the Sherman Anti-Trust Act in the service of those who would outlaw unions as unlawful "combinations in restraint of trade." Even the once-defiant voice of the Brotherhood of Professional Base Ball Players— John Montgomery Ward—had been so quieted that the National League in 1909, following the suicide of Harry Pulliam, nearly named him its new president. Preventing Ward's ascension, however, was AL president Johnson, still smarting six years later over his adversary's legal representation of player George Davis.

The rulings of the National Commission amply illustrated the gap in formal recognition and actual power between the baseball business's labor and management constituencies—a pattern frequently repeated throughout American industry. According to its first report, covering the period from its creation in September 1903 through the year 1904, the panel received nearly 2,000 inquiries and complaints and issued 110 rulings and findings. Forty-two of the cases involved player-management confrontations, with twenty-seven of them complaints brought by the player side. In these twenty-seven grievances, the commission ruled against the player on two-thirds of the occasions. In marked contrast, of the fifteen complaints raised by management against players, the body sided with the owners twelve times, while two cases were set aside and only one was adjudicated in the player's favor. Also in sharp juxtaposition were the commission's rulings in majors-versus-minors management disputes, where the need to placate both sides resulted in a nearly even division of outcomes. In fifty-four such cases, the panel ruled in the minors' favor twenty-five times and for the majors in twenty-nine instances. The tendency to rule arbitrarily on the basis of constituent clout rather than strict adherence to baseball "law" was fostered additionally by the confusion of the statutes themselves, which, in the words of NL president Pulliam, required a "Pinkerton detective" to find them and a "Philadelphia lawyer" to interpret them. In 1905, the commissioners fined Brooklyn $100 for use of an ineligible player but let St. Louis off with a warning for the same offense when it threatened to bring a lawsuit against them.[24]

By 1909, little had changed. That season, the number of inquiries to the commission rose to 6,220, and rulings to 126. As before, when the cases involved a minor league management claim against a major league one, the group "split the difference." Thirteen complaints were resolved in favor of the majors, twelve for the minors, and one ended in a compromise finding. At first glance, the commission's treatment of player complaints now also seemed more sympathetic. Of seventy player-versus-management cases, sixty-five were initiated by players, who "won" thirty-three of them. Management brought only five appeals and won four. But of the thirty-three player victories, twenty-six were requests by suspended players for reinstatement. Commission leniency in such cases reflected the self-interest of owners generally to augment the labor pool and to enhance their teams' pennant prospects by reinstating former jumpers and rules violators, although often at lower salaries and with reduced fines remaining. The "typical" reinstatee saw the commission restore his eligibility and reduce his fine from $200 to $50. In nonreinstatement grievance cases brought by players, however, management won on thirty-two out of thirty-nine occasions.[25]

Taken in their entirety, the owners' methods of labor control once more had proved most successful in rebuilding short-term industry profits. The majors and minors alike also benefited from the remarkable double-figure percentage growth of the urban population, which resulted in a rise in the urban share of Americans from 40 percent in 1900 to 46 percent by 1910. NL and AL gate totals also gained from the on-field success of the big-market teams in New York (with the notable exception of the lowly Highlanders) and Chicago. Combined with rising concession fees from vendors supplying refreshments ranging from beer to "temperance drinks," such as five-cent bottles of Coca-Cola, operating receipts rose while labor costs stabilized. With attendance up from 4.75 million fans in 1903 to 7.25 million in 1909, the major leagues earned $17 million dollars in operating income from 1901 to 1908. The Giants alone averaged annual profits of over $100,000 in the decade's last five years. World Series revenues boosted profits further. Following an "unofficial" series in 1903 and the refusal of the NL champion Giants to participate in one the next season, from 1905 to 1909 the World Series between the AL and NL winners earned an average of another $100,000 per year (varying with the number of games played). Shares to players on the two squads also helped ease their salary discontents, with the 1905 Giants receiving winners' shares of $1,142 each. In 1906 the victorious Chicago White Sox received a $15,000 bonus on top of their individual shares, and the rival Cubs in 1908 did the same with a $10,000 pot.[26]

Owners still complained about operating costs, but with continuing price deflation in the overall economy and effective labor suppression, the rising expenses were now more often the voluntary capital investments of an expanding industry. A building boom in the major leagues was ushered in by the replacement of wooden ballparks or their conversion to steel and concrete facilities with far greater seating capacities. In spite of poor-mouthing by owners, their franchises—worth from $50,000 to $100,000 at the beginning of the decade—soared in value to from five to ten times that amount by 1910. Nonetheless, the moguls refrained from injecting more offense into the game both because attendance was good and because they feared that doing so would escalate salary pressures while they were taking on new capital expenditures. Since the owners did not experience an immediate drop-off at the gate from low-scoring baseball (an unexpected windfall, given past experience), they felt little pressure to "juice up" the game to stimulate additional spectatorship (see Appendix, Fig. 4). With the owners having established a minimum fence distance of 235 feet in 1904, pitchers' earned run averages fell until 1908. Batting averages tailed off, and in 1905 the American League contained only two .300 hitters. Batters hit but 126 home runs in the National League in 1906 and 101 in the American League the next season. The National League's composite batting average plummeted to .239 by 1908, while the American League recorded its lowest hit totals the same year. The 1908 season saw the lowest combined batting average in the major leagues until 1968.

In response to the decline in offense in major league baseball, purists in the journalistic community, led by the venerable Henry Chadwick, urged another progressive-style "process" reform to address the issue. In an open letter to the owners, Chadwick urged creation of a new ten-member rules panel, half of which would constitute an advisory, or "consulting" committee, the other five an actual voting committee. The voting group, made up of the American League, National League, and National Association presidents and two "college men" to represent amateur baseball, would have the power to select the members of the consulting body and to adopt playing rules changes for the entire sport. Even though Chadwick left no room in his proposal for any player representation on the rule-making bodies, the owners still rejected his suggestion. Instead, in 1908 they belatedly attempted to mollify critics of low-scoring, "boring" baseball by extending the ban on deliberate dirtying of baseballs specifically to pitchers (although hurlers continued to "load up" or deface them without effective restraint) and adopting the rule of not counting a sacrifice fly as an at bat.[27]

If in this period of labor captivity, rising profits, and falling offense the game's on-field rules changed minimally, the same also could be said of the playing force's composition (see Appendix, Fig. 2). Because big league owners held such leverage over their players' job security and wages, the additional mechanism of labor cost containment through the broadening of the ethnic and racial pool of employment was not needed. As for the "new" immigration from Southern and Eastern Europe, it had only begun to provide a trickle of ballplaying aspirants from among its American-born descendants. Of 462 entry-level major leaguers from 1900 to 1909 whose bloodlines were identified later by Lee Allen, non-Irish descendants of the British Isles, including English, Scotch, Scotch-Irish, English-Irish, and Welsh players, accounted for about 40 percent of the total stock. Germanic entrants (Germans, Pennsylvania Dutch, Swiss, and Dutch) added another 28 percent, while the Irish share stood at 23 percent. The remainder made up less than 10 percent, with the largest shares being French and Eastern European (Bohemian, Russian, Slovak, Polish, or Lithuanian) with around 3 percent each, Scandinavians (Norwegian or Swedish) and American Indians at 1 percent each, and Spanish or Mexican players at .4 percent. As a product of the "organized play" movement of the Progressive Era, which sought to control delinquency and promote assimilation through organized, regulated clubs and leagues, more of the ethnic newcomers to professional baseball drew upon formal youth training. For the Irish it might be the "SACs" (social and athletic clubs), for the Germans the "turners," for Wasp public schoolchildren such organizations as New York's Public School Athletic League (PSAL), for Bohemian enclaves (especially in Chicago) the "sokols," for Indians the mission schools and Carlisle Institute, and for blacks "colored" YMCAs. Jewish youths as yet did not have as systematic an exposure to baseball as their Christian and nonsectarian counterparts, and accordingly stereotypes that characterized them as "temperamentally unfit" and lacking physical courage persisted. So pervasive were such perceptions, and management's fear of fan anti-Semitism, that owners "suggested" or ordered players with characteristically Jewish surnames such as Cohen to change them to Kane or Cohan. One individual found himself barred from the Eastern League in 1904 for refusing to do so. The irony was that American Jews already had broken into the ownership ranks in the persons of Freedman, Dreyfuss, and Louis Kramer, among others.[28]

For ballplaying aspirants of color, the barriers to the major league playing field were even more impenetrable. Cubans still found it nearly impossible to make it into the big leagues, even though American awareness and cultivation of the island's playing talent had increased dramatically because of the Spanish-American War of 1898 and the continuing U.S. presence on the island. One sportswriter described Cuba's developing stars as "natural-born artists." Indians entered the majors in small numbers (at least eight by 1909), with John McGraw—who, after all, had earlier contemplated smuggling a black into the majors as an Indian—a leader in their recruitment. One of his discoveries, Chief Meyers, praised McGraw for his insistence upon fair treatment for all his players, but he noted that in general others treated him as an inferior foreigner. For African Americans, Jim Crow rigidly held. The few black professional clubs in existence found difficulty even scheduling games with white opponents, and they often suffered financial collapse as a result. By the latter part of the decade, for example, the Leland Giants remained the lone black entry in Chicago's City League. Despite acquitting itself well against the Cubs in a 1909 postseason series, the team folded the next year.

The 1890s trend toward recruitment of college players also continued in the next decade—testament both to improved collegiate baseball programs and to the owners' continued desire to maintain a respectable image for their largely middle-class spectatorship. Lee Allen identified 485 major league entrants of the 1900–1909 period whose educational levels could be traced, and found that an astonishing 43.5 percent attended an institution of higher learning for at least some brief time. Although other data for the entire 1900–1920 period suggests that this figure is too high (given that the educational levels of lower-status ballplayers are less easily traceable), it is certainly safe to say that the "average" major league ballplayer was far better educated than the average American. Nonetheless, nearly a quarter of the sample had failed to progress beyond some stage of secondary school, and about a third had never reached high school, figures consistent with impressionistic accounts of a heterogeneous player force of college men, midwestern and southern "country boys," sons of middle-class and professional families, and products of blue-collar mill and factory towns.[29]

Like Progressive Era politicians, businessmen, and civic leaders, baseball's executives sought to promote self-images and public perceptions of themselves as individuals instilling in their charges greater efficiency and morality. For a club owner this meant erecting a more complex, specialized administrative bureaucracy ranging from a treasurer, road secretary, business manager, field manager, coach, players, and scouts down to groundskeepers, ushers, ticket takers, special policemen, and youthful scorecard hawkers. It also meant the incorporation of the lessons of Taylorism—of industrial time/motion studies and scientific management of production processes—on the ballfield. In spring training and after, manager and coach now conducted, albeit still crudely by today's standards, more specialized sessions for hitting, pitching, and fielding and drilled players to remove wasted motion from cutoffs, rundowns, and double plays. Rosters expanded, strategies were refined, and players became more specialized in their roles and contributions to team success—whether as platoon hitters, pinch runners, or relief pitchers. At the same time that the game became more "scientific," however, the work rituals of some players continued to show a rebellious disposition toward folklore and superstition in the pursuit of successful performance and its individual rewards. Ty Cobb, the "Georgia Peach" whose "scientific" hitting and fiery determination had made him the American League's biggest star by decade's end, nonetheless in 1908 kept in hiding in the dugout a black urchin he called "Li'l Rastus," whose head he rubbed for good luck. When Cobb and the club entered a protracted slump, he booted out the good luck charm only to see him land with the Cubs, who then defeated the Tigers in the World Series. The Philadelphia Athletics similarly discovered a hunchbacked dwarf named Louis Van Zelst, whose good luck powers concentrated in his hump led to his being made a batboy the next year.[30]

Whatever their individual backgrounds and peculiarities, now more than ever players were expected to project a public image of propriety— so long as it did not interfere with winning. Managers, whether the gentlemanly Mack or the combative McGraw, required their charges to wear suits while traveling. Owners eliminated such "carnival" aspects of the game as parading their uniformed players from the hotel to the park. Facilitating the change was a 1906 rule mandating dressing rooms, lockers, and running water in all stadiums. Baseball's former titan Spalding praised the removal of the "cheap circus act," but his words also conveyed the era's stark bigotry when he added, "'Coons' can do these things and feel proud of it but it is the most servile thing to compel gentlemanly players to do so." To police players' off-field behavior, clubs paid detectives at different rates—$5.00 a day for "shadows," $6.00 for "investigators"—and imposed curfews and bed checks. Clubs assessed fines for such offenses as tardiness, drinking, dice-playing, and challenging the manager's disciplinary authority.[31]

On the diamond, the main burden of regulating the players' conduct fell upon the umpires. Aiding modestly in the effort to secure player cooperation was the fact that Irish and German arbiters now were part of the umpiring fraternity, although it remained true that few umpires were college-educated. In the National League, umpires faced more obstacles to the enforcement of their authority because of the lack of a strong hand at the league helm to back them up. Under both the Fleischman Resolution of 1902 and the Brush amendments to it in 1904, the National League empowered umpires to expel players, with a league fine of $10 accompanying each ejection. If the NL president opted to add suspension to the penalty, an extra $10-per-day levy would be assessed. But owners anxious not to lose the services of their stars often undermined discipline by secretly paying the fines and forcing cancellation of suspensions. As catcher Buck Weaver put it, "They want you to get out there and fight, don't they, and do you think that we pay for that privilege?" While a 1904 study suggested that 85 percent of on-field incidents were no longer physical but merely verbal altercations, umpires still risked physical harm at whatever level of league, with the threat from players and spectators alike probably worse in the minors. In one 1907 example, a soda bottle hurled from the stands nearly killed an umpire.

The National League's reputation for standing by its umpires and policing its employees' on-field conduct plummeted to a new low in 1905, with the "Hey, Barney!" incident. At a game in May, John McGraw publicly accused the umpire of being a lackey of Pittsburgh owner Barney Dreyfuss and of owing money to a local bookie. When Dreyfuss filed formal charges against McGraw with the National League's board of directors, the Giants' skipper denied having made the accusations. After berating league president Pulliam over the telephone and demanding a hearing, McGraw still drew a fifteen-day suspension, a $150 fine, and a $10 levy for the May 20 ejection. The board, in turn, exonerated the manager but nonetheless upheld his fine and suspension in light of his subsequent conduct. Taking the matter to court, McGraw won a judge's verdict in his favor on the grounds that he (à la Pete Rose years later) had not received due process, which carried with it an injunction against the National League's collecting the fines. In a theatrical gesture, President Pulliam, on the grounds that he had treated McGraw's case the same as any other disciplinary case, then ordered all fines above $10 on 1905 NL offenders remanded—amounting to a $490 rebate. At the league's winter meetings, Pulliam barely survived an ouster attempt, and a "supporting resolution" passed at the meeting mandated board ratification of any subsequent presidential expulsion orders.

In the American League, Ban Johnson proved more willing to face down recalcitrant owners and performers in behalf of his umpires. In early 1905, in an incident that helped erode his friendship with Charles Comiskey, Johnson not only upheld umpire Frank "Silk" O'Loughlin's suspension of Chicago outfielder James "Ducky" Holmes but had his ruling delivered by special messenger so as to avoid delay. The league president infuriated the White Sox owner even more when in the midst of the 1907 pennant race he upheld the suspension of player-manager Fielder Jones. With the major league standard before 1906 being four umpires per circuit (since no more than four games per day could occur in an eight-team league), Johnson added a fifth arbiter that year and moved to a rotation system. But even his league did not pay umpires' travel expenses, and salaries continued to lag. Arbiters in the majors earned $1,500–2,000 in the early 1900s, but by decade's end four of the seven NL umpires still made less than $2,000, with $3,000 the top salary. The fortunate umpire selected to work the World Series gained more than notoriety for his opportunity, for the assignment carried with it an extra $400.[32]

The most alarming moral crisis within the playing fraternity, however, was the proliferation of contacts with, and payoffs from, gamblers, pool sellers, and game-fixers. As the "Hey, Barney!" incident revealed, players could be understandably cynical, even cavalier, about the matter because of similar contacts on the part of owners and managers. John McGraw, a victory junkie seemingly in constant need of a fix, admitted being an "inveterate gambler," though few could ever imagine him arranging his own club's defeat. National Commission chairman and Cincinnati president Herrmann in 1906 admitted that he bet $6,000 against $2,000 that Pittsburgh would not win the pennant, only to "ask out" of the wager later. Still, some wondered if he had traded Cy Seymour to the Giants to protect his money. As for player malfeasance, in one example, the Cubs' James Hart, a year after a 1903 postseason series with the team's intracity rivals, charged former player John Taylor with laying down to help the White Stockings win. Although the National Commission failed to find sufficient evidence on that charge, it did unearth a second instance of suspicious behavior on Taylor's part in a St. Louis–Pittsburgh game of July 1904 and fined him $300 for "prejudicial conduct." Despite urgings from Pittsburgh owner Dreyfuss that Taylor and cohort Jake Beckley of the Cardinals be fired in a way that would not competitively weaken St. Louis, Taylor remained in the league for several more years.

Fearing that unhappy traded players might fix games to help former teammates, the National Commission adopted rules barring the awarding of World Series shares to players dealt away beforehand. Signs of a game-fixing epidemic, however, resurfaced in 1908. One center of suspicion was the graceful, and completely unethical, first baseman Hal Chase. In September, accusations of throwing games from his manager on New York's AL team prompted Chase to jump to "outlaw ball" in California. Amazingly, not only did club management fire Chase's accuser, but the National Commission reinstated the renegade with only a $200 fine. In what should have been no surprise, the next season Chase drew renewed charges of laying-down, this time supposedly to get his new manager fired. In the other circuit, a suspicious Phillies-Giants series in 1908 bred rumors that someone had tried to bribe Philadelphia players, and another accusation stemmed from rumors of offers to umpires Bill Klem and John Johnstone before the Giants-Cubs tie-breaker game at season's end. The fact that Giants owner Brush headed the league's investigating panel did nothing to inspire confidence. The inquiry fixed blame on the New York team "masseur," Joseph Creamer, who had been brought into the organization at friend McGraw's specific insistence. As his sentence, organized baseball barred him from all its parks. No other individuals, however, were charged or penalized. Over a decade later, after the 1919 "Black Sox" scandal, Phillies catcher Charles "Red" Dooin additionally disclosed that he and others had been offered $40,000 to throw five games but had refused. According to his recollection, "the money was placed in my lap by a noted catcher of the New York Giants while I was in a railroad station."[33]

By the end of 1909, storm clouds had gathered over baseball's profitable monopoly, an industry itself standing on a shaky moral foundation of labor suppression. The injustices of the two-tier wage structure had multiplied, as had the abuses of the reserve system and the number of player grievances filed with the National Commission. Given the continuing relative homogeneity of professional baseball's work force in its ethnic makeup and skill requirements, player pride and resentment of abuses could yet embolden them once again to organize collectively if offered the slightest breathing space by renewed industry trade war. Worst of all, the economic repression of the player, combined with the self-interested reinstatements extended by management to those who had jumped their contracts or even fixed games, had laid the groundwork for future scandal. The continuous squeezing of players' legitimate incomes had made illicit avenues of alternative pay more and more alluring. At the same time, ironically, the absence of certain and meaningful punishment encouraged players to assume that even their worst transgressions still would not, at bottom, cost them a baseball livelihood. The seeds of 1919 and baseball's most notorious scandal, in short, already had been sown by the labor policies of a decade earlier.

 SEVEN

The Players' Fraternity and the Federal League, 1910-1915

The major league owners' financial bonanza came to an abrupt close with the start of the new decade. The slowdown provided an omen of renewed labor crackdowns, player turmoil, and union organization soon to follow. Attendance, which had peaked in 1909, began a drop that continued through the 1912 campaign. The American League's turnstile counts fell from 3.75 million to 3, and the National League's dropped by a similar amount. Contributing to the economic fallout from the revenue decline was the fact that it hit just as the surge in new concrete-and-steel stadium constructions began. From 1909 to 1914, the majors presided over the erection of seven new parks, including Philadelphia's Shibe Park, New York's Polo Grounds, Chicago's Comiskey

Park and Wrigley Field, Detroit's Tiger Stadium, Boston's Fenway Park, and Brooklyn's Ebbets Field, each at a cost of over $2 million. Another complication stemmed from yet another NL leadership crisis, forced by Harry Pulliam's suicide in 1909. On a temporary basis, John Heydler—former Washington *Post* sports editor, NL statistician, and league secretary—took over as the loop's president. But an opposing bloc of owners, led by Garry Herrmann, preferred Louisville's Robert W. Brown as a permanent replacement. After an awkward deadlock, the owners opted for compromise in the person of Thomas J. Lynch, a former major league umpire, Brush protégé, and theatrical manager. With the magnates persuaded that the former "King of Umpires" would better perform the presidential task of supervising and supporting the men in blue, they tabbed Lynch, and Heydler returned to his secretarial duties.

The cartel soon passed its hard times on to the players, although given their meager position during the past half dozen years, they could hardly be cited as the cause. Assisting the major leagues' intensified economic crackdown upon the player force was the substantial growth of the minors as a replacement pool. By 1910 the National Association claimed forty-four leagues and approximately 8,000 players. Nonetheless, to control franchise operating costs the leagues now enforced limits in each classification on the number of active players per team and on club monthly payrolls. The AA leagues limited rosters to twenty, and the Class A Southern Association maintained a fourteen-man limit. B, C, and D circuits averaged team caps of fourteen, thirteen, and thirteen respectively. The Southern's ceiling for a team's monthly payroll, $3,200, translated into an average player salary of under $230 a month, or $1,600 a year. At B level, figures averaged $1,825 per team and $130 per player per month, or $910 per season. C players earned $1,671 per team and $129 per individual a month, or about $900 a year; and in the D leagues teams received an average $851 a team and $65 a player, or an individual season salary of a little over $450. Even with larger rosters on the higher-classification teams, the fact that twenty-four of the forty-four minor leagues performed at D level meant that about half of minor league professionals made money at or around the bottom figures.[1]

Minor league limits did not rise appreciably the next year, although some shifting occurred within classifications. By 1911, the minors included forty-nine circuits, with five at AA or A level, eight B leagues, ten C aggregations, and twenty-six at D level. AA rosters remained at twenty, while Southern Association clubs were now permitted sixteen actives. With team payrolls capped at $3,500 per month, however, individual pay in the Southern actually shrunk to $219 a month and $1,533 a year to accommodate larger rosters. B squads rose on average to fifteen men, with the typical monthly team cap at $2,269, translating into individual figures of $151 a month and $1,057 a season. C teams stayed at thirteen players, with team payroll limits averaging $1,500, $171 less than the previous year. For the individual player this translated into monthly pay of $115, or about $800 for the season, $100 less than in 1910. D leagues economized by cutting rosters to an average of twelve men, while paying teams about $900 a month, producing individual increases to $75 a month and $525 a year.[2]

Without adopting official salary caps, major league magnates already had imposed a two-tier wage system in the previous decade that kept most ballplayers at a pay level little higher than that of the high minors, while pacifying the game's biggest gate attractions. Given that fact, broad-based additional economies on the wage front would be hard to find, and new savings likely would have to be obtained from the higher pay levels of the high-profile stars. Owners rejected raising additional revenues through lengthening the season to 168 games, both because of the weather impracticalities and the additional two weeks of player pay it might carry with it. Although one estimate pegged the average major league salary at $5,000, the figure more likely resembled $3,000, and even that average was inflated by the small number of highly paid stars and player-managers (see Appendix, Fig. 1). Rookies and fringe players probably earned $1,500–2,000. If the 1910 Cincinnati Reds can be claimed as typical, nineteen players split a $51,000 payroll, averaging $2,684. Salaries ranged from $1,500 to $4,200, with two men making $4,000 or more, eight earning in excess of $3,100, and the two lowest coming in at salaries of $1,500 and $1,800. Underscoring the manager's importance and official authority over the players, he drew $10,000. Across the majors only ten stars garnered five-figure pay in 1910. Player-manager Honus Wagner earned $18,000, Nap Lajoie $12,000, and Christy Mathewson $10,000. Younger, but equally if not more gifted, stars made less, with Ty Cobb at $9,000 or $9,500 depending on the source, and fireballing Walter Johnson at $6,500 or $7,000.[3]

The owners' immediate responses to the revenue-expense squeeze were twofold. First, they sought an immediate injection of offense to reverse the attendance decline of 1910 (see Appendix, Fig. 4). The most important change was the introduction of a "cushioned-cork" baseball—a ball whose cork now was encircled by a one-eighth-inch layer of rubber. The 1910 World Series provided a test run for the new ball, which passed with flying colors, as the two teams hit twenty points higher during the series than they had managed in the regular season. In 1911, the number of .300 hitters jumped by 30, led by Cobb with .420 (.035 higher than his previous best) and Shoeless Joe Jackson's .408. In the National League, the new stadiums also boosted power because of convenient outfield dimensions for pull hitters. The right field bleachers in the Polo Grounds stood but 258 feet from home plate, and the same foul line in Ebbets Field measured but 301 feet. Home runs jumped to 2,433 for the decade in the National League, over 1,000 more than in the previous ten-year period.[4]

At the same time that they loosened up on offense to attract fans, the owners attempted to tighten the screws on their top-end salaries, risking player outrage and holdouts over unrewarded on-field "improvement." Hal Chase received $6,000 in 1911 but still found himself at that level three years later. Ty Cobb's 1910 pay remained constant through 1912. Owners did try to sugarcoat the pill of salary restraint for pennant winners and top stars by increasing World Series shares to $3,000 and more—which they could afford to do with gate receipts for the fall classic rising tenfold from 1905 to 1912—and by creating special individual awards. As early as 1910 the Chalmers Motor Company awarded an automobile to the batting champion of each league. As the season ended that year, however, the St. Louis Browns' defense allowed Lajoie to "bunt his way" to the title in order to thwart the hated Cobb. The American League ordered the Browns to fire manager "Peach Pie" Jack O'Connor, along with a scout who had tried to coax an official scorer into awarding Lajoie even more hits. Ironically, O'Connor sued and won back $5,000 in salary initially lost by his firing, and no players were penalized at all. The car manufacturer awarded prizes to both hitters, only to scrap the award for 1911 in favor of most valuable player awards selected by a panel of writers. Reflecting the growing player-management tension, however, were the selection criteria, which now included not only on-field brilliance but also "loyalty," "integrity," obeying of training rules, and prompt reporting to one's club (the latter stipulation representing a threat to periodic holdouts such as Cobb).[5]

The desire for cheaper playing labor also strengthened the hand of those who wanted, albeit modestly and quietly, to tap into the growing Cuban talent market. Clark Griffith pioneered in the effort for Cincinnati and then carried the interest with him to Washington in 1912. Public racial sensitivities remained so acute, however, that Reds president Herrmann sought special reassurances from the team's scout in Havana.

His correspondent replied in fractured English, "I know personally both parents of our great players Marsans [and] Almeida and guarantee that none of them have other but pure caucasion [sic] blood in their veins, their claim to members of the white race is as good as yours and mine." A local sportswriter satirically mimicked the club's soothing public statements, writing, "Ladies and gentlemen, we have in our midst two descendants of a noble Spanish race, with no ignoble African blood to place a blot or a spot on their escutcheons. Permit me to introduce two of the purest bars of Castile soap that ever floated to these shores, senors Alameda [sic] and Marsans."[6]

During the ever more contentious salary negotiations with star players in 1911, public attention centered upon the case of Walter Johnson. The "Big Train" threatened to buy up his own option for $1,000 in order to secure free agent status, but *Sporting News* reported that other clubs had colluded not to bid on him or even to make fair trade offers to Washington for him. In retaliation, the pitcher let fly in print for *Baseball Magazine* in its July issue. The journal, begun in 1908, prided itself upon being the sport's only true muckraking publication, committed (among other things) to "knock the bald-headed magnate who sits on his piles of long green, grasped from the poor downtrodden player." Johnson entitled his contribution, "Baseball Slavery: The Great American Principle of Dog Eat Dog." Although he did not demand a salary equal to that of Mathewson, a nine-year veteran making $10,000, he argued his comparable worth to Cobb. Answering arguments that a pitcher was not worth as much as an "everyday" player, Johnson pointed out that owners already claimed that pitching constituted "80% of the game" (usually in negotiations with nonpitchers) and that he, in marked contrast to a position player, handled the ball 150 times or more in each game he started. Johnson finally received a $1,000 raise, only to see his salary frozen once more at its new level for the next campaign.[7]

Pay was the main, but not the sole, source of player grumbling. The increasingly lengthy, intrusive, and mechanistic regimen of spring training seemed to some performers needless drudgery. Despite the introduction of "safety spikes" in 1910, players still risked serious injury on the field, and clubs refused to provide pensions or health insurance. More immediately unsettling, however, was the Addie Joss tragedy. Joss, a star pitcher with Cleveland, had won 160 games in nine seasons, with a 1.88 ERA. When he complained of weakness during spring training, doctors misdiagnosed his malady and simply ordered rest at home in Toledo, Ohio. There Joss died of spinal meningitis. As an example of player determination and a tribute to their fallen comrade, Joss's team-mates, led by first baseman George "Firebrand" Stovall, boycotted the second game of a series with Detroit to attend the funeral. League president Ban Johnson, whose own pleas for a modest pension funded from World Series receipts had been rejected by the owners, prudently opted not to order the players to play, but instead rescheduled the missed game. Stovall became the club's field manager later in the season, and a host of major league stars organized an exhibition game that garnered $12,931.60 for Joss's widow.[8]

Having anticipated that increased player hostility springing from management belt-tightening might spill out onto the field, the magnates in 1911 irrevocably abandoned the one-umpire-per-game system and even paid umpires' travel expenses on a reimbursement basis. The National Commission also attempted to remove a few of the worst abuses of players' reservation and option status. Under a new ruling, a club president's expressed desire to reserve a player had to be genuine, and if it proved otherwise, he would be fined the amount of the player's previous draft price. The commission also placed a limit of eight on the number of players upon which a club could exercise its options at any one time. The pressure from the National Commission to draft only those players a club really intended to use, combined with the financial squeeze the majors were experiencing, resulted in a drop in the number of draftees from 117 in 1907 to but 68 by 1912. Nonetheless, Chicago's Comiskey reported to the governing panel in late October of 1911 a reserve list of forty and five others on his ineligible list.[9]

With the new squeezing of top-end major league salaries, the stars scrambled all the more for supplementary and off-season income through endorsements, hitting and pitching exhibitions, and barnstorming expeditions. They understandably became even more miffed when owners, fearing both player injury and reduced economic leverage in their negotiations with their charges, attempted to close off some of these money-making avenues. In 1910, some clubs unsuccessfully experimented with twelve-month contracts. The National Commission also blocked a Cincinnati promoter's efforts to organize two barnstorming all-star teams by offering $500–1,000 advances, closing all National Agreement parks to the tour's use. The majors, besides making hundreds of thousands of dollars on the World Series, also sold motion picture rights for fees that rose in one year's time from $500 to $3,500 in 1911. But the owners repulsed all requests by players to allocate the movie fees specifically to a pension fund. With all of the accumulating points of irritation, it is no surprise that the number of complaints filed with the National Commission rose from 7,610 in 1910 to 8,772 in 1911, and the number of rulings from 125 to 152.[10]

Player-management relations continued to worsen in 1912, as the offensive surge failed to reverse immediately the declining turnstile counts. In an effort at additional economies, the new National Agreement limited major league teams to twenty-five active players per roster and thirty-five individuals on each club's reserve list. The figures represented ratification of the higher levels of actives that teams had been moving toward for a decade but an accompanying reduction in the reserve numbers from the recent past. Given owners' fears that the rapid jump in offense in 1911 would trigger more holdouts and salary squabbles, their decision to increase to twenty-five actives made sense only if most of the additions were pitchers. Fresh arms would moderate the offensive escalation, and appearances and victories spread out among more pitchers would also help restrain hurlers' top-end salaries by making thirty-victory seasons rarer. Reducing the number of reserves a team could claim enabled the majors to raise individual draft prices to the minors to $2,500 at AA level, $2,000 at A, $1,500 at B, $750 at C, and $500 at D. At the same time, limiting the overall number of draftable players from each AA squad to one helped hold down the majors' total draft outlays. Under the new pact the minors followed suit in restraining payrolls, with Class AA active rosters held at twenty, A clubs limited to a maximum of twenty-eight reserves and eighteen actives, B teams to twenty-six and sixteen, C franchises to twenty-four and fourteen, and D to twenty-two and fourteen.[11]

The minors' new limits that applied across the board in each classification merely supplemented earlier league-sponsored caps on rosters and monthly payrolls, which still continued. Although the AA clubs did not reveal their salary limits, the Class A Southern Association, with sixteen-man rosters, adopted a $3,500 monthly team ceiling, and the Western Association, with eighteen-man squads, chose a $3,000 limit. The two circuits' combined averages for individual pay worked out to $191 a month and $1,337 for the season. The Southern Association additionally imposed an individual salary cap of $200 a month, which remained in place until 1921. B clubs averaged monthly payroll limits of $2,250 (down $19 for rosters typically still at fifteen men), C teams $1,360 (down $140 for rosters still at thirteen), and D squads $1,154 (up $254 for average rosters one player larger at thirteen). Such figures translated into individual pay of $150 a month (down $1), or $1,050 a season at B; $105 a month (down $10), or $735 yearly at C; and $89 (up $14), or $623 for the season at D. The figures for the lower classifications meant that a professional ballplayer at those rungs toiled at a limited-duration career for pay that was less than that of the average worker in manufacturing. Under the new National Agreement, draft prices were established and capped even for promoted umpires, with a $500 maximum and $75 minimum figure for elevation to a higher league. Although the National League and American League did not sign on as official parties to that particular pact, they did use the numbers as guidelines when they reached into the minors for new arbiters.[12]

Most of the public's attention in the spring of 1912, however, again focused on the salary tug-of-war between big league stars and their owners (see Appendix, Fig. 1). According to subsequent figures supplied by David Lewis Fultz, a former major leaguer and lawyer in 1912 who before year's end would become leader of a new players' organization, some major leaguers still received contracts offering but $900 for 1912. One pitcher with a winning record claimed only $1,200. Mordecai "Three-Finger" Brown, the Chicago Cubs' pitching ace, still earned only $7,000 after nine years of service and contributions to four NL pennants. In addition to frozen salaries, the owners' tendencies to raise capital in time of fiscal hardship by selling off players at prices of $50,000 and more without the affected performers' consent and without giving them a share of the gain, rubbed raw nerves. By season's end, in a "fire sale," Cubs owner Charles W. Murphy dismantled his high-priced but highly successful team, firing manager Frank Chance and arranging his exodus to the New York Yankees, selling pitcher Big Ed Reulbach to Brooklyn and shortstop Joe Tinker to Cincinnati, and humiliating Brown by sending him to the Reds only after an interval in the minors.[13]

With such ongoing frictions as context, angry players became more and more willing to resort to collective action. Ironically, it was the controversial Ty Cobb who became the rallying point of the most publicized incident of the 1912 season. Cobb had held out briefly year after year during spring training in order to avoid its drudgery and to protest over his static salary, only to report belatedly. 1912 proved to be no exception. That spring, Detroit refused to yield to the "Georgia Peach's" demand to renegotiate the last year of his 1910 three-year deal for an increase to $15,000 (about $175,000 in today's dollars). On May 12, a still-disgruntled and much-heckled Cobb attacked a fan in the stands during a game with the Yankees. When Ban Johnson suspended the Tigers' star for ten days without pay, his teammates, despite their decidedly

Walter Johnson and Ty Cobb. The salary holdouts of these two stars in the early 1910s prompted tremendous public attention and, in Cobb's case, a congressional investigation.

mixed feelings toward Cobb, threatened a strike unless he was reinstated pending a formal hearing by the league. With the players having informed manager Hughie Jennings of their plans to sit out their scheduled game on Saturday, club management desperately scrambled to avoid a walkout and cancellation that would carry a $5,000-per-game AL fine.

When second baseman Jim Delahanty and other Tigers proved true to their strike pledge and either went home or watched from the stands, Jennings recruited semipros and even spectators to play the game. By the third inning, with the match a rout, angry fans demanded their money back. With no game scheduled for Sunday, Ban Johnson created a forty-eight-hour cooling-off period by canceling the Tigers' Monday tilt but also fined the players $100 each and ordered them to show for their game in Washington on Tuesday or face suspensions. At Cobb's urging, tney returned and Johnson reduced their fines to $50 each, although he ordered Detroit owner Frank Navin not to pay his charges' levies for them. The AL president reinstated Cobb on May 26, and, in an additional sop to the disgruntled player, the league announced that henceforth special policemen would be installed in all ballparks to ensure improved spectator control. Among steps taken by the administrators of organized baseball to siphon off other possible catalysts of player protest in 1912, the National Commission belatedly declared that injury did not provide just cause for owner retention of a player without pay and required that such performers either receive their money or be released. The commission also carried out the readmission of past jumpers to the outlaw California State League, completing the process in 1913. The latter hardly constituted a selfless act of generosity, however, as the additional players made available through reinstatement only increased the size of the player pool available to management.[14]

Despite these meager steps, the frequency of management abuses of players' rights continued to increase. Only about 10 percent of major league players in 1912 actually received personal copies of their contracts from their clubs. During the year, the number of complaints to the National Commission climbed to 11,546, and the number of rulings reached 153. Despite the fact that a player could be optioned out only once in a season, Brooklyn dispatched outfielder Henry "Hi" Myers three separate times. Boston Red Sox player Kurt "Casey" Hageman, having signed a $400-a-month contract with the club, found himself optioned to minor league Jersey City in May. He agreed to report, and signed a new contract with the Jersey City club at the same salary, when assured that he would soon be called back up to the majors. But a month later, when Jersey City reversed itself and claimed it had no use for his services, Boston assigned Hageman to Denver without his consent at a lower pay level ($250 a month). Denver expressed a willingness to release the unhappy ballplayer, but only if another club would pay $1,500 for him. When Hageman instead reported back to Boston and appealed his case to the National Commission, the panel ruled against him and ordered him to report to Denver.

In similar fashion, Arthur Hofman, who had signed a $5,000 contract with the Cubs for 1912, was ordered to a minor league franchise at lower pay after being "laundered" through Pittsburgh. Hofman pursued his case not only with the National Commission but also in the courts, and after three years of litigation, he won $2,944.47 in the Illinois State Court of Appeals in 1915. Along with all the other disputes, perhaps most troubling for the health of the game, however, were the continuing accusations of players and even managers laying down for revenge and money. Philadelphia Phillies president Horace Fogel, urged on by financial backer Charles P. Taft of Cincinnati and Cubs president Murphy, publicly accused St. Louis manager Roger Bresnahan, previously a player for the Giants, of having helped his former teammates by instructing his club to "take it easy" on them. Despite the similarity to 1908 accusations of bribery and game-fixing against the Giants, it was Fogel, not Bresnahan, whom the National League "indicted" on seven counts of false accusation and "convicted" on five. Fogel found himself banished from league councils as a consequence, and other backers soon edged him out of his office and franchise stockholdings.[15]

With player discontent increasingly visible, in September 1912 major leaguers chartered under New York state corporation law a new union, the Fraternity of Professional Baseball Players of America. The Players' Fraternity, as it became publicly known, tabbed David Fultz as its president and selected four players, two from each league, to serve as vice-presidents and another veteran as organization secretary. Fultz and his vice-presidents served as an initial advisory board, later supplemented by a board of directors consisting of player representatives from each team. Charging $18 annual dues, the fraternity quickly signed up 288 players, representing a majority of every big league club save the two Boston teams and Cleveland. In November, Fultz outlined the union's objectives in *Baseball Magazine*. In the conciliatory language of a moderate trade unionist, the president offered his organization's services in policing contract compliance on both sides, and he pledged to help protect players from abuses and eradicate rowdyism. Fultz also promised to extend financial assistance and advice to needy members and to promote professional pride within the union.

However noble Fultz's pronouncements, he brought to the job of Players' Fraternity leadership an altogether mixed bag of personal assets and liabilities. After graduating from college, he had entered the majors as an outfielder with the Phillies in 1898 and witnessed firsthand the grim realities of that era for players. Having signed what he thought was a contract for $2,400 a season, Fultz learned from club president Rogers that only half that amount was actual salary and the other half merely a one-shot signing bonus. In mid-season Philadelphia had traded the disgruntled rookie center fielder to Baltimore, where he began a seven-year career that peaked in 1902 with his leading the American League in runs scored with 109 for Connie Mack's Athletics. Besides bouncing around with several teams, Fultz had suffered from chronic leg problems stemming from his undergraduate football days. In September 1905, a broken jaw resulting from an outfield collision hastened his retirement from the game. Receiving his law degree at New York University, Fultz set up a Wall Street practice, ironically within a few blocks of that of John Montgomery Ward, and began representing player clients. Having turned down a suggestion to lead a players' organization two years earlier, by 1912 he had changed his mind.

Although Fultz's own experiences dovetailed with those of many of the players he now led, he was of an earlier generation and personally knew few of the current actives. As such he was less "one of them" than their "hired gun" in their legal battles with management. His own approach toward his membership suggested a leader more like a well-bred Progressive Era social worker than a hard-bitten union boss—one intent upon "uplifting" his charges both materially and morally from "above." Some remembered that even as a player he had been known for refusing to play on Sundays. Others questioned his "highbrow" education at Brown and NYU and his Wall Street address. In personality something of a dour loner, Fultz occasionally lectured members on their moral habits, and he permitted others to launch a Prohibition effort within the fraternity. Well-intentioned though he was, it remained an open question whether or not Fultz could secure and retain the trust of the majority of the player force and call upon it for collective action. Such doubts magnified when observers factored in circumstances that divided players, such as league, classification, region, seniority, pay, and level of education.[16]

A spirit of confrontation between player and owner, meanwhile, continued to build, aggravated by yet more spring training salary showdowns in 1913. In the new issue of his *Spalding Guide*, the retired Chicago magnate sounded the alarm at a growing "selfish coterie of players." In February's *Baseball Magazine*, Fultz strongly defended his membership from a similar diatribe presented in the pages of *Sporting Life*. Once more, at the top of management's least-favorite player list stood Ty Cobb. With his salary still stuck at its 1910 level of less than five figures, Cobb and three disgruntled teammates refused to sign their new contracts with the Tigers. By the time spring training camps opened, the others had signed and reported—but not Cobb, who again demanded $15,000 a year. In hindsight, the demand does not appear excessive, given that the Detroit star had won five straight AL batting titles. Even with the increase, the pay would not have been the highest

David Lewis Fultz, president of the Players' Fraternity, 1913–17

ever awarded. Nonetheless, owner Frank Navin refused to budge, bolstered by other AL owners who in secret session discussed the cases of Cobb and teammate Wahoo Sam Crawford. After weighing privately the likely effects on public opinion of an unyielding stand, the owners directed their colleague to stand firm out of fear of what doing otherwise might mean for their own salary scales. When Cobb refused to report, Navin suspended him, and the National Commission placed him on the ineligible list.

Because of Cobb's tremendous notoriety, Congress jumped into the melee in the persons of U.S. Senator Hoke Smith and Representative Thomas Hardwick, both from Cobb's home state of Georgia. The two demanded a copy of the Detroit contract and pressed for a broader muckraking investigation of baseball's status under the antitrust laws. Shortly into the regular season, Cobb signed with the Tigers for $11,332.55 and was reinstated by the National Commission effective May 1, leaving a verbal reprimand and a token $50 fine as punishment. In the aftermath, Congressman Thomas Gallagher of Illinois pushed ahead with an investigation of baseball he had launched in 1912 and introduced a resolution calling for the creation of a seven-member blue-ribbon commission to examine professional baseball's actions as a "predacious and mendacious trust." Hoping to kill any such proposal through kindness, the National Commission issued public relations statements denying that its industry needed such scrutiny but claiming that it "welcomed" any investigation. Ironically, at the same time, however, John Montgomery Ward, former brotherhood leader now turned club executive, testified before Gallagher's committee against an inquiry on the grounds that while baseball was a monopoly, it could not successfully operate otherwise. Less charitable toward the politicians was the pro-management *Sporting News*, which blasted the political motives of those pressing for an investigation. The magnates' strategy worked, as Gallagher's resolution died in committee.[17]

Major league owners' determination to prevent a new round of salary escalation had been underscored by the continued drop in attendance totals in 1912. Hoping to redirect fan attention and appreciation toward pitching, and thereby deflate the batting-driven pay demands of Cobb and other position players, the National League rediscovered the earned run average statistic, which it had not officially kept since the 1880s. Ban Johnson admired the statistic so much he urged his circuit to promote it instead of won-lost records, and the American League did through 1919. On the salary front, among the new contract offers reported in the press was $2,400 to the Yankees' Roger Peckinpaugh. Teammate Ray Fisher, who had been signed five years earlier as a rookie for $7,500, now received $3,000. Although stars' pay inflated the averages even in a time of owner recalcitrance, a typical player's salary probably stood at about $2,800 (see Appendix, Fig. 1). Defenders of management fairness pointed to individual cases such as that of Ed Sweeney, who had signed in 1900 at $1,500 and now made $5,300 despite never hitting over .270, while the average American worker earned less than $1,500.

Even *Baseball Magazine*'s Francis C. Lane reported that fifty players now made more than $4,500 a year. But this, of course, represented only 9 percent of the 560 players under major league reserve. Fultz countered the "high-priced ballplayer" claim by pointing out the misleading picture painted by stars' salaries while others still earned less than $1,000. To arguments that even that level of pay was generous for playing a "kid's game," the fraternity president responded that a fairer comparison of major league baseball salaries would be with those of the top 300 individuals in a comparably sized industry. Contradicting owner poor-mouthing, Fultz also noted that the magnates had generated enough money for their new stadium constructions. The entire discussion, in any event, ignored the pay of thousands of minor leaguers, which remained capped. For 1913, Class A players could only earn on average $200 a month, or $1,400 a year. At the B level, the cap of $2,417 per team per month, worked out to individual amounts of $161 a month and $1,127 a season. C pay averaged $108 dollars per individual per month, or $756 a year, and D players earned $83 a month and $581 for the year, a drop of $42 from the previous year.[18]

Fultz's indictment of baseball's labor practices extended beyond salaries to other collective concerns, including contract abuses, arbitrary disciplinary actions, and safety issues. He pointed out that players demoted to the minors, in addition to the humiliation they suffered from the action itself, had to pay their own travel expenses. While the number of draftees to the majors rose by twenty in 1913 to eighty-eight, owners also were misleading them through the use of so-called "probationary contracts." Under these pacts, a major league club retained a rookie for a forty-five-day trial period at pay up to 25 percent higher than his previous minor league salary (although usually less than this percentage). If the club decided to keep the player, it was obligated to issue him a standard major league contract. But in some cases owners refused to do so, retaining the player at lower pay than he was entitled to or misleading the player at the time he initially signed the probationary contract into believing that it guaranteed him 25 percent more money if he made the club, when it actually did not. Studies also showed that job security in the majors had not improved much, with a 90 percent player turnover in the previous ten years. Given the precariousness of the security of a major league income, Fultz also objected to ownership practices of issuing 50 percent salary cuts to unsigned players in their option year, and he pressed for a clear, finite reserve period of perhaps five years which could be extended only by mutual agreement. (The proposal bears a striking similarity to today's length of service required before a player may obtain free agent status.)[19]

With the Players' Fraternity peppering the National Commission with complaints, the panel's workload rose to 11,859 inquiries in 1913, but only 139 findings resulted. Grievances included complaints against spectator abuse of players, demands of hearings for ejected players prior to the announcement of their penalties, and salary guarantees for transferred players. During the 1913 season, for example, the admittedly wild-living Rube Waddell ended the year in debt because of $1,000 in fines billed him for alcoholism, $700 in other levies, and a $750 deduction by his club for an alimony payment. The National Commission, however, refused to recognize the fraternity as a plaintiff in good standing before its tribunal. When Fultz accompanied player Ad Brennan, charged with assaulting manager John McGraw, to his hearing, the commission upheld the fine and told the union president his presence constituted an "intrusion." Undeterred, Fultz took up the case of Kurt Hageman in public courts, seeking for his client $1,480 in back salary. After five years, Hageman finally won a judgment in a New York appellate court for $2,348.56 but collected it only after Boston owner Harry Frazee faced a contempt citation if he did not pay up.[20]

Official spokesmen for the majors did their best to undercut Fultz's legitimacy in the eyes of the public. National Commission chairman Herrmann avoided direct denunciation of the Players' Fraternity, but he emphasized how little the membership had in common. As he put it, the player force consisted of those "on the make," those at the top, and those on the down side, with little shared interest. Others labeled Fultz an "outsider" lawyer, "out of touch" with present player circumstances. Athletics owner-manager Connie Mack even smuggled player-coach Ira Thomas into the fraternity as a company spy. Thomas, who eventually rose to a vice-presidency in the union, asserted late in 1913 that in the case of Mack's employees at least, they had no grounds for complaint because of their boss's fairness. Fultz bitingly quipped that for anyone who believed that, Mack's nickname of Connie had become even more appropriate. Under pressure from the fraternity, and fearing legal actions, more clubs secured accident insurance for their players. The Aetna insurance firm alone claimed eight major league clubs and one minor league franchise as clients. But Fultz pressed for greater precautions, including protective equipment and the painting of outfield fences green so as to provide hitters with better sight backgrounds and reduce beaning incidents. Even a minor league umpire, ex-player Edward Hugo Cermak, had been killed in 1913 when struck in the throat by a ball.[21]

At season's end, a new furor arose over attempts by the owners to ban yet another form of postseason compensation. Under pressure from regular sportswriters, who did not welcome the competition, the National Commission issued a directive barring any players eligible for the World Series or any other postseason city series from writing "insider" accounts for sale to newspapers. Already several players had been invited by various publications to provide such diary accounts and had signed contracts to do so. The owners disliked most sources of player income outside their licensing or control—including the "pitching" of products that ranged from soft drinks, gloves, and gum all the way to paint, fearing that it loosened their hold on the player at contract time. But cigarette cards with players' likenesses had existed since the 1880s, and companies welcomed players as visible champions of their particular wares. After heated exchanges and threats of fines and cancellation of the World Series by the commission, it relented to the extent that it permitted player "scribes" who had already signed contracts to receive payment for their accounts in 1913 but it prohibited such arrangements by anyone else in the future. The ban on World Series participants serving as journalists was, however, largely ignored by the players and unenforced by the commission in the coming years.[22]

Despite their irritation at the fraternity's unwelcome presence, the major league owners finally enjoyed a better year financially in 1913. But even before the magnates could count up their full take for the year, they faced the challenge of a new outlaw league. The new circuit, the Federal League, was in fact merely the latest in a string of opponents since 1910. As with the two-party political system at certain intervals, public dissatisfaction with the status quo, registered in the form of low turnout of an expanded base of potential "customers," invited third-party challenges. Businessman Daniel Fletcher, whose plans for an all-star barnstorming tour had been thwarted by the owners, had tried unsuccessfully to mount a challenge to the existing cartel in 1911, and the

Pennsylvania-based U.S. Baseball League similarly had folded after only a month in operation. At the beginning of 1913, the Federal League had emerged as a minor league, with Chicago's John T. Powers as president. Featuring teams in Cincinnati (actually Covington, Kentucky), Chicago, St. Louis, Cleveland, Pittsburgh, and Indianapolis, the "mushroom league" had to transfer its Queen City team to Kansas City in midseason, and *Sporting News* gleefully predicted that the league would need a "pulmotor" to survive much longer. But using free agent youngsters and former major leaguers, it staggered through the season and then received a major new injection of financial backing. James Gilmore, a wealthy Chicago stationer, became FL president, and the circuit lured away St. Louis Browns club secretary Lloyd Rickart to be league secretary. The heaviest financial hitters, however, were Chicago cafeteria owner and millionaire Charles Weeghman; brewer and park director Otto Steifel and ice manufacturer Phillip DeCatesby Ball, both of St. Louis; and the Ward brothers, entrepreneurs of Brooklyn's Tip-Top Bread firm.[23]

The new claimant to major league status, ironically, organized itself as a single trust along the lines of Andrew Freedman's rejected NL scheme. Club owners divided stock among themselves in parcels of ten at $100 each, and each team also posted a $25,000 guarantee. In order to deter desertions by individual clubs, the league held team leases on parks. The Victor Sporting Goods Company of Springfield, Massachusetts, provided the official baseball used by the circuit. The league's teams, following the addition of Baltimore and Brooklyn members and relocation of the Cleveland club to Buffalo, would compete in four cities with either the National League or the American League and with both circuits in St. Louis and Chicago. Clearly pivotal to the success of the Federal League effort, however, would be the contest for the loyalties of the major league players in the National and American leagues. Accordingly, the new league's pronouncements were designed to make it appear more generous to its employees. FL club owners would hold player options for the season following their active contracts but would be required to notify players of their intent to exercise those options no later than September 15. The Federal League offered long-term deals instead of the reserve, with guaranteed increases of 5 percent above each previous year's pay. Salaries would be paid beginning at spring training rather than at the start of the regular season. Ten-year veterans could demand their unconditional release and become free agents. Although the Federal League indicated that it would sign reservists but not major leaguers under active contract, their inking of George Stovall, organizer of the Addie Joss walkout, as Kansas City player-manager sent the message that disgruntled major leaguers would find a happy home with the Feds.[24]

The Federal League's emergence supplied the Players' Fraternity with immediate new leverage in its dealings with the established majors. In order to drive home the lesson that the fraternity now could play the leagues off against each other in behalf of the players, Fultz instructed members to hold off on signing any new contracts yet. Adding to the pressure upon the NL-AL cartel were rumors that the Federals' counsel, Edward E. Gates, planned an antitrust lawsuit against the National Agreement partners. Attempting to split off the fraternity's membership from its leadership, as it had done earlier to the Protective Association, National Commission chairman Herrmann, speaking for the cartel, announced to minor league executives at their November convention being held in Columbus that while the fraternity's representatives would be welcome before his panel, Fultz would not. According to Herrmann, Fultz was an "outsider" bent on stirring up "strife and dissension." The moguls also floated rumors claiming that the union president's actions were motivated by "private ends"—in particular, his interest in the presidency of the Federal League.[25]

In truth, however, the major leagues could not afford to antagonize Fultz and his organization completely, for with the fraternity's open opposition the owners might suffer wholesale player desertions to the Federal League. On the one hand, Herrmann partially reversed himself by allowing Fultz to appear before the National Commission—if he was accompanied by a player committee rather than appearing alone. On the other, Ban Johnson threatened jumpers—both those under contract and those held in reserve—with permanent banishment from National Agreement leagues. Nonetheless, in December star shortstop Joe Tinker shocked the owners by jumping to the Chicago FL entry. Tinker had chafed at the restrictions placed upon him as Cincinnati player-manager and had been sold at season's end to Brooklyn with the promise of $10,000 of his $25,000 sales price. But instead of receiving the $10,000 immediately, Tinker learned that Ebbets had only sent Cincinnati's Herrmann $15,000. Despite Ebbets's promise to give him the $10,000 as a belated bonus on top of a more modest regular salary of $7,500, Tinker bolted in favor of an FL three-year offer of $12,000 a season plus expenses and stock ownership rights.

Soon after Tinker's desertion to the Federals, Three-Finger Brown joined him by signing a pact to become the league's St. Louis field manager. Next in line stood another Cubs star, Johnny Evers, who had managed Chicago to third place in 1913 despite owner Murphy's personnel auctions and had been signed to a new four-year pact at $10,000 a season. When Evers entertained offers from the Federals, Murphy threatened to tear up the contract and suspend him without pay, saying that the player-manager effectively had "resigned" without providing the requisite ten-day notice. The Evers crisis presented a major challenge to the National League's new president, John Tener, who had replaced Lynch. Tener, a former major leaguer in the 1880s, loyalist of the Penrose political machine in Pennsylvania, and the Keystone State's governor, attempted to orchestrate a trade to Boston in order to keep Evers in his league. After initially balking at the deal, Evers, with his new salary guaranteed, relented and went to the Braves for not only his contract pay but an NL-paid bonus as well. Signaling his criticism of the arrangement, AL president Ban Johnson stated that the "evil practices and reckless extravagance" of some owners had brought the current crisis upon the cartel, and he opined that the new rival league might actually end up useful as a "cleansing agent" ridding the established circuits of "undesireable elements."[26]

Nonetheless, others were less sanguine about the possible loss of star players to the Federal League and reluctantly made concessions to the Players' Fraternity to hold off the eventuality. In early January, the National Commission attended an open meeting of some 200 to 300 players and received a seventeen-point set of demands. Private sessions followed between the commission and the fraternity's five-member advisory council, resulting in commission approval of eleven of the proposals. Management accepted responsibility for paying for players' uniforms (except shoes) and travel expenses to spring training, and agreed to painting outfield fences green in the majors and high minors. (Nonetheless, by 1915 fifty-nine professional and semipro players in the United States died as a result of on-field accidents, and thirty-eight of them died as a result of head injuries received while in the batter's box.) Players were promised written notification and explanation of suspensions or releases and nondiscrimination against fraternity members. Ten-year major league veterans, in a change dubbed the "Brown rule" in honor of the veteran pitcher, received the right of unconditional release. Fultz also pushed for free agency for players with twelve years' combined seniority in major league and AA ball but settled for a fifteen-year deadline. Released players also now could negotiate immediately for a new job rather than have to wait ten days. In the case of A and AA leagues, owners now had to provide, with pay, five days' advance notice of release, but lower classifications did not, despite some clubs having "fired" players even between innings of a game. Transferred players also won the right to written explanations of their sale or option terms, and all players were promised actual copies of their contracts. As for the "probationary" player, he benefited from the requirement that if the club in question decided to keep him, it had to provide him with a legitimate major league contract at the end of the trial period or else forfeit to him free agent status.[27]

On other issues, however, the National Commission refused to yield. The management panel, despite the ongoing Hageman lawsuit, rejected fraternity calls for the contracts of transferred players to follow them as binding pacts upon their new employers. At most, the commission consented to provide a "fair hearing" for complaints lodged on the basis of the issue. Similarly, management refused to provide enforcement of individual clubs' "side agreements" with players. The commission argued that such under-the-table pacts, although widely ignored by it in its past rulings, were illegal, with participating owners subject to $500 fines. It also refused player demands to require written advance notice to players for whom waivers were to be asked, which would have given them more opportunity to market themselves openly. Finally, when the owners unveiled their new version of the standard contract for 1914, it included new language specifically barring players from participating in unauthorized off-season athletic exhibitions such as softball, baseball, or football games.

Having given as much ground as they dared, the magnates now pressured Fultz for his reciprocal cooperation against the Federal League. Seeking fraternity help in preventing player jumping, Garry Herrmann bluntly asked the union president, "What are you going to do for us?" All Fultz proved willing to offer was a lifting of the earlier freeze on his members' signing new contracts with their clubs. He refused to order the expulsion of jumpers from the fraternity, arguing in the case of players under reserve or option that he could not demand adherence to a rule that the courts might well find illegal or unenforceable. The union's leader did say that he condemned the breaking of active contracts and would recommend to his colleagues the expulsion of contract breakers from the fraternity, but he did so knowing that the membership likely would not concur. The union did adopt rules to expel a jumper who refused first to consent to an examination of his grievances by, and receive permission from, its advisory board. But such steps seemed to the owners wholly inadequate. In revenge, Ban Johnson claimed that the grievances Fultz had presented to the National Commission had been fictitious and simply a ploy to justify his union salary. *Sporting News* again labeled the fraternity president an "outlaw" and a "baseball anarchist," and the secretary of the minors' National Association similarly called him a "professional agitator."[28]

Most major leaguers recognized the low odds of Federal League success and accordingly used the jumping threat to secure higher pay without usually following through on it. To deter actual jumping, Herrmann, while stating that "proper" FL contracts would be honored along with the National Agreement clubs' player pacts, promised "vigorous defensive measures." Typical of player reaction was the response of catcher Bill Killefer of the Phillies, who leaped to the Chifeds (as Chicago's FL club was called) only to return to his former team within twelve days. The year before, Philadelphia had paid him $3,200, and the club had notified him that his contract would be renewed with a pay increase. After giving his verbal acceptance, Killefer then had accepted the FL offer for three years at $17,500, accompanied by an immediate $525. Once he pocketed the advance, however, he re-signed with the Phillies at $18,500 spread over three years. While Ban Johnson rejected overtures to his circuit from FL president Gilmore for a compromise that would grant the rival major league standing, a pundit quipped:

> Weeghman, Weeghman, Federal man,
> Make me a contract as fast as you can.
> Pad it and sign it and mark it OK,
> And I'll go to the majors and ask for more pay.[29]

In what became known as the "Battle of the Dock," prior to 1914 spring training Federal League agents established a vigil in New York, hoping to sign returnees from an all-star world exhibition tour sponsored by Comiskey and McGraw. But the Feds only managed to secure the services of two players, the Phillies' Mike Doolan and the Cardinals' Steve Evans. Given the Phillies' own earlier disregard of a signed FL contract in the Killefer matter, the new circuit now felt free to raid not only reservists but also NL and AL performers under current contract. FL scouts prowled major league camps in Georgia, Florida, and Arkansas, hoping to pick off unhappy players. Echoing the continuing refrain that the Federal League understood players' contributions to the game better and would act accordingly, John Montgomery Ward, who had been signed on as business manager by the FL team in Brooklyn, courted players and sportswriters alike by asserting that the game's progress to date owed 25 percent to the players, 75 percent to the press, and nothing to the owners.[30]

Attempting to blunt such appeals, the majors had redrawn the standard contract, which previously had stated that 25 percent of a player's salary actually was compensation in consideration of his "acceptance" of the club's right to reserve him. Under the earlier version, however, the player still did not receive this partial sum if the club then decided to dump him the next spring. Under the new language, the contract was made to appear fairer to reservists by designating a specific sum of money as the "option payment" for the next year's services. Although it did not constitute an actual addition to the next year's salary if the player was kept, it did promise some compensation if the club chose not to exercise its option on the player. In the owners' judgment, it also made the reserve clause less indefinite and more mutual in the eyes of the law, and therefore less subject to court challenge during the trade war. Club officials pointed out this new generosity to players contemplating jumping and usually followed up their pitch with a new contract offer at higher pay if the player remained loyal. In another move designed to reduce legal vulnerability, the owners also struck out the language that stipulated only ten days' notice by management before releasing a player while giving the player no similar power to abruptly and unilaterally terminate his contract. The owners did not intend actually to equalize the right of contract termination, but they judged that greater ambiguity in the standard language would serve them better than specifics so clearly skewed against the player.[31]

With the bidding war underway, even cheap owners such as Connie Mack found it necessary to tear up old contracts and offer players multiyear deals at substantial increases. One scribe summed the situation up this way:

> Sing a song of dollars,
> A pocketful of kale;
> See the players jumping,
> Hear the magnates wail.
> Soon the season opens,
> Salary coming due.
> If it's not forthcoming,
> Jumpers will be blue.

Most were not. During the two years of the Federal League war, only 18 men actually jumped active major league contracts and 63 ignored club reserves to join the Federals' total of 264 players. But many more were bought off with huge pay increases (see Appendix, Figs. 1 and 4). Walter Johnson, who had won 36 games in 1913, became one of what were known as "rubber legs"—players who made a double jump to the Federal League and back to their old clubs. The White Sox' Comiskey actually paid a $6,000 signing bonus to entice the "Big Train" back to his AL rivals, the Washington Senators, in order to prevent the player from joining up with the Chicago FL entry. Johnson also received an increase in base salary to $10,000 for 1914 and $12,500 for the next year. Among other examples, Ray Caldwell inked a four-year pact raising his annual salary from $2,400 to $8,000 a year. Walter "Rabbit" Maranville's pay jumped from $1,800 to $6,000. Brooklyn's Jake Daubert received a five-year deal with an immediate annual pay boost from $5,000 to $9,000. White Sox infielder George "Buck" Weaver went from a $2,500 salary to a three-year contract at $6,000 a season. For his part, Boston hitting sensation Tris Speaker garnered an aggregate $35,000 over two years for not jumping to the Feds. According to historian Harold Seymour, the average pay of twenty major league regulars rose from $3,800 in 1913 to $7,300 by 1915. In 1913, the clubs with the biggest payrolls had spent $75,000 at most. Within a year, the average major league payroll nearly equaled that amount.[32]

In the pursuit of talent, owners, agents, and players performed subterfuges worthy of espionage rings. In May, the Chifeds wired $1,000 to their Seattle agent, Tim O'Rourke, to secure the services of local pitcher Pete Schneider. O'Rourke received instructions to give the player $500 as an immediate signing bonus, along with $71 to cover train fare to the Windy City. But when Schneider learned of his contemporaneous purchase by the National League's Cincinnati club, he honorably attempted to return the Federals' bonus money. When O'Rourke refused to accept it, the player left it with his Seattle club president and prepared to depart for the Queen City. Desperate to stop him, O'Rourke then dispatched ex-player toughs from his "dive saloon" to kidnap Schneider before he boarded a train, and a scout assigned to accompany the player was nearly shot as the toughs tried to follow through on their orders. In another tangled case, veteran pitcher Rube Marquard demanded a $1,500 advance on his two-year Giants contract and then, when the advance was refused, jumped to the Brookfeds, telling them that he had been released by New York. For legal protection John Ward made the player sign an affidavit to that effect before inking him to a two-year, $10,000-per-season deal. When he discovered Marquard's lie, Ward did the honorable thing and returned him to the Giants. A grateful McGraw even offered to cover any debts the Brooklyn executive had incurred, in exchange for Ward's promise not to prosecute the pitcher for fraud.[33]

Other cases required final settlement in the courts. Tacitly recognizing the legal vulnerability of the reserve clause, the National League and American League usually sought redress only when players broke active contracts. In the Bill Killefer matter, federal courts in June upheld the Phillies' claim, accepting attorney George Wharton Pepper's argument that the Chifeds had been the first party guilty of "seducing" the player into breaking contract obligations. The National League also won in the case of Armando Marsans, who skipped Cincinnati for the St. Louis FL entry. The Reds first tried to coax the Cuban back by appealing to his "true Spanish chivalry" and then threatened him with loss of his earnings from cigar endorsements and the club's termination of future dealings in Cuba. When these threats failed, Cincinnati sought and won an injunction against Marsans in court. In a less favorable outcome for the Reds, when pitcher George "Chief" Johnson jumped to the Chifeds, Cincinnati again obtained an injunction from a Chicago court, but an appellate court overruled the earlier decision. When Hal Chase turned the tables on the White Sox by issuing them ten days' notice of his jump to the Buffalo FL team on June 15, New York State Supreme Court Justice Herbert Bissell also ruled in the Federals' favor.[34]

With all of the maneuvering, the main institutional victims of the player shifting during the Federal League war were franchises in the high minors. As early as January, minor league clubs found it necessary to offer under-the-table deals in violation of their salary caps to keep players from jumping. In retaliation, the fraternity's Fultz redirected minor league members of his organization not to sign their contracts unless such extra provisions were clearly spelled out in writing, since the National Commission had refused to enforce undocumented side arrangements. Of the 264 men on FL rosters in 1914 and 1915, 25 were minor league jumpers from active contracts, and 115 more were reserve jumpers, for a total of 115 compared to but 81 major leaguers who jumped. (The remaining 43 came as free agents, 18 of whom claimed no professional experience at all.) The majors did offer limited assistance, but they found their ability to shore up their feeder clubs decreased by a 1913 National Commission edict requiring divestiture of minor league holdings by January 1, 1914. The National League and American League continued the minor league draft at reduced levels, but the total compensation to the minors for the selected players fell from $264,000 to $231,000. The National Commission also permitted covert collusion between the minors and majors to "cover" talent from the Federals. Major league teams drafted players from the Class A level and then "demoted" them to needy AA clubs.[35]

Nonetheless, the high minors faced the dilemma of losing their main gate attractions to the Federals or bankrupting themselves through higher salary offers in order to keep their talent. Given that the phenomenon of the "career minor leaguer" with ten years' service but no big league break was already well known, management could hardly expect its players to sympathize. Facing the grim realities, some clubs sold their best players to the established majors for the best prices they could get in order to balance their books. Jack Dunn, owner of the International League's Baltimore Orioles, sold the rights to the talented pitcher and slugger George Herman "Babe" Ruth to the Boston Red Sox for only $2,500. The National Commission itself "loaned" the International League $30,000, and Ban Johnson personally extended $3,200 to Buffalo president Ed Barrow. Given the overriding every-man-for-himself mentality induced by the financial strains of trade war, however, it is not surprising that of eight commission rulings in disputes between major league and minor league claimants, seven found the panel siding with the majors. As if the minors' plight were not severe enough, a spiking victim from one of the lesser circuits even won a $1,000 judgment in a Holyoke, Massachusetts, court.[36]

One case involving the struggle for labor between clubs at different classifications nearly triggered a strike by the Players' Fraternity. In midsummer, Brooklyn owner Ebbets sent Clarence Kraft, a Class A draftee from New Orleans of the Southern Association, to Class AA Newark. However, months earlier another Southern Association club, Nashville, had filed formal notice of its desire to claim Kraft if he failed to catch on in the majors. When the National Commission upheld Nashville's claim on the player, the fraternity protested Kraft's demotion to a lower level as a violation of its January pact with organized baseball. Ban Johnson, however, maintained that the Class A club's claim on the player had been filed prior to the labor agreement and therefore took precedence. Fultz retaliated by threatening to take his members out on strike after the games of Wednesday, July 22. *Sporting Life* labeled the strike threat an "insolent ultimatum," and Johnson, threatening to lock players out of parks, cut off their salaries, and fine strikers, blasted Fultz as a "menace to the game." The AL president also covertly urged Mack lieutenant Ira Thomas to start up a rival company union. NL president Tener weighed in, pronouncing that "professional men do not strike." But the majors desperately needed to avoid a strike, and the crisis was averted when Ebbets paid $2,500 in compensation to Nashville in exchange for its allowing Kraft to go to Newark. *Sporting Life* conceded that the National League had been forced to "quit cold" out of fear.[37]

Because minor league rosters were the primary targets of Federal League raids, the trade war altered little the ethnic or socioeconomic character of the major league player force. The big league playing fraternity continued to be dominated by American-born performers of Western European ancestry, especially those whose ancestors came from the British Isles or Germany. Baseball literature, such as the *Baseball Joe* series inaugurated in 1912, continued to display hostility toward Jewish ballplayers ("low, greasy specimens") and a preference for college-educated Anglo-Saxons ("natural scholars"). A 1915 study of 146 "crack" players by a criminologist claimed the average player measured 5'9½" tall and pitchers and catchers 5'11", but that the shorter men made better hitters and fielders. From Lee Allen's data, of 720 entry-level players from 1910 to 1915, "non-Irish" sons of the British Isles (English, Scotch, Welsh, Scotch-Irish, and English-Irish) made up about 39 percent of the total player force, with Germanic stock contributing nearly 32 percent. The Irish added 18 percent, and about 12 percent claimed other ancestors, ranging from French (under 4 percent) and Scandinavians (2.5 percent) to Southern and Eastern Europeans (including Poles, Czechs, Bohemians, Slovaks, Italians, Yugoslavs, and Serbs, totaling 2 percent), Canadians and Cubans (each under 1 percent), American Indians, and even a Canary Islander and a Hawaiian. In regard to education, Allen's figures on 755 entering players suggested a more equal division than before between those claiming some college experience (39 percent), some level of high school training (33 percent), and just elementary schooling (28 percent), with the high school cohort rising and the lowest-level category declining.

Among nonwhites, Cubans and Indians continued to trickle into the majors, but their initial entrance had preceded the trade war and was not dramatically accelerated by it. The Boston "Miracle Braves" of 1914 did retain a Cuban witch doctor, however, whom they dubbed the "Black Pope." The New York Giants signed the renowned Indian athlete Jim Thorpe. But still the majors and the National Agreement minors, despite their labor problems, could find no room for African American talent. Smokey Joe Williams, a black hurler who bested Walter Johnson and other star major leaguers in postseason exhibitions, found no takers for his skills in organized baseball. Even more egregious was the refusal to hire shortstop John Henry Lloyd, labeled the "black Wagner" for his dazzling abilities. Years later, in 1938, Wagner himself would tell a sportswriter that Lloyd had been the greatest ballplayer he had ever seen, greater even than Babe Ruth.[38]

The minor leagues, despite the strains upon their relationship with the majors, recognized that they could not stand alone against the Federal League and therefore, through their National Association, pledged continued fealty to the National and American leagues at their November convention in Omaha. Signaling the greater solidarity, in December an expanded Joint Committee on Playing Rules, with three representatives each from the National League and American League and one National Association member, began operation. Estimates by the *New York Times* placed season losses at $150,000 for the International League and $90,000 for the American Association. The number of minor leagues, forty-four at the beginning of 1914, fell to twenty-eight. AA teams enforced team limits of thirty reservists and twenty actives. Class A clubs reduced active rosters from eighteen to fifteen, and reserves from twenty-eight to twenty-six, which enabled them to lower team monthly payroll caps from $3,600 to $3,000 while maintaining individual salaries at competitive levels. B clubs pared team rosters and monthly payrolls from fifteen to fourteen actives, twenty-six to twenty-four reserves, and $2,450 to $2,050 and cut individual pay from $163 per month to $146. C leagues held the line on team and individual pay by keeping active rosters on average at thirteen but reducing reserve lists from twenty-four to twenty-two. At D level, reserve numbers stayed at twenty-two and active rosters generally at thirteen, but individual monthly pay dropped $7, and monthly team payroll limits fell from $1,142 to $1,059. Given the hard times, it came as no surprise that a survey of Atlanta Cracker ballplayers showed that all fourteen men had to secure off-season employment, ranging from blue-collar work to winter ball to postal jobs to engagements with vaudeville troupes.[39]

If the minors had been buffeted, the Players' Fraternity now also found its own temporary clout running into limits. In October the membership reelected Fultz president, and with its spirits boosted by the Clayton Act's exemption of unions from antitrust scrutiny, its numbers and treasury receipts grew to 1,100 men and over $10,000. Flexing the organization's newfound muscle, Fultz pressed nine demands upon the National Commission, most of them extensions of or variations on earlier requests. But the Commission rejected all save one, claiming either that they had already been addressed or that they dealt with strictly major league matters outside the panel's purview. The fraternity did not fare notably better in 1914 grievance rulings by the commission. Out of one hundred findings issued, forty-eight were in cases involving player claims and appeals against management. Discounting four reinstatement requests that were granted (which could be expected, given clubs' need to secure players), players won but seven of the remaining forty-four cases. Perhaps to bolster the minor league National Association's governance structures, in cases involving owner appeals to overturn labor rulings issued by the minors' National Board, they too won but three out of eleven judgments. In cases brought by umpires and managers against management (six in each category) the commission ruled against the plaintiffs four times each.[40]

The ultimate fate of each of the combatants in the Federal League war, including the Players' Fraternity, would be determined at the turnstiles. The National Commission's cold shoulder to the union's demands at year's end suggested that while the National Agreement parties had been wounded, the Federals were near death. NL and AL attendance did plummet to 4.1 million, a loss of 1.9 million. The National League bravely claimed a leaguewide profit of $115,000, and the American League $58,000, but even by their own assertions only half of the clubs made money. The Federal League, with smaller fiscal reserves, fared far worse, with a loss of $176,000. In steps designed to shore up paid attendance, the American League instituted a two-pass limit for players, and the National League set a cap of 6 percent of the total attendance on its free admissions. Individual teams in some cases sold off high-priced talent to richer clubs in anticipation of even darker days ahead at the gate. Connie Mack's Philadelphia Athletics, embarrassed by the Braves in the 1914 World Series, sold Eddie Collins to the White Sox for over $50,000 and, with other sales added, raised $180,000. Chief Bender and Eddie Plank avoided the auction block only by jumping to the Federal League. The Athletics plummeted to last place, where they remained for the next seven years. In contrast, Brooklyn's Charles Ebbets retained his talent at higher salaries in hopes that a successful season on the field would best minimize financial woes.

As financially strapped as they were, FL owners had particular reason to wish that there would not be a second year of war. Ironically, just as the real fighting of World War I began in August 1914, peace rumors first circulated within baseball circles. Herrmann and Weeghman even held truce talks, but the established leagues still saw the Federal League's demand for equal status as too high a price for armistice. So, in preparation for 1915, the Federals switched their Indianapolis franchise to Newark, and Indy's star outfielder Benny Kauff was reassigned to Brooklyn to help shore up that ailing club. Kauff, after signing a three-year deal with his new club, proceeded to jump to New York's NL team, which did not know he was already under contract. With characteristic bravado, Kauff announced, "I'll make Cobb look like a bush leaguer if I can play for the Giants!" With NL rival and defending World Series champion Boston refusing to play New York if it retained Kauff, however, the Giants returned him to the Brookfeds. A parallel effort by Brooklyn's Harry Sinclair to hire away manager John McGraw for $100,000 also failed, with the Giants' skipper honoring a five-year deal at $30,000 a season he had signed at the end of 1912. Federal League demands for a three-way World Series or a Chicago-area series similarly fell on deaf ears.[41]

Because of the loyalty of the minors to the National Agreement, the Federal League could not draw upon a feeder system of deserter clubs. As a consequence, its teams had to maintain expensive thirty-man rosters in an attempt to stash away talent where the National and American leagues couldn't get to it. The Federals did manage to infiltrate the Colonial League of New England, only to have the National Association lift that circuit's reserve protections. For several months in 1915, rumors also floated of a Pennsylvania farm system for the Federal League, with the Players' Fraternity planning cooperation for its own sake. One informer relayed to Garry Herrmann, "None of the players will tell me what action they are taking but Fultz is framing up something." Nothing came of the scheme, however. Signs of easing pressure upon the National Agreement partners and greater passivity by the Players' Fraternity included a drop in inquiries filed with the National Commission to 8,153. Rulings also fell, from 100 to only 36.[42]

The Federal League's last real hopes lay with the antitrust lawsuit its lawyers filed in January 1915 in the U.S. District Court of Northern Illinois. The upstart circuit hoped that the presiding judge, Kenesaw Mountain Landis, would be sympathetic, basing their hope upon his famous 1907 verdict of $29 million against Standard Oil (which a higher court subsequently had overturned). The lawsuit named as defendants all sixteen NL and AL club presidents, along with the National Commission.

In defense, Herrmann submitted a forty-seven-page affidavit. A worried Clark Griffith openly criticized the Players' Fraternity for refusing to take sides with the National Agreement partners in the action. Nonetheless, Landis indicated his leanings against the Federals early on, when, in an exchange with their attorney, he pointedly queried, "Do you realize that a decision in this case may tear down the very foundation of the game?" Cutting off the plaintiffs' attempts to introduce evidence on players' working conditions to support the antitrust suit, Landis insisted upon seeing organized baseball as a "national institution" rather than a monopolistic industry. Clearly hoping for an out-of-court surrender by the Federal League, the judge stalled the case for over a year. During that span, the league gave indications that it might indeed surrender by retracting legal reprisals against a half dozen of its players who had jumped to the other side.[43]

Landis's postponement of a decision in the antitrust suit bought time for the Federal League's opponents to bankrupt it at the gate in 1915. Combined attendance in the American and National leagues increased by over 400,000, while the Federals lost an estimated $2.5 million. Talks resumed between executives of the rival leagues as early as the start of the regular season. In April, Ban Johnson met with Phillip Ball at a private dinner arranged by *Sporting News* editor Taylor Spink. By October, with the World Series offering the backdrop, the National Commission was discussing peace with Gilmore, Sinclair, and Ball in Philadelphia. The Federal League's position eroded further with the death of one of the Ward brothers, its chief backers in Brooklyn. On December 13, NL owners received Gilmore and Sinclair at league president Tener's office, and the conferees presented a rough outline of a settlement that evening at a gathering in the Republican Club. To cement AL agreement, the National League dispatched a committee of owners to meet a counterpart AL panel on December 17 and then solicited final acceptance from Federal League, International League, American Association, and National Association representatives.

The Federals were now ready to surrender, so they designated a new committee to sound out Landis regarding the proposed peace agreement. With the judge agreeing to dismiss the suit if the parties came to an out-of-court settlement, the "treaty" was signed in Garry Herrmann's Cincinnati office on December 22, 1915. Under its terms, the victors bought out the Federal League for $600,000 and amalgamated two of its franchises with existing clubs while jettisoning the rest. The Ward family received $400,000 in twenty annual payments of

$20,000, Sinclair garnered $100,000 in ten $10,000 increments, and investors in Pittsburgh's FL club gained another $50,000 (infuriating Pirates owner Barney Dreyfuss). Charles Weeghman and his associates purchased the Chicago Cubs, with the National League chipping in $50,000 of the sale price, and Phillip Ball secured the St. Louis Browns. Organized baseball seized the parks in Pittsburgh, Newark, and Brooklyn, while it left FL interests in Kansas City and Buffalo stranded. Besides his other gains, Harry Sinclair received the rights to auction off seventeen FL players unclaimed under National Association contracts and uncontrolled by Weeghman and Ball, netting the oilman another $129,150 in sales ($35,000 for Benny Kauff alone). Unpurchased players reverted to their old clubs if they wanted them or were abandoned if their former clubs did not. Garry Herrmann, anxious to tie up another loose end, paid Ball $2,500 in damages for having prevented the jumper Marsans from performing for the St. Loufeds.

The only thread that could not be secured immediately lay in Baltimore, whose ignored FL directors sued the major leagues, Weeghman, and Gilmore for engaging in a conspiracy to reestablish a monopoly and shut them out of professional baseball. The lawsuit contained echoes of the old Players' League war of 1890, for Ned Hanlon was one of the plaintiffs and John Montgomery Ward a supporting assistant counsel. Major league owners rejected adopting a Baltimore franchise, with Ebbets defending their stance by observing that the city contained "too many colored population to start with."[44] The 1916 antitrust suit would drag on for six years until its resolution by the U.S. Supreme Court in a momentous 1922 decision by Justice Oliver Wendell Holmes, Jr., which exempted the major leagues from antitrust laws. For the present, with the Federal League but a memory, the Players' Fraternity now looked to its immediate future with justifiable foreboding. Even with its 1,200-man membership, the union could now expect the victorious cartel to come at it with renewed vengeance. Without the leverage provided by trade war, could the fraternity hope to hold its own against the new onslaught?

**EIGHT**

WAR AND THE QUEST FOR NORMALCY, 1916-1920

By 1916, while the nation nervously eyed the prospect of war "over there," baseball struggled with the problem of recovering from its most recent trade conflict. Owners pursued labor economies, as operating costs surged higher from intensifying inflationary pressures. For major league stars who had threatened to jump to the Federal League only to sign multiyear deals with their same clubs, postwar salary erosion might be a year or two away. But for those now seeking to return from the outlaw circuit, not even temporary mercy could be expected. Brooklyn owner Charles Ebbets lamented operating costs in the range of $250,000 and daily attendance that had plummeted to only 4,000. Contract negotiations took on a renewed air of bitterness on both sides.

When one pitcher sought a $2,800 raise to $6,000, only to be offered a $4,000 salary, he registered his opinion by telegram in no uncertain terms: "I see you want to give me a good f——g." He defiantly added, "I'll pick s—t with the chickens before I'll play for any less." Another holdout similarly fired back at management, "I won't stand to be f——d by no Jew s-b." In retaliation, owners threatened to deny recalcitrant players their transportation fees when they sought to report to spring training.[1]

Franchises explained that in the overall picture, team payrolls were not so much being cut as held at existing levels (see Appendix, Fig. 1). The Phillies' pay, for example, stood at $4,300 a man in 1916, some $900 above the 1914 figure. But real wages no longer kept pace with contract offers, and attempts to realize economies in the pay of individual stars drew heightened attention. In the face of the hard line taken by the Boston Red Sox, pitcher Smokey Joe Wood ended up holding out the entire season. Tris Speaker, another Boston star, refused to accept a 50 percent pay cut from $18,000 to $9,000, demanding $15,000 instead. Rather than pay up, Boston sold Speaker to Cleveland for $55,000 and two lesser players. Fearful that this stratagem would in roundabout fashion result in the pay cut, the outfielder demanded $10,000 of the sale price or else he would not report to his new club. When the owner balked, AL president Ban Johnson ordered the bonus paid, and Speaker reported. When star hitter Edd Roush held out, Cincinnati club president Garry Herrmann pulled out all the emotional stops. According to Herrmann, Roush owed it to his wife, his own future, and his teammates to sign his contract—one which offered him but $4,500. When the owner finally upped the amount to $5,000, Roush relented, only to be forced into repeating the scenario the next spring. One of Harry Sinclair's auctioned FL veterans, Jimmy Johnston, who had signed a two-year pact in 1915 at $4,000 a season, received a 1916 contract from Ebbets for $3,400. As the new owner of the Cubs, former FL magnate Weeghman also got into the spirit by slashing six of his players' salaries, each by $1,000 or more.

Salary reductions and freezes were not the players' only grievances in 1916. With the Federals' collapse, the number of major league jobs abruptly plunged by one-third. Safety concerns remained prominent, with John Dodge of the Southern Association a beaning fatality that season. Abuses of players' rights by the minors escalated as the junior circuits scrambled to recoup their personnel and gate losses from the Federal League war. Manipulation of talent by major league moguls continued, with Ebbets refusing to sell a particular minor league prospect but "loaning" him to another club. Yankees' co-owner Jacob Ruppert pressed for a relaxation of the eight-player limit on the number of players under option, calling for a figure of fifteen and the power to keep as many as five under that status for up to two continuous years. Lacking the leverage provided by trade war, the Players' Fraternity's demand for representation on the National Commission was rejected. Ban Johnson suggested the possibility of a player member, but only if the designee did not belong to the union. Nonetheless, the fraternity pressed ahead as litigant for the full restoration of Federal League jumpers and the fulfillment of multiyear contract agreements. Commission cases rose to 8,407, and findings to 73. The fraternity's own 1916 report claimed recovery of $7,521.98 from the owners and validation of contract claims worth $2,775 more. Offering Fultz hope of establishing his union as a permanent player in baseball's fiscal management was its expanding membership among minor leaguers. Overall union membership reached 1,215 by year's end.[2]

Part of the explanation for the relative mildness of the major league owners' immediate postwar actions came from improved attendance figures, which bounced back to 7.5 million. The minors, however, had suffered far more, and it was there that Fultz anticipated the fraternity's stiffest new tests. In 1916 the minors continued to falter, shrinking to twenty-five circuits and laying off entire rosters of players. While active and reserve lists remained steady from 1915 levels, team monthly payroll limits fell to a $2,700 average at Class A level, a drop of $300; $2,033 at B, down $17; $1,338 at C, $62 lower; and $1,025 at D, down $34 from 1915. Such figures translated into monthly and seasonal averages for individual players of $193 (down $7) and $1,351 at A level, $145 (down $1) and $1,015 at B, $89 (down $19) and $623 at C, and $68 (down $13) and $476 at D. With such patterns in mind, Fultz at the end of 1916 emphasized the plight of minor league players and recruited from their ranks, claiming "A minor leaguer is just as important to us as the biggest star." Expecting a hostile reception, the union head nonetheless presented a four-point program of demands to the National Association at its November convention in New Orleans. The package included abolition of the practice of suspending players without pay for injury, owner payment of minor leaguers' expenses in traveling to spring training, disclosure of the contents of management's briefs in grievance cases in which the National Commission ruled against the player, and enforcement of a five-day notice provision before release of a Class AA or A player, with provisions enabling the releasee to sign immediately with another club. Fultz implied that if the National Association rejected the platform, he would pressure the National Commission to impose it upon the minors. If that failed, he would advise his membership not to sign 1917 contracts and to be prepared to strike.[3]

Even Fultz, however, was taken aback by the vehemence of official denunciations of his proposals. Although *Sporting News* opined that the planks seemed reasonable, both the minors' own ruling National Board and the National Commission rejected them out of hand. The National Association accused the union of "violating the letter and spirit" of baseball law, and its secretary, J. H. Farrell, claimed that every point had previously been addressed or involved a fraternity misinterpretation of present rules. Farrell insisted that injury pay already existed and that in the matter of spring travel pay, most clubs already provided it and lower clubs should not be compelled. He maintained that Fultz misread the minors' release policy, and snubbed the union on the grievance disclosure issue by asserting that all genuine "interested-parties" to the action—pointedly excluding the fraternity—already had received copies of the arguments and rulings. Farrell concluded that Fultz's demands stemmed merely from personal pique at the National Board's dealing directly with individual players and labeled them as "schoolboy, Fourth of July oratory." Backing up the association, National Commission chairman Herrmann asserted that management's interpretations of the rules might have been in error occasionally but "not as badly" as Fultz's.[4]

Stung sharply, the fraternity's advisory board characterized the response to its proposals as "dictatorial in the extreme" and began canvassing its members in December regarding a possible strike. Central to the success of any such walkout would be the solidarity of major league and minor league players, and Fultz accordingly urged unity. Two weeks later, the fraternity leader announced that if his organization's demands were not met, it would authorize a strike. He indicated that some 600 to 700 members had pledged to go out if called upon, and he defended the threat by citing two years of frustrated "petition, argument, and appeals to public sentiment." In early January, Fultz held talks with the AFL's Samuel Gompers, and a *New York Times* story suggested that the Players' Fraternity was now prepared to affiliate with the labor federation. At the same time, independent of Fultz, some minor league umpires also consulted the AFL regarding formation of a union.[5]

The fraternity's hopes of bluffing management into surrender failed when the National Commission refused to meet Fultz or discuss the union's demands. NL president John Tener insisted he possessed no power to compel the minors. Indicating a willingness to meet with individual players but not fraternity representatives, he labeled the walkout threat "almost a conspiracy," and he warned potential strikers that by holding out they would "automatically suspend themselves." Pittsburgh owner Barney Dreyfuss blamed the fraternity's existence for excessive fraternization between teams that undermined on-field competitiveness. In his words, there was now "too much handshaking among players." Phillies' officials complained about strike threats and similar tactics being waged against their "sport," rather than upon a real industry. In similar vein, sportswriter John Foster, who had branded the earlier brotherhood as "bolshevik," characterized the fraternity as "foreign, hostile, and injurious to sport."

In the American League, Ban Johnson threatened preemptively to lock players out of his circuit's spring training camps and withhold travel payments if they tried to report without first signing their contracts. The International League's Ed Barrow echoed the AL position. Johnson ominously singled out the fraternity representative from Washington, John Henry, for special treatment, threatening to "lay a strong hand" on him. True to his word, Johnson and AL owners pressured the Senators to fire Henry on the grounds that "such persons are undesireable in our league." Washington subsequently waived him out under suspicious circumstances, and the circuit's other clubs compensated the Senators for the loss. The Yankees' "Colonel" T. L. Huston rationalized the owners' militance by pleading, "We cannot stand for the players taking such action as they contemplate. We must stabilize our business."[6]

Fultz as yet did not fully realize it, but he and his union had badly overreached themselves. The fraternity's leader had taken too literally his rhetoric of worker solidarity and had vastly overestimated the willingness of major leaguers, especially stars, to go to bat for the rights of those they considered the prime threats to their job security. Garry Herrmann drove a wedge between the Players' Fraternity and the AFL by describing Gompers as a fair main misled on the merits of the case by Fultz. At the same time, Ban Johnson exploited the breach between the union's leaders and its major league stars, claiming that Fultz's ultimate aims included the imposition of a wage scale for the entire industry and consequently the end of the star system. In response Fultz desperately tried to patch up union solidarity, calling such management assertions "bombastic," and charged the owners with being the ones who really intended to impose wage ceilings. At salary time, he insisted, players would remain free of industrywide dictates but, like actors, would continue to bargain individually. On common matters of player rights under the National Agreement, however, he argued that the members had every right to press collectively, since the owners themselves often acted in consort. Nonetheless, owners knew that the fraternity's major league members were unlikely to be willing to strike, and therefore risk banishment, for minor leaguers threatening to take away their jobs. Some stars already griped because the union had refused to flex its collective muscle for them in their individual contract battles, leaving them isolated in their salary negotiations for new pacts in addition to having failed to secure a collective pension system for them and other players.[7]

By the end of January, the owners warned Gompers that the AFL would look foolish if it backed a ballplayer strike to whose picket lines "nobody came." In response the federation head publicly backtracked, indicating now that the AFL had only taken fraternity affiliation "under advisement." Aware of the need to shore up popular and membership support, Fultz considered renting out a New York theater for a rally and a public presentation of the union's position. But he ruled it out on the grounds of his own oratorical inadequacies. The fraternity did hold smaller, covert membership sessions and solicited supportive telegrams from stars Tris Speaker and Al Demaree. Nonetheless, some members defied Fultz and signed new contracts, forcing the union to retaliate by expelling them. In turn, the National League, American League, and National Commission severed all official communications with the fraternity and its leaders. Too late sensing his organization's peril, Fultz sent a conciliatory note to AA and A level minor league officials, who ignored it. Rumored compromise talks between the fraternity head and NL emissary John McGraw also collapsed, and the senior circuit declared the January 1914 Cincinnati agreement with the union abrogated. Other signatories followed suit, and with all vestiges of prior official recognition withdrawn, the fraternity faced the prospect of open management warfare against its members.

In a last-ditch effort to protect his members from owner vengeance, on February 20 Fultz called off the strike threat and released his charges from their no-signing pledges. At the same time he sought guarantees from the major leagues that fraternity loyalists would not be persecuted and penalized for their steadfastness. Fultz knew, however, that the fraternity was beaten, probably for good. He admitted to *Baseball Magazine* that the outcome represented the "biggest disappointment of my life." Within a year he left American shores for France as an aviator, although he would return in 1918, ironically in a management role as International League president, a position he held for two seasons. Migrating subsequently to Florida, he established a law practice and remained far out of the baseball limelight for the rest of his life. As an organization, the Players' Fraternity lingered on until 1918, but its back had been broken by the abortive strike and membership desertions of the previous season.[8]

Once again unencumbered by a player association, and with more players with recently expired Federal League pacts due up for new contract negotiation, baseball's moguls in 1917 found more opportunities for economies in labor costs. More salaries were pared, and pared more severely (see Appendix, Fig. 1). When Edd Roush threatened to retire and buy a farm rather than accept the Reds' new contract offer, Herrmann retained agents to uncover the emptiness of the player's bluff. Pittsburgh offered Honus Wagner a pay cut of nearly 50 percent on the part of his salary derived from his nonmanagerial duties, from $10,000 down to $5,400. After a half year holdout, Wagner reported for a $6,000 figure prorated for the rest of the season. The National League also ushered in a new morals crackdown, drafting a revised uniform code threatening fines, suspension without pay, or both for such "gross misbehavior" as on-field intoxication, fighting, quarreling, and public indecency. Ironically, the most prominent "victim" of the new crackdown was manager McGraw, suspended for sixteen days and fined $500 for punching an umpire. Little Mac's subsequent diatribe to a reporter landed him before an NL board of inquiry, where he denied the quotes attributed to him but was contradicted by other witnesses. President Tener accordingly stuck on an additional $1,000 in fines.[9]

The heightened sensitivity of baseball to projecting an image of public probity and sacrifice owed much to events half a world away. America's entry into the First World War on April 6, 1917, led owners to sponsor on-field patriotic displays, including AL players engaging in pregame military maneuvers with bats positioned on their shoulders like rifles. The drills commenced as baseball's contribution to "preparedness" as early as spring training at southern camps, and Ban Johnson pledged a $500 bonus to the best-drilled squad. Although one suspects that more than martial crispness accounted for the prize going to the previous season's last-place St. Louis Browns, the *Spalding Guide* claimed the drills "anticipated" and "nullified" any public charges of "slackerism." Under the guise of patriotic interest in civilian morale, but more in line with profit restoration, teams maintained full schedules for 1917 and scheduled more

Sunday tilts and exhibitions, including some for military dependents. Clubs also urged star players to volunteer as Liberty Loan spokesmen. Putting a conservative baseball executive's particular ideological spin on the Great War, John Tener labeled it a "war of democracy against bureaucracy." The NL president, who criticized his owners for emphasizing baseball's business aspects too frequently in public, instead heralded his sport's role in American democracy. "There is no sport or business or anything under heaven which exerts the leveling influence that baseball does," he asserted. Tener added that even America's closest ally, Britain, lacked baseball's "finishing touch."[10]

Despite their patriotic emotings, the last thing baseball officials really wanted was to be called upon by the government to exhibit genuine sacrifice. Having already been buffeted by their version of war, owners did not look forward to having schedules reduced, attendance at games by war workers discouraged, or their playing labor lost for the sake of military victory. In the short run, the industry proved lucky, for despite the beginning of draft registration on June 5 and the first drawings on July 20, in 1917 few ballplayers actually received the call from Uncle Sam. Attendance did drop by over 1.25 million in the majors, however, and war-accelerated price inflation began pushing up club operating expenses. Fearing worse consequences the next season, in December the owners nonetheless deferred action to reduce the playing schedule, but Ban Johnson pressed the Wilson administration to permit clubs eighteen draft exemptions each. The move brought ridicule from the National League's Tener, who labeled such special pleading "preposterous" and cited his owners' resolution urging their playing men to volunteer.[11]

In 1917 it was the minors who continued to be hit hardest by the shifting economic realities. Despite average reductions in C and D club active rosters from fifteen to thirteen in order to trim payrolls (AA and B squads respectively stayed at twenty and fourteen, while A teams typically increased by one, to fifteen), the number of surviving leagues continued to shrink. In Class A ball, individual monthly average salaries fell $13 to $180, or $1,260 a year. Elsewhere, trimmed rosters enabled individual pay to rise modestly. B incomes rose $9 monthly to $154 and $1,078. C salaries went up the same monthly amount, to $98 and $686, and D individuals' pay averaged $560 for the season, a gain of $84. But even without adjusting the salary figures downward to reflect players' real income in light of higher wartime living costs, as a whole individual salaries still stood at levels lower than those of five years earlier, before the onset of the Federal League war (see Appendix, Fig. 5). At year's end, the surviving franchises tried to absorb some of the players from the defunct rosters, collecting extra talent as insurance against anticipated personnel losses to the military in 1918. Reserve and active-roster maximums rose from twenty-six and fourteen to twenty-eight and eighteen in Class A, from twenty-four and thirteen to twenty-six and sixteen in B, from twenty-two and thirteen to twenty-four and fourteen at C (although no Class C leagues actually opened for business in 1918), and from twenty-two and thirteen to twenty-two and fourteen at the D classification. Pay also rose modestly. Individual average salaries increased $20 a month in Class A ball to $200, or $1,400 for the year; $25 to $179 and $1,253 in B; and $16 to $96 and $672 in D. Despite the advance moves, however, the number of minor leagues fell another 50 percent to only ten by the start of the season. The result was a minor league component of the industry employing far fewer players, despite the surviving clubs' roster increases, and paying out much less in total salaries.[12]

Attempting to anticipate their own troubles ahead, major league owners for 1918 also abolished their player limits and stockpiled reserve talent insurance. In addition, some clubs chose spring training sites closer to home in order to save transportation expenses and juggled playing schedules for the same reason. Not surprisingly, they also cut salaries again. In defending his economies, Connie Mack claimed that if the club turned out to make money, he would share it with his players. Branch Rickey, the new president of the St. Louis Browns, sent his players new contracts accompanied by the demand that they be signed and returned to him within ten days or else the players would be susceptible to additional cuts. Twenty of his performers managed to beat his unilaterally imposed deadline. Owners' revenue concerns were heightened by the Wilson administration's levy of a 10 percent entertainment admissions tax, which translated into ticket price supplements of three, eight, and thirteen cents for each seating category if passed on exactly to the customer. The magnates instead opted to raise the gate prices by higher five-cent increments, from $.25 to $.30, $.75 to $.85, and $1.25 to $1.40. Having made their decision, they also quietly voted not to donate the difference to patriotic charities but to keep it.

Following the start of the regular season, on May 1 *Sporting News* reported that some 560 professional ballplayers from all levels had left their clubs for the armed forces. The real crunch, however, came three weeks later, on May 23, when the office of the U.S. Provost Marshal issued a "work or fight" order. The edict set July 1, 1918, as the deadline by which able-bodied men between the ages of twenty-one and thirty had to enter essential civilian employment or face military induction. Although owners immediately offered supportive bromides, barely a month later Ban Johnson again pressed for special relief, citing the tax revenues and charitable contributions baseball generated and the boost to civilian morale it provided. Besides, he argued, if theatrical performers could be exempted on the latter grounds, why not ballplayers? *Sporting News* pointed out one basic difference—that in contrast with most other entertainers, ballplayers worked in the daytime and therefore drew more spectators away from civilian work.[13]

In July, club officials sought further clarification of the "work or fight" directive. Washington owner Clark Griffith drafted an appeal for exemption for his catcher, Eddie Ainsmith, and by implication for others as well. Its three main points were that the baseball industry included substantial physical properties not adaptable for other purposes, whose tax value would plummet if not in use; ballplayers lacked the alternative skills to enter war-related employment without severe economic regression and family hardship; and baseball's continued operation as the "national sport" would promote domestic harmony and civilian morale. Not only did the appeal to Secretary of War Newton Baker fall on deaf ears, but Baker extended the "work or fight" policy to other, previously exempted entertainments. In what seemed to owners to be a contradictory signal, the White House on July 27 issued a statement in which President Woodrow Wilson indicated that no need existed to shut down baseball per se. What the Wilson administration was giving baseball, however, was a choice between shutting down completely or continuing with makeshift teams that, save for underage and overage players, ran the risk of frequent disruptions through military induction.

As clarified by the War Department, "work or fight" triggered a massive exodus of players from major and minor league rosters in 1918: 124 AL and 103 NL "veterans" entered the armed forces. Others continued to ply their trade on overseas training camps, or on American bases, or in the Navy's yeoman's branch. Many more evaded the risk of induction by finding employment in war industries at home, especially in steel mills and shipyards. Often these "camouflaged players" actually did little hard labor but were hired by employers to perform on company teams under the cover of another job—evoking memories of mid-nineteenth-century "amateur" baseball. Some companies even actively "scouted" for additional prospective talent. Critics charged that the most-sought-after ballplayers might be hired as painters, for example, only to carry paint to the real workers and then play ball all day for as much as $500 a week. At one Philadelphia shipyard, such practices led to vocal complaints by regular workers striking for comparable rewards. Although the Emergency Ship Corporation dismissed such stories as exaggerations, under pressure individual shipyards limited the allowable number of professionals on its company teams to from two to five players each.[14]

For franchise owners within organized baseball, the war labor policies resembled other trade wars in that outside raiders were bidding for their talent, but with the added handicap that the government's "work or fight" edict barred them from the immediate opportunity of retaining their players through better offers. Some embittered owners even talked of blacklisting those who had "jumped" into civilian "work" rather than sign up for the draft. Ban Johnson openly blasted businessmen, most notably Bethlehem Steel's Charles M. Schwab, for "drafting" players onto their industrial league teams. The steel executive, who presided over the so-called "Schwab League," promised to halt further raids but did not offer to return any of his acquisitions. If the magnates were frustrated at the lack of loyalty shown by their players, they should not have expected better, particularly since they had shown no reciprocal loyalty prior to the war. Before their own crisis had struck, for example, they had released or farmed out employees at substantial pay cuts and had discarded the "ironclad" contract of the Federal League era that had omitted language permitting such unilateral releases after ten days' notice.[15]

Now that they faced a labor emergency rather than a surplus, clubs "exhumed" retired players, plucked talent from the struggling minors, and muddled through. With the renewed abuses by the majors compounding the deleterious effects of "work or fight," only one minor league—the International League—managed to complete its full season. More typical was the Southern Association, whose attendance fell from 789,190 to 279,737 when the schedule had to be abbreviated to only seventy games. Caught under falling attendance, labor desertions, and cost pressures aggravated by inflation, many minor leagues disintegrated, triggering additional tugs-of-war between major league owners over the disbanding teams' players. In the most publicized case, involving Pacific Coast League pitcher Jack Quinn, Comiskey obtained National Commission approval to sign Quinn to play for the White Sox for the remainder of the season. But before the Chicago president could actually secure Quinn's signature, the New York Yankees did so. To Ban

Johnson's satisfaction, and Comiskey's outrage, the National Commission contradicted itself and validated the new transaction.

Despite owners' maneuvers, even the major leagues proved unable to complete a full schedule. Apparently attempting to make up for lost time in demonstrating his circuit's patriotism, Ban Johnson even urged in response to the Baker pronouncement that the American League immediately suspend further games for the duration of the war. Johnson's owners responded by ignoring him. In a reversal of previous positions, the NL office now seemed more eager to continue indefinitely with overage and underage talent. Both circuits again sought a special exemption from the Wilson administration, this time one allowing players to delay compliance with the "work or fight" order until October 15. But Baker yielded only as far as to September 1, a two-month extension of the War Department's earlier deadline. Owners continued to squabble over the end date of the abbreviated season and over whether to reschedule the World Series for sometime prior to September. The decision they reached—a season of approximately 125 games, ending on Labor Day and followed immediately by the World Series—still put the ending day of the regular schedule one day past Baker's deadline.

Players booked for games on the holiday, or those on pennant-winning squads, nervously sought management reassurances that their further participation would not trigger induction. When owners relayed the concerns to the War Department, the "half-a-loaf" answer they received extended the exemption for World Series performers, but not other players, beyond September 1. Despite the inadequate assurances, all games scheduled for the day after the deadline day went ahead except in St. Louis. Many Cleveland players, having been mistakenly assured by their owner that the Labor Day tilts would have to be canceled, had lined up war industry work to begin as early as the Tuesday morning after Labor Day. As a result, when they learned instead that their season-ending Sunday and Monday series in St. Louis was still on, they refused to make the trip and jeopardize their civilian jobs. With no possibility of rescheduling, Ban Johnson wisely refrained from penalizing the players or mandating forfeits by Cleveland.[16]

Faced with an abbreviated season and determined not to pay their charges for services not rendered, owners availed themselves of the opportunity to collect more wage savings by issuing players notice of their release up to ten days before the new schedule's end, then colluding among themselves not to bid for each other's releasees during the interval. As a consequence, the clubs claimed some $200,000 in additional payroll savings from the contracts of the players. In retaliation, some of those so manipulated sued for the balance of their salaries. Brooklyn first baseman Jake Daubert, for example, took his club to court for the remaining $2,150 of his $9,000 contract. When he won an out-of-court settlement, owner Ebbets then turned around and traded him to Cincinnati. When Washington's Burt Shotton similarly sued for $1,400, club spokesmen labeled him a "Bolsheviki" and waived him. Although major league attendance in 1918 plummeted by over 2 million, the owners had survived on the backs of fans and players through their higher admission rates and by retracting some six weeks' worth of payroll.

Additional economy moves imposed by owners on financially squeezed players almost provoked the cancellation of the fall classic. The American League and National League already had agreed to change the allotment of World Series bonuses between winning and losing rosters from a 75-25 division to a 60-40 split. The wider discrepancy in the past had encouraged covert side arrangements between opposing players to "hedge their bets" on the series outcome, which in owners' fears undermined the games' integrity. But the moguls now also announced, in a move designed to boost series attendance, that admission rates would be kept at regular-season levels rather than, as in the recent past, at marked-up figures. They also declared, in a move intended to pacify a broader segment of the players in light of the salary withholding effected at the end of the season, that bonus moneys from the championship series also would be shared with each league's second- through fourth-place regular-season squads. Angry AL and NL pennant winners, who already had voted to donate 10 percent of their shares to the Red Cross, now saw their anticipated individual takes diminished to around $1,000 instead of the expected $2,000–4,000 of previous contests. When the participants threatened not to play game six of the series and remained in their clubhouses, Ban Johnson personally appealed to their patriotism and persuaded them to start the game after an hour's delay. Per-player shares for the champion Boston Red Sox, led by Babe Ruth, amounted to $1,102.51, while the defeated Chicago Cubs players received $671.09 each. Perhaps as a sign that the owners had feared on-field disciplinary trouble, the one participant in the World Series contracted at noticeably higher pay was star umpire Bill Klem. Klem, who had demanded and gotten $650 as the highest-paid arbiter working the 1917 classic, successfully pressured owners for $1,000 in 1918. As for the players, despite promises that their brief "sit-down" would not be punished, the National Commission "fined" them by refusing to send them their championship emblems that winter.[17]

Although the Great War created great havoc on baseball's labor front, producing among other things a shrinkage in clubs, jobs, salaries, and real wages, it did not significantly alter the demographic patterns of the player force. The impact of "work or fight" forced many players to abandon their professional jobs in organized baseball, but—especially in the minors—produced a short-term shrinkage in the number of jobs rather than a massive turnover of job occupants. Since many of those inducted or absorbed into civilian work continued to ply their baseball wares, they also remained in a position to attempt to reclaim their baseball posts after the armistice of November 11. Perhaps the most noteworthy "nonevent" of the war, from the perspective of its impact on baseball, is the failure of patriotic popular hostility toward the Central Powers and their sympathizers to result in a narrowing of the avenues of access for players of German or Irish descent, at least at the major league level (see Appendix, Fig. 2). Even though both groups clearly were associated in the public mind with America's military adversaries, of 342 entrants into the American League or National League between 1916 and 1920 identified by Lee Allen, fully 31 percent claimed "Germanic" extraction, and another 19 percent were Irish. With eleven out of sixteen major league managers in 1915 already of Irish ancestry, the Great War did not reverse such gains within the sport's post-playing-career opportunities, either. Among nationality groups identified with the Allies, "non-Irish" descendants of the British Isles contributed 36 percent of the newcomers to the player force, while players of French heritage added about 4 percent. Scandinavians, at another 4 percent; Southern and Eastern Europeans, at 4.5 percent; and a handful of American Indians, Cubans, Canadians, and a Portuguese rounded out the total. Virtually all claimed American birth, and while the trend of growing contributions from the South and West continued, the Northeast and Midwest still generated a strong majority of major league actives.[18]

The Great War similarly did little in the short run to retard or accelerate existing socioeconomic or educational patterns within the player force. Historian Steven Riess has shown in his study of a sample of ballplayers from 1900 to 1920 that about two-fifths of them, a ratio double the national average, came from white-collar families, while a little over one-third were from manual-trade backgrounds and over one-fifth from farmsteads. Lee Allen's data on educational attainment for his 1915–20 cohort indicates that over two-fifths of those identified claimed some college attendance, and 37 percent went only as far as high school, while those failing to advance past elementary school fell to less than one-fifth of the total. Whether or not the college segment actually was that high (other estimates suggest a share only half as large), even the lower figure put the percentage of college boys in baseball at no less than twice their numbers in the population as a whole. Paired with the findings from earlier cohorts, these figures suggest continuing declines in illiteracy and in low levels of schooling within baseball that paralleled similar declines in the larger society during the era.[19]

Although careers on average remained brief, the evidence also suggests that the generally higher wages players earned compared to most American workers and the long-term growth in postcareer baseball-related employment meant that by the era of World War I players suffered less postcareer socioeconomic "slippage" than had nineteenth-century performers. According to Riess, while over a third of players examined from the 1870s and early 1880s had fallen from white-collar status into manual trades, only about one in seven of the 1900–20 group experienced a similar decline. Few landed in extreme destitution, and most wound up in middle-class occupations, many of them sports-related or client-based spinoffs from earlier ballplaying notoriety such as real estate and insurance brokerages. Among the college-educated segment, an impressive number entered the swelling ranks of the professions. A sizable and growing minority, even with the hard times of the minor leagues, now secured post-playing-career opportunities at other tiers of the baseball industry as managers, coaches, scouts, and umpires. At the lower levels of baseball management, according to one source, the average minor league skipper by the late 1910s had been a professional player for over nine years, and one-third of major league managers claimed prior experience as a minor league field boss. Virtually without exception, major league managers without similar experience came from the ranks of veteran star players, showing how the owners utilized these opportunities to buttress further their two-tier wage system.[20]

Following the armistice, owners desired as rapid a return to prewar economic realities as possible, especially on the labor and attendance fronts. Major league officials appealed to the War Department to release drafted players from their military obligations in time for the 1919 season. Fearing that attendance might be slow to bounce back, however, they secretly arranged for additional payroll reductions and cutbacks for active rosters to twenty-one players per team, as well as operating an abbreviated schedule of 140 games. To secure as many ballplaying returnees as possible in the talent pool, they delayed spring training until late March. For similar reasons, the National Commission issued no rulings on any grievances filed against players by management, but of twenty-six cases initiated by players (nineteen being reinstatement requests), the panel sided with the players twenty-three times (including all of the reinstatements). Returning star Ty Cobb remained the game's highest-paid player at $20,000, but that figure represented no change in his salary since 1915. In general, player pay remained capped at the levels it had reached after the Federal League war. The minors maintained the same reserve and active roster limits they had had at the start of 1918, and the number of circuits bounced back to fifteen. Individual salaries continued to fall, however, as owners tried to regroup from the calamity of the previous season. Permitted levels of Class A individual pay averaged $189 a month (down $11), or $1,323 for the year. Class B minor leaguers made an average of $144 a month (down $35) and $1,008. Class C players drew $131 monthly and $917 for the season, up substantially from the levels of 1917, the nearest available comparison year. But at D level, no leagues survived to post full-year salary numbers through 1919.[21]

In their fears of sluggish attendance, the major leagues proved both overly pessimistic and financially shortsighted. Having adopted a shortened schedule out of premature caution, the owners then discovered that they had cost themselves hundreds of thousands of dollars in additional revenues. Attendance jumped from 3 million to over 6, and projected figures for an additional two weeks suggest that the majors missed out on approximately 600,000 fans because of the 140-game schedule. And since owners had delayed the start of the season, they could not adjust the schedule in midstream. Even worse for the major leagues, however, was the legacy of their abuse of the minors during the war. Minor league executives bitterly remembered the mid-season cancellations and bankruptcies of 1918, and they partly blamed the majors for their plight by doing little to bail them out and by raiding their rosters for their own benefit following the initial "work or fight" order. With their operating costs still soaring because of escalating price inflation, they demanded more major league compensation in the form of higher draft prices for 1919. When the major league owners—acting under their own cost pressures and in keeping with their pessimistic revenue assumptions for the upcoming season—refused, the minors broke ranks. Following the expiration of the National Association's January

17, 1919, deadline for adjustment of the draft prices, its member clubs suspended the majors' draft and optional-assignment rights with them for, as it turned out, two years. National Commission chairman and major league club executive Garry Herrmann managed to preserve the mutual territorial and player-reservation guarantees of the shattered National Agreement but could do nothing to reverse the severance of the draft and optioning procedures. As a consequence, the majors now faced grave uncertainties in the procurement of new, cheap replacement ballplayers.

As ominous as was the breakdown of majors-minors cooperation in talent acquisition, it was but one immediate example of how divisive wartime labor competition and financial strains had torn at prewar industry governance structures. As early as August 1918, NL president John Tener had resigned following disputes with the American League over the case of pitcher Scott Perry. The National League's Boston franchise had purchased Perry from the Atlanta minor league club for $2,800 on a thirty-day trial basis, with Atlanta receiving $500 down. After seventeen days, however, Perry had jumped to an outlaw team, resulting in his name appearing on Atlanta's ineligible list. When the National Commission ordered his return to the Boston Braves if the Braves paid an additional $2,000 balance, Atlanta turned around and sold him again, this time to the American League's Philadelphia Athletics. Defying the National Commission, Connie Mack, with Ban Johnson's approval, secured an injunction blocking the panel from implementing its order to deliver Perry to Boston. Tener's successor as NL president, the functionary John Heydler, did manage to secure Boston $2,500 in exchange for the Athletics' retaining Perry.[22]

Ironically, Ban Johnson was next to find his authority undermined by rogue owners in a player dispute. On July 13, 1919, Boston Red Sox hurler Carl Mays received an extended disciplinary suspension from the American League. Under Johnson's edict, Mays could not be traded or sold to another club until he had completed his sentence. Nonetheless, Yankees owners Ruppert and Huston arranged for the purchase of the penalized pitcher. When Johnson ordered the deal voided, the Yankee magnates charged the league president with acting self-interestedly to aid the pennant chances of rival Cleveland, in which Johnson reportedly held some stock. Not only did the Yankees obtain an injunction preventing Johnson from enforcing the suspension upon Mays, but they secured another one preventing him even from using league funds to fight the first. Additional confusion followed when Ruppert tried to convene an AL owners' meeting without Johnson and when Detroit protested at season's end that it deserved third-place money on the grounds that without Mays the Yankees would not have finished ahead of them.

With the National Commission withholding payment of the disputed shares until the Mays matter had been conclusively resolved, in late October New York state judge Robert Wagner's grant of a permanent injunction against Ban Johnson resulted in a legal victory for the Yankees and the end of the AL president's effective authority over his circuit's club owners. By February 1920, Johnson and five "loyalist" AL owners faced off against an opposing camp of three clubs, led by New York, wanting to oust him. Ruppert and Huston even filed a damage suit against Johnson, charging him with attempting to manipulate Polo Grounds rental negotiations with the NL Giants to drive the Yankees out of the majors. Their suit did not lack merit, for Johnson had tried to persuade the Giants either to cancel the Yankees' lease or to hand over control of it to him. The American League's internal standoff came to an end with the "caving-in" of the loyalists in the face of the market power of the Yankee bloc. The owners created a two-man board of review with the power to reconsider and overturn presidentially imposed penalties of over $100 and suspensions of over ten days, pending rulings by a Chicago federal judge (presumably the previously "tested" Landis).[23]

Even the National Commission, the final panel of arbitration of disputes between the major leagues and between the majors and minors, now crumbled in the face of bitter opposing claims to player talent. While the minors' blow in withdrawing draft and option privileges had undermined the administrative "ligaments" of the National Agreement, the commission's chairman suffered an erosion of personal prestige, as owners continued to attack Herrmann for his George Sisler ruling. Pittsburgh had purchased the rights to the young Sisler from a minor league club that had signed him out of high school, only to have the player request that the National Commission disallow the claim so that he could play for the University of Michigan. The panel granted the request, with Pittsburgh led to believe that it still would enjoy "first rights" of signing the star youngster when he opted to leave college. However, Sisler signed with the St. Louis Browns when his college coach, Branch Rickey, joined that same organization's front office. Infuriating Pirate owner Barney Dreyfuss, the National Commission upheld the new signing and denied Pittsburgh's complaint. Dreyfuss and other NL owners nursed additional, longstanding grievances against Herrmann for the generous player-auctioning rights offered FL magnate Harry Sinclair and for the perception that Herrmann remained under the thumb of the American League's Ban Johnson. In late 1919, Herrmann lost an owner vote of confidence to remain on the National Commission, and he submitted his resignation effective February 1, 1920. Sensing in Herrmann's departure the wolves circling closer around his own door, Ban Johnson managed to use his remaining power as AL president to block the appointment of a new chairman, and the National Commission drifted aimlessly through the 1920 season.[24]

In spite of all the internal bickering, major league management enjoyed an attendance and revenue resurgence in 1920. Facing no threats from unions or rival circuits, and thus able to maintain the requisite salary discipline in preseason contract negotiations, the magnates helped along the rush to the turnstiles by injecting more offensive excitement into the game (see Appendix, Figs. 3 and 4). Major league head counts reached a record level of 9 million. The New York Yankees alone earned $373,000 in profits in 1920, aided in no small measure by the slugging feats of Babe Ruth, whom they had secured from Boston for a record $125,000. Ruth himself received a $20,000 salary. More typical of the owners' continued salary firmness were the lowly Philadelphia Phillies, whose individual salary average, $3,300, stood at $1,000 less than it had in 1916. Major league umpires split a total payroll of $41,000, or about $2,500 per man. Pundits attributed the attendance surge to a "lively ball" caused by tighter winding, different wool, or an altered center, although the manufacturer denied it. What could not be denied was another pro-offense change adopted by the magnates' Joint Committee on Rules, which made it illegal throughout organized baseball for a pitcher to tamper with the ball; the new rule formally outlawed the spitball, although it excluded seventeen major league veterans for whom a "grandfather clause" exemption applied.[25]

With customers finally returning to the ballparks in prewar numbers, the minors also enjoyed a financial recovery year. Twenty-two circuits, with perhaps 2,500 players or more, started the year, and twenty-one finished it. The Southern Association, which had drawn under 300,000 fans only two years earlier, now attracted over 1.2 million spectators. Minor league clubs on average also increased their team rosters by one, and player pay levels rose. Monthly team payroll limits surged from $2,650 to $3,500 at Class A, $1,867 to $2,004 at B, and $1,700 to $2,000 at C. Class D showed a two-year jump from $1,250 in 1918 to $1,729 in 1920. The team figures translated into individual monthly increases over 1919 levels of $44 in Class A ball, a drop of $1 in B leagues, a $12 jump at C, and a $37 rise for D players from 1918, their nearest comparison season given the circuit collapses of 1919. The individual season salaries for the four rankings, $1,631, $1,001, $1,001, and $931, meant, however, that only in 1920 did minor leaguers' pay finally surpass its previous highs during the Federal League period. But given the precipitous wartime reductions in the number of circuits and the fact that the minors had recovered only partially by this time, fewer players enjoyed those fruits than had in 1914 or 1915, and the inflation-reduced real wages of players at all levels meant that their living standards still trailed those of five years earlier.[26]

Even the owner's changes in rules to facilitate offense and fan excitement proved not without unanticipated—and in at least one case, tragic—flaws. In mid-season Carl Mays, one of the veteran pitchers exempted from the anti-spitball rule, beaned Cleveland's Ray Chapman, who died the next morning as a result of his skull injuries. In the aftermath of the Chapman tragedy, which was attributed to the batter's "freezing" at being unable to pick up the sight of the soiled ball, additional rules modifications enforced the substitution of a new, clean ball for a used one whenever it became even slightly discolored or defaced. This change, combined with those made in preseason and perhaps a lingering shortage of quality pitchers caused by war and draft interruption, boosted major league batting averages. By season's end, averages, led by Sisler's .407, stood thirty points higher than they had in 1915 and thirteen points up from the year before. Home runs, led by Ruth's leap from 29 in 1919 to 54 in 1920, soared to 631, up from 384 in 1915. Despite the continuing practice of dividing up World Series shares with second- and third-place clubs, in 1920 victorious Cleveland and losing Brooklyn still split impressive team bonuses of $93,697.24 and $67,464.82 in the most popular fall classic to date.[27]

Dark clouds of scandal had, however, already begun to overshadow the return of good times at the gate. For many years baseball management had not only largely ignored the problem of player gambling and game-fixing, but unconsciously had encouraged it through the combination of salary penny-pinching and automatic reinstatements of suspended employees. By the late 1910s, aggravated by lagging real wages, player wagering to boost one's income had become such a part of the game's work culture at all levels that one source estimated a typical semipro could raise his take to the $2,000–4,000 range through bets. Back in 1916, Giants manager John McGraw had accused his own players of quitting during a late-season series with Brooklyn, and sportswriters had speculated that the behavior stemmed either from misguided comradeship with former teammates Chief Bender, Rube Marquard, and Fred Merkle or the desire to deny the pennant to the hated Phillies. The next year, St. Louis Browns owner Phil Ball suspected members of his team of similarly laying down against the Chicago White Sox. When his double-play combination, John "Doc" Lavan and Del Pratt, sued him for slander, Ball accepted an out-of-court settlement arranged by Ban Johnson and Clark Griffith that resulted in Lavan's shipment to Washington and Pratt's to New York. Both men, however, remained active major leaguers for many years.

The champion among cheaters and game-fixers, however, remained Hal Chase, who had worn out his welcome in the American League only to land with the Cincinnati Reds in the National League in 1916. Two years later, manager Christy Mathewson suspended the nefarious Chase for what he labeled "indifferent play and insubordination." What the manager suspected his player of doing went far beyond that—to arranging widespread fixes of games for his betting profit. Chase sued the club for $1,650 in back salary, and the National League five months later cleared him without even a reprimand. Aiding Chase was the fact that by the time his hearing took place, Mathewson had been sent to France with the U.S. Army's Chemical Warfare Service and could not testify to what he knew. Unfazed by the continuing stream of accusations directed at the first baseman, the Giants signed him as part of an NL deal to get Chase to drop his demand for back pay. Making their action all the more incredible was the fact that one of the charges against Chase had been his alleged attempt to bribe a Giants pitcher into throwing a game. The primary accusation that had been levied, however, involved the suspicious laying of $500 bets by Chase and Reds teammate Lee Magee (real name Leopold Hoernschemeyer) with a local gambler before a road series with the Boston Braves. Rumor had it that the two had bribed Braves pitcher Pete Schneider (who was waived quietly out of the league at season's end) to throw the first game of a scheduled doubleheader. Chase's reputation already preceded him by 1918, and throughout the road swing hecklers had shouted, "Well, Hal, what are the odds today?"[28]

Antagonists Mathewson and Chase were reunited in 1919, when the Giants hired the returning veteran as a coach. By September, Chase's corrupting influence had led McGraw to lift him and Heinie Zimmerman out of the lineup, although Chase remained on the roster at full pay until the end of the season. NL president Heydler later revealed that the two had been accused of offering fellow Giant Benny Kauff $500 to help throw a game to the St. Louis Cardinals. With National League cooperation, the Giants quietly eased the two suspected cheaters out of the majors. Chase landed on his feet, however, continuing to play winter ball and becoming part-owner of the San Jose club in the semipro Mission League. From that vantage point, he continued to corrupt professional ballplayers, particularly in the adjoining Pacific Coast League. With no small contribution from Chase's illicit activity, by October 1920 a deputy district attorney in Los Angeles concluded that gambling interests controlled five of the Class AA circuit's eight teams, and at least six players were known to have laid down for money. Combined with evidence of a $2,000 slush fund for Portland and Salt Lake City players, the other information led to the impaneling of a county grand jury. Although the proceedings failed to produce indictments, three Pacific Coast League veterans, all former major leaguers, were expelled, and the Mission League belatedly tossed Chase out.[29]

Meanwhile, the smell of scandal continued to haunt the majors. Subsequent allegations even hinted at a possible game-fixing scandal late in the 1919 season involving the illustrious Ty Cobb and Tris Speaker. According to the charges, which did not surface until after the 1926 season with the mysterious and sudden "retirements" of both Cobb and Speaker as managers, prior to a September 25 game between Detroit and Cleveland the Indians (already assured of second place) had arranged to lose on purpose a game on which player bets had been placed. Hal Chase's old partner, Lee Magee, also was busy in 1919, having been traded to Brooklyn early in the year, passed on from there to Chicago, and then released by the Cubs, always with gambling rumors never very far behind. To "grease" Magee's "skids," Garry Herrmann and Charles Ebbets even chipped in $2,500 compensation in persuading Chicago to take him off Brooklyn's hands. When the Cubs let him go, however, Magee took them to federal court, suing them in Cincinnati in June 1920 for back pay and threatening to blow the lid off baseball's seamy underworld if he lost. By the 1920 stretch run, new rumors circulated that a Cubs pitcher, Claude Hendrix, intended to lose intentionally to the last-place Phillies. In an effort to thwart the scheme, the club replaced him with Grover Cleveland Alexander, who pitched honestly but lost anyway, 3-0. During the off-season, the Cubs suspiciously released Hendrix without explanation or public disclosure.[30]

The late-season Cubs rumor spawned a Cook County grand jury investigation, but as it turned out the most explosive revelations erupted from

Chicago's South Side, the home of the White Sox. Rube Benton, recounting a past offer from teammates Chase and Zimmerman to throw a game to the Cubs, revealed that White Sox infielder Buck Herzog had been allied with them in such fixes. That disclosure began to draw attention to Comiskey's club, which in the opinion of many had underperformed notably in losing to the Cincinnati Reds in the 1919 World Series. Several observers, most prominently Chicago wire-service reporter Hugh Fullerton, had identified examples of suspicious play by the White Sox. Soon the grand jury investigation uncovered evidence that pitcher Eddie Cicotte and first baseman Chick Gandil had approached gambler Sleepy Bill Burns (himself a former major leaguer) and solicited bribes of $100,000 to throw the series. Testimony pointing to overlapping efforts to secure a player fix by different groups of gamblers (including one led by Hal Chase), each claiming or possessing the support of New York kingpin Arnold Rothstein, indicated that the principal effort involved Burns's promise to deliver $20,000 via partner Abe Attell to the participants after each game. Ironically, another small-time gambler in Burns's circle, Billy Maharg, traced his relationship with the former pitcher back to the 1912 Detroit player walkout in support of Ty Cobb, for Burns had recommended him then to Hughie Jennings as a replacement third baseman. On September 28, Cicotte and star outfielder Joe Jackson admitted in sworn affidavits their acceptance of bribes the previous fall in exchange for agreeing to lay down against the Reds.

When the disclosure of the "Black Sox" scandal hit the newspapers in September, the White Sox were in the midst of the 1920 pennant race. Owner Comiskey, who later admitted that he had possessed secret information of his players' duplicity, supplied by gambler Harry Redmond, since the winter of 1919, nonetheless had retained most of the principals on his 1920 team. Chick Gandil had dropped out of baseball, but the other seven accused of either knowing about or participating in the fix—Jackson, Cicotte, pitcher Claude "Lefty" Williams, outfielder Oscar "Happy" Felsch, shortstop Charles "Swede" Risberg, third baseman George "Buck" Weaver, and utility man Fred McMullin—remained active players. Only when the scandal reached the press did Comiskey suspend the accused men, ensuring Cleveland the AL pennant. While baseball tried to carry on with the World Series, press accounts revealed that during the previous year's fall classic Cicotte had received $10,000 after game one, while Jackson, who had been promised $20,000, got but $5,000. Williams had "earned" $5,000, although he had been promised $10,000, after game four for laying down in the series's second contest. Risberg, for his part, tried to deflect attention by charging that in 1917 Detroit players had thrown a game to the White Sox in order to help them finish ahead of the Red Sox, and his teammates had put up a $1,100 purse to reward the Tiger pitchers. Bitter at Comiskey's new public relations gesture of paying retroactive bonuses to the presumably "honest" Sox players, Risberg accused two of them, second baseman Eddie Collins and catcher Ray Schalk, with contributing to the earlier Tiger pool, and he added that the White Sox had "returned the favor" to Detroit in 1919.[31]

Taken together, all of the disclosures suggested that in his own way Comiskey deserved as much or more condemnation than his corrupt players. In spite of his knowledge of their activity in 1919, he had concealed it for the sake of success on the field and at the gate in 1920. In some cases not only had he retained those implicated in scandal, but after the partial economic upturn of the 1919 season he had even given them substantial raises. Cicotte, with a $5,000 base salary in 1919, had received double that amount for 1920, plus a $3,000 bonus. Williams's pay had doubled to $6,000 plus incentive bonuses based upon his win total. Felsch's income had risen $3,000 to $7,000, plus a $3,000 bonus, and Jackson had received a three-year pact with a $2,000 annual raise to $8,000. Ironically, before the scandal occurred it could have been argued that of the White Sox stars, only Eddie Collins, earning around $15,000, had been receiving a salary commensurate with both his market value and Chicago's revenue potential. Other Chicago salaries in 1919 included Schalk's $7,500, Weaver's $6,500, Gandil's $4,000, and Risberg's estimated $2,500. At best, Comiskey paid his players more for 1920 in spite of their recent conduct because he could afford it and for the sake of holding together a "successful" team. At worst, he himself could be accused of bribing his players in order to maintain their public silence on the events of the 1919 Series.

More recent historians correctly have pointed out that the White Sox payroll in 1919, taken as a whole, had stood at a level comparable with those of most other franchises. By that standard, at least, Comiskey had not been uniquely penurious, although such practices of his as charging the players for their uniform cleaning bills grated upon them. What is more to the point is the fact that players' salaries generally had experienced no growth since the Federal League years, and with the ravages of wartime inflation the pay of veterans from those years had taken a severe beating (see Appendix, Fig. 5). It is noteworthy that the game-fixing ringleaders on the White Sox, Cicotte and Gandil, were thirteen-

Charles Comiskey, owner of the Chicago White Sox. Ironically, once a jumper to the Players' League, Comiskey became known for his frugality toward his players as well as the disgrace of eight of his employees in the 1919 "Black Sox" scandal.

and nine-year major league veterans, whose incomes had been boosted by the Federal League war only to fall precipitously in real terms. As for Joe Jackson, what message had it sent him that back in 1915 he had been sold from Cleveland for $65,000, but his 1919 income still represented less than one-tenth that amount? The conspirators' lot had not differed from that of many other teams' veterans, just as the proclivity toward gambling associations was not unique to the White Sox. What proved different had been the unique opportunity presented to them for a last chance to "cash in" before retirement because of their appearance in the World Series. And even if caught, the pattern of disciplinary action by baseball officialdom had suggested that they might well receive a financial slap on the wrist, followed after a "decent interval" by reinstatement, if they desired it, or at worst an unpublicized, graceful exit from the game. What in hindsight is more surprising than the Sox players' solicitation and acceptance of bribes is the apparent refusal of the Reds players to do likewise. Given the Sox' status as series favorites, however, far fewer gamblers would have perceived much "action" in trying to induce the Cincinnati players to lay down. By the time the odds had shifted, it probably had been too late to arrange a Reds fix.[32]

Fears of the worsening scandal's impact upon the game's public image and fan attendance made it illogical to reverse immediately the forces released to boost offense, despite their likely impact upon salary demands for 1921 and beyond. Instead, the other immediate consequence of the Black Sox revelations was the renewed impetus it now gave the magnates finally to abandon their outworn and ineffectual governance structures. Hoping through the overhaul to restore an image of integrity to the industry and order to the majors-minors labor turmoil, big league owners approved a plan drafted by Cubs stockholder Albert D. Lasker for a new National Commission. Under the scheme, the new panel would consist of three nonpartisan figures unconnected to individual franchises. Ban Johnson, aware of the plan's implications for his own official future but also knowing that he could not block it, held out at minimum for the selection of his own candidate—Charles MacDonald, the presiding judge in the Black Sox grand jury investigation—for the commission chairmanship. His many adversaries among the owners, however, including Comiskey, did not want MacDonald and preferred Landis, who had proven himself to them by his handling of the Federal League litigation.

By early November, the Lasker plan had been altered to create not a three-man commission but instead a single chief executive. Like a single president of all of organized baseball, the new commissioner would be vested with unprecedented and far-reaching individual authority to arbitrate disputes between the industry's recognized constituencies and to regulate their behavior "in the best interests of baseball." On November 12, fifteen of the sixteen owners, with Phil Ball holding back out of loyalty to Johnson, offered Landis the position. Landis, in turn, demanded guarantees from them of his absolute and unchallenged authority. With the desperate magnates offering the necessary assurances, the judge accepted the appointment and the $50,000 salary that it carried, while still retaining his federal judgeship.[33]

The industry and the labor-management relationship that Landis now inherited had undergone many transformations over the past three-quarters of a century. It had emerged as a cultural offshoot of New England congregationalism, with antebellum northeastern Yankees forming clubs as one of many forms of voluntary association. By the 1850s it already had been heralded by its boosters as the national game, and that assertion fueled the pressures for access by the sons of pre-Civil War immigration, particularly the Irish and Germans. The currents of war and commerce carried it to new regions, but as its range of participants broadened, its more affluent and exclusive off-field custodians increasingly sequestered the reins of control to themselves. As individual clubs joined with each other in leagues and state associations, their officers and delegates extended the administrative instruments of control to regional and national levels.

Such forms of management segregation from on-field labor, initially justified by the desire to uphold ethnocultural traditions, had been refined further as club officers and stockholders gradually awakened to the full commercial possibilities of the sport. By the 1870s, at least one group of Gilded Age magnates, presiding over revenue-generating and wage-paying professional teams in the largest northeastern and midwestern markets, had turned to a blunter, more comprehensive model of control that acknowledged at its core baseball's primary identity as an industry. Under these self-conscious capitalists, led by Chicago's William Hulbert, baseball became still more dictatorial and exploitive in its dealings with its workers on the diamond. Over the next forty-five years, in various forms ranging from the coercive collusion of a dominant franchise to the solidarity of interlocking ownership arrangements to the regulatory curbing of intramanagement economic warfare, the National League and its accumulated partners sought to impose a system of labor

The new commissioner of baseball, Judge Kenesaw Mountain Landis, in December 1920

control unequalled in American industry for its thoroughness. Through the collusive interclub arrangements of their cartel they dictated their players' place of employment, freedom of occupational movement, salary, working conditions, and even their off-field conduct. They exercised unilateral control over the game's playing rules, utilizing that power to stimulate gate revenues or modulate the individual productivity statistics that served as the performance basis for player compensation. Headed by the deployment of the reserve clause, and enforcement of its reins on player mobility through the blacklist, baseball's web of player controls had been crafted to buttress an industry with such an all-encompassing system of labor serfdom that it would be guaranteed steady, massive growth.

Unfortunately for the owners, they had never been able to completely achieve their orderly utopia. The game's own growth in popularity and the dramatic increase in America's urban population created repeated opportunities for outside challenges to baseball's closed circle. Nor had the baseball cartel been able to find a permanent solution to the problem of internal factionalism and internecine economic warfare within its own management ranks. As a result, players sporadically were able to exploit management disunion and warfare to create more "breathing space" for themselves. Their own intermittent efforts, however, had failed to build the kind of long-term solidarity necessary to wrest back from the owners a greater permanent measure of industry control and workplace democracy. The delay in the development and introduction of new on-field talent, especially that of the descendants of Southern and Eastern Europe, preserved a greater degree of ethnic homogeneity among players, and the inability of high-skill employees to be replaced by machines in this entertainment industry also helped make possible a limited solidarity based upon professional pride. But the relative lucrativeness and brief duration of the typical baseball career had encouraged player individualism. Owners in turn had not hesitated to exploit the rivalries and tensions over pay and job security between stars and journeymen, veterans and rookies, and major leaguers and minor leaguers. Both sides, in other words, had preyed upon each other's tendencies toward individual acquisitiveness, competitive rivalry, and demographic division to deny the other the peace of mind that could only come with the attainment of a secure hegemony.

By 1920, the player force over which Landis had come to preside still consisted mainly of middle-class, relatively well educated descendants of Northern and Western Europe, especially Britain, Ireland, and Germany. The industry's "ground-floor" doors had been opened a crack to American Indians, Canadians, Cubans, and Southern and Eastern Europeans, but access to the higher levels and post-playing-career opportunities of coaching, managing, umpiring, and administration remained tightly guarded. As for African Americans, they had found the doors of opportunity slammed in their faces and were relegated to struggling clubs outside the sanction and protection of organized baseball. Those performers who made it into the cartel succeeded in reaching, albeit while enduring many peaks and valleys, higher levels of compensation and living standards. Their progress, however, had not been as rapid or massive as that of the industry itself, whether measured in profit figures or the declining percentage contribution of team payrolls to club operating costs. The players also discovered, as did American workers generally in the industrial age, that their greater material security had come at the expense of lessened personal control of the workplace and of their economic lives.

With the National Commission moribund and the National Agreement relationship between the majors and their minor league suppliers of cheap labor in jeopardy, players and owners alike waited to see what the new era—the "age of Landis"—would bring. Would his rule see a further broadening of the ethnic base of baseball participation? If it did, would one consequence nonetheless be an even more divided and diverse player force incapable of collective action? Would he seek to open wider the doors of upward occupational advancement within the industry, or would he prove an indifferent or vigilant maintainer of the status quo? Would he entertain thoughts of permitting greater player freedom of movement, salary leverage, job security, and workplace voice, or would he simply preside over the construction and administration of more effective methods of serfdom? For if he failed to do the latter, would not the owners challenge his newly won authority, in spite of their own tarnished reputations? Would they not seek to bypass his office and construct their own minor league labor chains, or "farm systems," to replace the defunct National Commission's prior draft relationship with the minors?

However the new pattern of baseball's labor-management relations might unfold, the fact remained that the sport's professional playing labor had been unable to maintain a collective instrument capable of withstanding the assaults of management and of seizing a role as a major "player" in the industry's operations. As a consequence, the players' hopes for a brighter day in economic rights and benefits lay far less in their own hands than in the intentions and paternalistic powers of the new commissioner. Given baseball labor's continuing "dependency" status in 1920, it did not bode well for the choices Landis would make in the years ahead that in the past he had been unwilling even to conceive of baseball as an industry, one as capable as any other of exploitive, monopolistic practices. Instead, he had insisted upon viewing the sport as a "national institution" somehow divorced from the economic realities of his time. In that regard at least, his view, however inaccurate, echoed the claims made long before in behalf of baseball by the industry's antebellum Yankee progenitors and illustrated the lingering imprint of their cultural legacy upon the sport as it entered a new, uncertain era.

APPENDIX

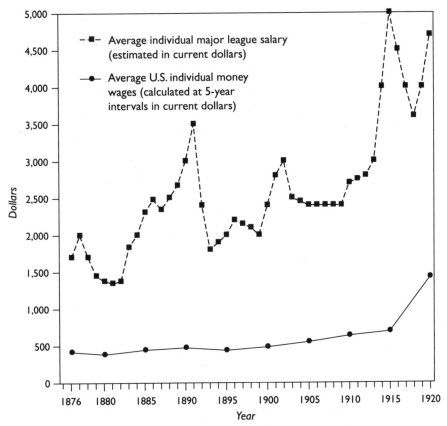

Figure 1. Players' Salaries vs. Average American Wage, 1876–1920
The long-term pattern of player salaries tended to reflect the rises and falls of American wages generally, but at significantly higher levels and with wider ranges of fluctuation. Sources: Player salary data from Harold Seymour, *Baseball: The Early Years* (New York: Oxford University Press, 1960), 67–68, 106, 117–20, 267; Harold Seymour, *Baseball: The Golden Age* (New York: Oxford University Press, 1971), 171–73, 206–7, 334–35; Peter S. Craig, "Monopsony in Manpower: Organized Baseball Meets the Anti-Trust Laws," *Yale Law Journal* 62 (March 1953): 605; Peter S. Craig, "Organized Baseball: An Industry Study of a $100 Million Spectator Sport" (B.A. thesis, Oberlin College, 1950), 49, 112a, 135; David Q. Voigt, *American Baseball*, vol. 1: *From Gentlemen's Sport to the Commissioner System* (Norman: University of Oklahoma Press, 1966), 56–57, 76–77, 234–35, and vol. 2: *From the Commissioners to Continental Expansion*, 65–66; Charles C. Alexander, *Our Game: An American Baseball History* (New York: Henry Holt, 1991), 92, 103, 106, 127–28; House Judiciary Committee, *Organized Baseball: Report of the Subcommittee on the Study of Monopoly Power of the Committee on the Judiciary*, House Report no. 2002, 82d Cong., 1st sess. (Washington, D.C.: Government Printing Office, 1952), 21–23; and *Spalding's Base Ball Guide* (1890), 19–21. U.S. individual money wages from Stanley Lebergott, *Manpower in Economic Growth: The American Record since 1800* (New York: McGraw-Hill, 1964), 524–28.

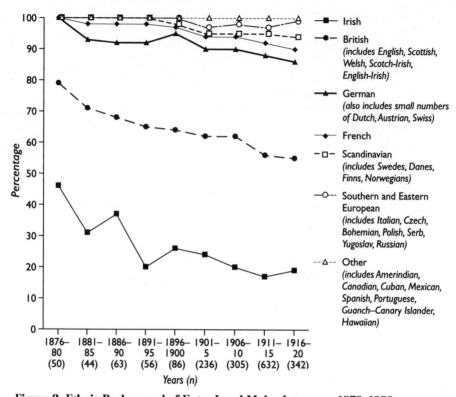

Figure 2. Ethnic Background of Entry-Level Major Leaguers, 1876–1920
As late as 1920, the overwhelming majority of major league entrants still were descendants of immigrants from the British Isles or Western Europe, especially Germany. The share of the total from other backgrounds gradually increased over this span of time, however. Source: Lee Allen Notebooks, National Baseball Library, Cooperstown, N.Y.

Rules Change	Year	Batting Average Change
Balls for a walk reduced to 8	1880	−.010
Pitcher's mound moved back to 50'	1881	+.015
Balls for a walk reduced to 7	1882	−.012
Balls for a walk reduced to 6; overhand delivery allowed	1884	−.014
Balls for a walk increased to 7	1886	+.002
Strikeout raised to 4 strikes; 5-ball walk is a hit	1887	+.025
Strikeout lowered to 3 strikes; walks no longer hits	1888	−.032
Balls for a walk reduced to 4	1889	+.024
Pitcher's mound moved back to 60'6"	1893	+.035
"Lively ball" used; spitball banned; soiled or defaced balls replaced	1920	+.013

Figure 3. Rules Changes and Their Impact on Batting Average

Prior to 1887, reductions in the number of balls needed for a walk lowered batting averages. No strike zone existed—instead batters called for a high or low pitch. As a result, the more pitches a batter could select from before swinging or walking, the more likely he would get a hittable one. After 1887, with a shoulders-to-knees strike zone in place, this was no longer true. Reducing the number of balls for a walk to four put pressure on pitchers to avoid "nibbling" and to "groove" pitches if behind in the count in order to avoid walks. Also, note the frequency with which rules were fine-tuned in the tumultuous 1880s. Source: Information on change in batting average from Gerald W. Scully, *The Business of Major League Baseball* (Chicago: University of Chicago Press, 1989), 64; rules changes from Thomas R. Heitz, "Rules and Scoring," in *Total Baseball*, ed. John Thorn and Pete Palmer (New York: Warner Books, 1989), 2222–30.

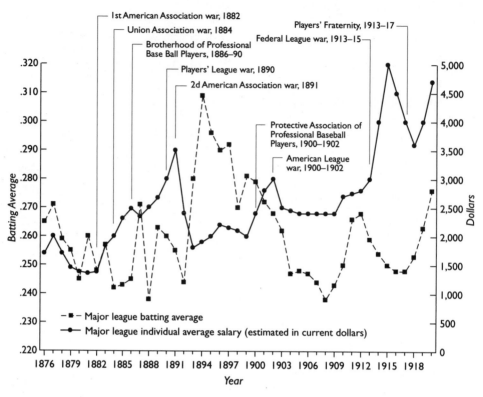

Figure 4. Major League Batting Averages and Players' Salaries, 1876–1920

In their search for fiscal order, major league owners frequently changed playing rules to raise or lower offense (see Fig. 3). Raising offense increased attendance but, usually with a one-year lag, ratcheted up salary pressures. Then offense would be brought back down to cool off wage inflation. Longer lags between changes in offense and salaries occurred when trade wars and competitive bidding for player services mandated multiyear contracts at high salary figures or when players' unions possessed sufficient market power to extend wage gains. In contrast, the National League's period of major league monopoly and labor weakness from 1892 to 1899 saw owners elevate offense for attendance purposes without comparable pay raises for players. Sources: Major league salary data same as in Fig. 1; batting average data from Gerald W. Scully, *The Business of Major League Baseball* (Chicago: University of Chicago Press, 1989), 53.

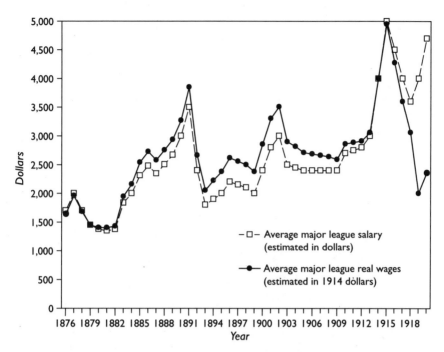

Figure 5. Players' Salaries and Real Wages, 1876–1920

Ballplayers' increases in real wages generally kept up with, or even exceeded, actual pay raises, given the prevalence of price deflation during much of the industrial era. After the pay hikes of 1913–15 resulting from the Federal League war, however, inflation during World War I and the immediate postwar period severely eroded the real earnings of players. Such trends made illicit outside earnings all the more attractive and encouraged developments such as the 1919 "Black Sox" scandal. Sources: Major league salary data same as in Fig. 1; real wage calculations derived from Stanley Lebergott, *Manpower in Economic Growth: The American Record since 1800* (New York: McGraw-Hill, 1964), 524–28.

NOTES

CHAPTER ONE

1. For recent examples of the application of social science theory to the historical study of sport, particularly baseball, see Melvin L. Adelman, *A Sporting Time: New York City and the Rise of Modern Athletics, 1820–70* (Urbana: University of Illinois Press, 1986), which relies heavily upon the modernization model of historian Richard D. Brown; and Stephen Hardy, *How Boston Played: Sport, Recreation, and Community, 1865–1918* (Boston: Northeastern University Press, 1982), and Steven A. Riess, *City Games: The Evolution of American Urban Society and the Rise of Sports* (Urbana: University of Illinois Press, 1989), which stress the interplay of urbanization and the institutional evolution of sport. These approaches contribute greatly to our understanding of the changing structure of baseball since the 1840s and to the role of the material and spatial environment in such adaptations; however, they also tend to obscure the human "trees" in a forest of abstract theories and fail to emphasize the unique ethnocultural origins and traditions within the sport. The thesis for the cultural origins of American baseball presented in my text is drawn from David Hackett Fischer, *Albion's Seed: Four British Folkways in America* (New York: Oxford University Press, 1989), esp. 3–11, 13–54, 146–51.

2. Fischer, *Albion's Seed*, 151.

3. Ibid., 146–51, 158; Gerald Astor, *The Baseball Hall of Fame 50th Anniversary Book* (New York: Prentice Hall Press, 1988), 2; Riess, *City Games*, 21. For an instructive discussion of the Puritan outlook on recreation, see Nancy L. Struna, "Puritans and Sports: The Irretrievable Tide of Change," *Journal of Sport History* 4 (Spring 1977): 1–21.

4. Harold Seymour, *Baseball: The Early Years* (New York: Oxford University Press, 1960), 5; Harold Seymour, *Baseball: The People's Game* (New York: Oxford University Press, 1990), 40, 131–32; Astor, *Baseball Hall of Fame*, 2; Warren Goldstein, *Playing for Keeps: A History of Early Baseball* (Ithaca, N.Y.: Cornell University Press, 1989), 12; George B. Kirsch, *The Creation of American Team Sports: Baseball and Cricket, 1838–72* (Urbana: University of Illinois Press, 1989), 53; Akron *Beacon-Journal*, June 10, 1991.

5. Seymour, *Baseball: The Early Years*, 15; Kirsch, *Creation of American Team Sports*, 6–12; Goldstein, *Playing for Keeps*, 12; James M. DiClerico and Barry J. Pavelec, *The Jersey Game: The History of Modern Baseball from Its Birth to the Big Leagues in the Garden State* (New Brunswick, N.J.: Rutgers University Press, 1991),

5-19; Elsdon C. Smith, *Dictionary of American Family Names* (New York: Harper and Bros., 1956).

6. Seymour, *Baseball: The Early Years*, 16; Adelman, *A Sporting Time*, 121–23.

7. Goldstein, *Playing for Keeps*, 17–20, 34–35; Seymour, *Baseball: The Early Years*, 17; Adelman, *A Sporting Time*, 124.

8. Seymour, *Baseball: The Early Years*, 17–18.

9. Ibid., 18–23; Goldstein, *Playing for Keeps*, 12, 30; Adelman, *A Sporting Time*, 278. A new work describing the growing cult of material comfort among the antebellum middle classes, and their defensiveness toward the claims of their ethnic and class "inferiors," is Richard L. Bushman, *The Refinement of America: Persons, Houses, Cities* (New York: Alfred A. Knopf, 1992).

10. Adelman, *A Sporting Time*, 91–118, 135–37; Kirsch, *Creation of American Team Sports*, 92–95, 123, 149, 173; Riess, *City Games*, 15.

11. Seymour, *Baseball: The Early Years*, 24; Adelman, *A Sporting Time*, 125–26; Kirsch, *Creation of American Team Sports*, 131–32.

12. Goldstein, *Playing for Keeps*, 25–27; Adelman, *A Sporting Time*, 138; Kirsch, *Creation of American Team Sports*, 131–32, 149.

13. Seymour, *Baseball: The Early Years*, 24–25; Kirsch, *Creation of American Team Sports*, 69–70; Adelman, *A Sporting Time*, 127, 139–40.

14. Seymour, *Baseball: The Early Years*, 26–30; Kirsch, *Creation of American Team Sports*, 70; Adelman, *A Sporting Time*, 134; New York *Clipper*, September 8, 1860, 164. The thesis that antebellum Yankees employed voluntary organizations to assert control over other ethnic, working-class Americans is strongly argued in Clifford S. Griffin, *Their Brothers' Keepers: Moral Stewardship in the United States, 1800–1855* (New Brunswick, N.J.: Rutgers University Press, 1960). A modified, later version of the "social control" thesis is in Paul Boyer, *Urban Masses and Moral Order in America, 1820–1920* (Cambridge, Mass.: Harvard University Press, 1978).

15. Seymour, *Baseball: The Early Years*, 35; Kirsch, *Creation of American Team Sports*, 14–15; Seymour, *Baseball: The People's Game*, 6; *Porter's Spirit of the Times*, June 20, 1857, 245, and November 27, 1858, 196.

16. Adelman, *A Sporting Time*, 139–41. For keen insights into ethnic stereotyping by the press in the antebellum period, and a methodology for content analysis research into such stereotyping, see Dale T. Knobel, *Paddy and the Republic: Ethnicity and Nationality in Antebellum America* (Middletown, Conn.: Wesleyan University Press, 1986).

17. Seymour, *Baseball: The Early Years*, 35–36; Goldstein, *Playing for Keeps*, 44–45; Adelman, *A Sporting Time*, 127–28; *Porter's Spirit of the Times*, March 20, 1858, 337.

18. Seymour, *Baseball: The Early Years*, 36.

19. Ibid., 36–37; Goldstein, *Playing for Keeps*, 40–41.

20. Adelman, *A Sporting Time*, 129–31; Goldstein, *Playing for Keeps*, 48–49.

21. Seymour, *Baseball: The Early Years*, 38.

22. Ibid., 38–40, 50; Kirsch, *Creation of American Team Sports*, 55–61, 69; Goldstein, *Playing for Keeps*, 38–39; Adelman, *A Sporting Time*, 137.

CHAPTER TWO

1. Bill Felber, "The Changing Game," in *Total Baseball*, ed. John Thorn and Pete Palmer (New York: Warner Books, 1989), 263; Gerald Astor, *The Baseball Hall of Fame 50th Anniversary Book* (New York: Prentice Hall Press, 1988), 4.

2. Harold Seymour, *Baseball: The Early Years* (New York: Oxford University Press, 1960), 40–41, 48; Paul Dickson, ed., *The Dickson Baseball Dictionary* (New York: Facts on File, 1989), 44; Felber, "Changing Game," 261–62; Warren Goldstein, *Playing for Keeps: A History of Early Baseball* (Ithaca, N.Y.: Cornell University Press, 1989), 108–11.

3. Seymour, *Baseball: The Early Years*, 40, 50; Melvin L. Adelman, *A Sporting Time: New York City and the Rise of Modern Athletics, 1820–70* (Urbana: University of Illinois Press, 1986), 146; Goldstein, *Playing for Keeps*, 49, 72.

4. Seymour, *Baseball: The Early Years*, 48; Adelman, *A Sporting Time*, 146–48, 151.

5. "A Sermon on Baseball," ca. 1865, in Henry Chadwick Scrapbooks, vol. 10, Albert G. Spalding Collection, microform copy at National Baseball Library, Cooperstown, New York (hereafter, NBL). All references to the Spalding Collection are to the microform copy at the NBL (the original materials comprising the collection are in the New York Public Library).

6. Adelman, *A Sporting Time*, 155–56.

7. Seymour, *Baseball: The Early Years*, 42, 50, 328.

8. Ibid., 43–45.

9. Ibid., 48, 51–52; Charles C. Alexander, *Our Game: An American Baseball History* (New York: Henry Holt, 1991), 14; Adelman, *A Sporting Time*, 160.

10. Seymour claims the Mutuals garnered $38,000 annually from the New York City treasury, a figure Adelman insists is vastly inflated. Seymour, *Baseball: The Early Years*, 52–53; Adelman, *A Sporting Time*, 160–61; Goldstein, *Playing for Keeps*, 91–92.

11. Seymour, *Baseball: The Early Years*, 53–54; Adelman, *A Sporting Time*, 163–67; Goldstein, *Playing for Keeps*, 90.

12. *Wilkes' Spirit of the Times*, July 6, 1867, 347; Seymour, *Baseball: The People's Game* (New York: Oxford University Press, 1990), 27–28; Dale A. Somers, *The Rise of Sports in New Orleans, 1850–1900* (Baton Rouge: Louisiana State University Press, 1972), 117–21.

13. Adelman, *A Sporting Time*, 175–78; Stephen Freedman, "The Baseball Fad in Chicago, 1865–1870: An Exploration of the Role of Sport in the Nineteenth-Century City," *Journal of Sport History* 5 (Summer 1978): 56; Steven A. Riess, *City Games: The Evolution of American Urban Society and the Rise of Sports* (Urbana: University of Illinois Press, 1989), 35.

14. Seymour, *Baseball: The Early Years*, 45, 52.

15. Ibid., 42–45; Goldstein, *Playing for Keeps*, 72; *Wilkes' Spirit of the Times*, May 4, 1867, 150.

16. Goldstein, *Playing for Keeps*, 73–74, 86–88.

17. Ibid., 88; Somers, *Rise of Sports in New Orleans*, 120; Adelman, *A Sporting Time*, 176; Seymour, *Baseball: The People's Game*, 534–37; George B. Kirsch, *The*

Creation of American Team Sports: Baseball and Cricket, 1838–72 (Urbana: University of Illinois Press, 1989), 124–28, 149–53.

18. Goldstein, *Playing for Keeps*, 83; Seymour, *Baseball: The Early Years*, 55.

19. Seymour, *Baseball: The Early Years*, 56; Goldstein, *Playing for Keeps*, 88, 98.

20. Seymour, *Baseball: The Early Years*, 56–57, 71; Goldstein, *Playing for Keeps*, 104–7, 112–14; David Q. Voigt, *American Baseball*, vol. 1: *From Gentlemen's Sport to the Commissioner System* (Norman: University of Oklahoma Press, 1966), 27; Cincinnati Red Stockings Scrapbook, Chadwick Scrapbooks, vol. 7, Spalding Collection, NBL.

21. Goldstein, *Playing for Keeps*, 100, 136–41. See Steven M. Gelber, "Working at Playing: The Culture of the Workplace and the Rise of Baseball," *Journal of Social History* 16 (Summer 1983), 3–22.

22. Goldstein, *Playing for Keeps*, 115–19.

23. Ibid., 93–94; Seymour, *Baseball: The Early Years*, 59; Adelman, *A Sporting Time*, 153.

24. Goldstein, *Playing for Keeps*, 97, 120–35; Seymour, *Baseball: The Early Years*, 59–60; Steven A. Riess, *Touching Base: Professional Baseball and American Culture in the Progressive Era* (Westport, Conn.: Greenwood Press, 1980), 153, 157–60; Adelman, *A Sporting Time*, 169–72, 178–79.

25. Adelman, *A Sporting Time*, 173, 179–80.

26. Ibid., 180–83; Riess, *Touching Base*, 158–59, 201.

27. Lee Allen Notebooks, 1871–75, NBL; Bill Deane, "Foreign-Born Players," in Thorn and Palmer, *Total Baseball*, 414–15.

28. Somers, *Rise of Sports in New Orleans*, 125; Seymour, *Baseball: The Early Years*, 62–66.

29. Goldstein, *Playing for Keeps*, 142–46; Thorn and Palmer, *Total Baseball*, 679.

30. Seymour, *Baseball: The Early Years*, 60, 67–68; Voigt, *American Baseball*, 1:36–42, 56–57; Goldstein, *Playing for Keeps*, 135–39; Peter S. Craig, "Organized Baseball: An Industry Study of a $100 Million Spectator Sport" (B.A. thesis, Oberlin College, 1950), 112a.

31. Seymour, *Baseball: The Early Years*, 68; Voigt, *American Baseball*, 1:57–59; Gerald W. Scully, *The Business of Major League Baseball* (Chicago: University of Chicago Press, 1989), 1.

32. Voigt, *American Baseball*, 1:47.

33. Ibid., 48–51.

CHAPTER THREE

1. Harold Seymour, *Baseball: The Early Years* (New York: Oxford University Press, 1960), 77–78, 80; Steven A. Riess, *City Games: The Evolution of American Urban Society and the Rise of Sports* (Urbana: University of Illinois Press, 1989), 67; David Q. Voigt, *American Baseball*, vol. 1: *From Gentlemen's Sport to the Commissioner System* (Norman: University of Oklahoma Press, 1966), 60–62; Albert Spalding Scrapbooks, vol. 1, Albert G. Spalding Collection, National Baseball Library, Cooperstown, N.Y. (hereafter, NBL). For a fine biography of Spalding detailing his relationship with Hulbert, see Peter Levine, *A. G. Spalding and the Rise of*

Baseball: The Promise of American Sport (New York: Oxford University Press, 1985).

2. Spalding Scrapbooks, vols. 1–2, Spalding Collection, NBL; Seymour, *Baseball: The Early Years*, 79–80.

3. Voigt, *American Baseball*, 1:64–66; Gerald W. Scully, *The Business of Major League Baseball* (Chicago: University of Chicago Press, 1989), 2; Seymour, *Baseball: The Early Years*, 80–85.

4. Seymour, *Baseball: The Early Years*, 176; Scully, *Business of Major League Baseball*, 59; Bill Felber, "The Changing Game," in *Total Baseball*, ed. John Thorn and Pete Palmer (New York: Warner Books, 1989), 264; Thomas R. Heitz, "Rules and Scoring," in Thorn and Palmer, *Total Baseball*, 2221.

5. Seymour, *Baseball: The Early Years*, 86–88; Scully, *Business of Major League Baseball*, 89; Voigt, *American Baseball*, 1:68–70, 76; Gerald Astor, *The Baseball Hall of Fame 50th Anniversary Book* (New York: Prentice Hall Press, 1988), 12.

6. Seymour, *Baseball: The Early Years*, 89–92.

7. Ibid., 94–100; Voigt, *American Baseball*, 1:73, 122; Neil J. Sullivan, *The Minors: The Struggles and the Triumph of Baseball's Poor Relation from 1876 to the Present* (New York: St. Martin's Press, 1990), 12–14.

8. Seymour, *Baseball: The Early Years*, 86, 106; Voigt, *American Baseball*, 1:76.

9. Voigt, *American Baseball*, 1:70; Seymour, *Baseball: The Early Years*, 121; Scully, *Business of Major League Baseball*, 1.

10. Seymour, *Baseball: The Early Years*, 87, 121; Voigt, *American Baseball*, 1:71–73; Heitz, "Rules and Scoring," 2221; Charles C. Alexander, *Our Game: An American Baseball History* (New York: Henry Holt, 1991), 30.

11. Seymour, *Baseball: The Early Years*, 86; Voigt, *American Baseball*, 1:74.

12. Scully, *Business of Major League Baseball*, 32–33; Voigt, *American Baseball*, 1:77; Seymour, *Baseball: The Early Years*, 87, 106.

13. Scully, *Business of Major League Baseball*, 2; Seymour, *Baseball: The Early Years*, 105–9.

14. Cleveland *Plain Dealer*, October 10, 1879; Seymour, *Baseball: The Early Years*, 111–14.

15. Voigt, *American Baseball*, 1:77; Seymour, *Baseball: The Early Years*, 127; House Judiciary Committee, *Organized Baseball: Report of the Subcommittee on the Study of Monopoly Power of the Committee on the Judiciary*, House Report no. 2002, 82d Cong., 1st sess. (Washington, D.C.: Government Printing Office, 1952), 21–23.

16. Seymour, *Baseball: The Early Years*, 117; *Spalding's Base Ball Guide* (1890), 19; Steven A. Riess, *Touching Base: Professional Baseball and American Culture in the Progressive Era* (Westport, Conn.: Greenwood Press, 1980), 159, 201; Lee Allen Notebooks, 1876–84, NBL.

17. Larry R. Gerlach, "Umpires," in Thorn and Palmer, *Total Baseball*, 465; Heitz, "Rules and Scoring," 2221–22.

18. Seymour, *Baseball: The Early Years*, 125–26; Voigt, *American Baseball*, 1:79.

19. Seymour, *Baseball: The Early Years*, 130–31; Stephen S. Hall, "Scandals and Controversies," in Thorn and Palmer, *Total Baseball*, 438; Levine, *A. G. Spalding*, 52.

20. Allen Notebooks, 1876–84, NBL; Alexander, *Our Game*, 32–33.

21. Voigt, *American Baseball*, 1:105–6, 205; Scully, *Business of Major League Baseball*, 53–54, 64; Heitz, "Rules and Scoring," 2222. The relationship between on-field rules changes, the business context in which they were made, and their economic consequences has been largely neglected by both narrative historians of baseball and "sabermetricians." Admittedly, no paper trail in which owners directly state the purposes behind their rules changes has survived. But a considerable chain of circumstantial evidence points to the conscious use of such tinkering to improve clubs' economic position. First, baseball management consistently fought efforts to include other constituencies within the sport in the rule-making process—suggesting that it was a power of value to them. Second, the timing of rules changes that either boosted or lowered offensive production bears a marked correlation to the presence of particular economic concerns, specifically disappointing attendance and gate receipts or serious salary escalation. Third, baseball executives came to the sport from other economic fields in which firms, motivated by cutthroat competition, tried to adjust worker production levels, lower labor costs, and attract more customers. It seems unlikely that they would not attempt to take similar measures in the baseball industry.

What is also very clear is that increases in offense, if designed to boost fan attendance, usually also led to growing salary pressures, and that cuts in offense diminished such forces. By using the information in Figure 4 in the Appendix, the yearly direction of change in batting average in the major leagues from the previous season can be paired with the direction of salary change in the following year. Forty-four such batting average/salary pairs for the years 1877–1921 result, and in thirty-one of them, the direction of change of each statistic is the same: when offense goes up, salary follows, and when batting averages decline, so do salaries. Of the thirteen "deviant" pairs, nine involved batting average declines but salary increases (1881–82, 1884–85, 1888–89, 1890–91, 1895–96, 1900–1901, 1901–2, 1913–14, and 1914–15). In all but one of these (1895–96), the deviation coincided with an interleague trade war or strong union activity, circumstances that operated as overriding inflationary counterpressures. In the four cases in which batting average increase was trailed by salary decline (1877–78, 1886–87, 1897–98, and 1905–6), the salary movement in the first and third pairs occurred at times when not only was there no effective threat of a trade war or a players' union but even the monopoly cartel consisted of a single league rather than two. The smaller number of major league clubs in the cartel, then, would be expected to offer even less than the "usual" level of interclub salary-bidding pressure. In the other two cases, the amount of batting average movement was so tiny as to exert negligible influence upon salaries, and in the 1905–6 pairing the salary change also is virtually undetectable.

22. Seymour, *Baseball: The Early Years*, 102–3, 135–39; Voigt, *American Baseball*, 1:106–7, 122–23; Sullivan, *The Minors*, 14–17; Gerlach, "Umpires," 465.

23. Seymour, *Baseball: The Early Years*, 139–43.

24. *Spalding's Base Ball Guide* (1890), 19–20; Spalding Scrapbooks, vol. 4, Spalding Collection, NBL; Seymour, *Baseball: The Early Years*, 117–18; Peter S. Craig, "Organized Baseball: An Industry Study of a $100 Million Spectator Sport" (B.A. thesis, Oberlin College, 1950), 41.

25. Seymour, *Baseball: The Early Years*, 119, 143–45; Voigt, *American Baseball*, 1:124–25, 130.

26. Seymour, *Baseball: The Early Years*, 145–46; A. G. Mills to O. P. Caylor, March 1, 3, 1883, A. G. Mills Correspondence, vol. 1, NBL.

27. Scully, *Business of Major League Baseball*, 2–3; House Judiciary Committee, *Organized Baseball*, 153; Seymour, *Baseball: The Early Years*, 109, 119, 146–47.

28. A. G. Mills to Denny McKnight, December 8, 1883, Mills Correspondence, vol. 1, NBL; Scully, *Business of Major League Baseball*, 60, 64; Felber, "Changing Game," 264–65; Heitz, "Rules and Scoring," 2222, 2245.

29. Seymour, *Baseball: The Early Years*, 114, 148–49; Voigt, *American Baseball*, 1:130–32. A summary history of the Union Association is Joshua B. Orenstein, "The Union Association of 1884: A Glorious Failure," *Baseball Research Journal* 19 (1990): 3–6.

30. Seymour, *Baseball: The Early Years*, 149–50; Voigt, *American Baseball*, 1:133–35.

31. Seymour, *Baseball: The Early Years*, 151–52; Alexander, *Our Game*, 38–39.

32. Seymour, *Baseball: The Early Years*, 110, 126, 130, 153–56; Harold Seymour *Baseball: The People's Game* (New York: Oxford University Press, 1990), 547–48; Levine, *A. G. Spalding*, 43, 47.

33. Voigt, *American Baseball*, 1:107–8; *Spalding's Base Ball Guide* (1890), 20.

34. *Spalding's Base Ball Guide* (1890), 19–20; Craig, "Organized Baseball," 41, 112a; Seymour, *Baseball: The Early Years*, 157, 186.

35. Seymour, *Baseball: The Early Years*, 158–61.

CHAPTER FOUR

1. For a general overview of the business struggle for market stability in the era of industrialization, see Robert H. Wiebe, *The Search for Order, 1877–1920* (New York: Hill and Wang, 1967). Studies of the labor implications of this "search" include David Montgomery, *The Fall of the House of Labor: The Workplace, the State, and American Labor Activism, 1865–1925* (New York: Cambridge University Press, 1987); Herbert G. Gutman, "Work, Culture, and Society in Industrializing America, 1815–1919," *American Historical Review* 78 (1973), 531–87; and, focusing specifically upon the steel industry, David Brody, *Steelworkers in America: The Nonunion Era* (Cambridge, Mass.: Harvard University Press, 1960).

2. Neil J. Sullivan, *The Minors: The Struggles and the Triumph of Baseball's Poor Relation from 1876 to the Present* (New York: St. Martin's Press, 1990), 20–22; Harold Seymour, *Baseball: The Early Years* (New York: Oxford University Press, 1960), 190; David Q. Voigt, *American Baseball*, vol. 1: *From Gentlemen's Sport to the Commissioner System* (Norman: University of Oklahoma Press, 1966), 220; Peter Levine, *A. G. Spalding and the Rise of Baseball: The Promise of American Sport* (New York: Oxford University Press, 1985), 37.

3. Seymour, *Baseball: The Early Years*, 162–70.

4. Ibid., 217–18.

5. *Sporting Life*, October 28, 1885; *Sporting News*, October 11, 1886; Seymour, *Baseball: The Early Years*, 109–10, 117, 119–20; *Spalding's Base Ball Guide* (1890), 19–20.

6. Seymour, *Baseball: The Early Years*, 110, 170; Voigt, *American Baseball*,

1:110; Gerald W. Scully, *The Business of Major League Baseball* (Chicago: University of Chicago Press, 1989), 3.

7. Seymour, *Baseball: The Early Years*, 110–11, 127; Voigt, *American Baseball*, 1:111, 176; Charles C. Alexander, *Our Game: An American Baseball History* (New York: Henry Holt, 1991), 42.

8. *Sporting News*, January 15, 1887; Voigt, *American Baseball*, 1:171–72; Seymour, *Baseball: The Early Years*, 192–93.

9. *Sporting Life*, November 18, 1885; Harold Seymour, *Baseball: The People's Game* (New York: Oxford University Press, 1990), 539–43, 548–49.

10. Seymour, *Baseball: The Early Years*, 126, 179, 181, 187–88; Voigt, *American Baseball*, 1:138–41, 209; Stephen S. Hall, "Scandals and Controversies," in *Total Baseball*, ed. John Thorn and Pete Palmer (New York: Warner Books, 1989), 438, 441; Lee Allen Notebooks, 1885–90, National Baseball Library, Cooperstown, N.Y. (hereafter, NBL).

11. Levine, *A. G. Spalding*, 43–44; Seymour, *Baseball: The Early Years*, 128–29; Voigt, *American Baseball*, 1:104.

12. Larry R. Gerlach, "Umpires," in Thorn and Palmer, *Total Baseball*, 466; Alexander, *Our Game*, 29; Seymour, *Baseball: The Early Years*, 177, 179; Scully, *Business of Major League Baseball*, 64; Thomas R. Heitz, "Rules and Scoring," in Thorn and Palmer, *Total Baseball*, 2222, 2245.

13. Voigt, *American Baseball*, 1:142–43, 220; Peter S. Craig, "Organized Baseball: An Industry Study of a $100 Million Spectator Sport" (B.A. thesis, Oberlin College, 1950), tab. 8; Seymour, *Baseball: The Early Years*, 118, 186–203.

14. Seymour, *Baseball: The Early Years*, 178, 181; Voigt, *American Baseball*, 1:174–76.

15. Seymour, *Baseball: The Early Years*, 221–22; Lee Lowenfish, *The Imperfect Diamond: A History of Baseball's Labor Wars*, rev. ed (New York: Da Capo Press, 1991), 28–29. For a comparison with the assault upon ethnic and skill solidarity in another industry's work force, see Brody, *Steelworkers in America*, 50–111.

16. New York *Clipper*, February 14, 1885; *Sporting Life*, November 17, 1886; Lowenfish, *Imperfect Diamond*, 28, 31; Voigt, *American Baseball*, 1:155, 157; Seymour, *Baseball: The Early Years*, 221.

17. Seymour, *Baseball: The Early Years*, 108–9, 223; Scully, *Business of Major League Baseball*, 5, 33.

18. John Montgomery Ward, "The Base-Ball Player: Is He a Chattel?," *Lippincott's*, August 1887, 310; Lowenfish, *Imperfect Diamond*, 31–32. A study of reform unions of the Gilded Age, especially the Knights of Labor, with suggestive parallels to the brotherhood as regards the composition and aim of union membership is Gerald N. Grob, *Workers and Utopia: A Study of Ideological Conflict in the American Labor Movement, 1865–1900* (Evanston, Ill.: Northwestern University Press, 1961), esp. 43–52.

19. Lowenfish, *Imperfect Diamond*, 28, 30; Seymour, *Baseball: The People's Game*, 547–53; Seymour, *Baseball: The Early Years*, 177–79, 277; Voigt, *American Baseball*, 1:112; Scully, *Business of Major League Baseball*, 54, 61, 64; Heitz, "Rules and Scoring," 2223.

20. Voigt, *American Baseball*, 1:113, 144–45; Seymour, *Baseball: The Early*

Years, 201, 208–9; Dale A. Somers, *The Rise of Sports in New Orleans, 1850–1900* (Baton Rouge: Louisiana State University Press, 1972), 131.

21. *Spalding's Base Ball Guide* (1890), 19–20; Gerlach, "Umpires," 466; Sullivan, *The Minors*, 22–23.

22. Seymour, *Baseball: The Early Years*, 109–10, 208–10; Scully, *Business of Major League Baseball*, 61, 64; Heitz, "Rules and Scoring," 2224; Voigt, *American Baseball*, 1:111–12.

23. *Sporting Life*, December 7, 1887; Voigt, *American Baseball*, 1:201–2.

24. Somers, *Rise of Sports in New Orleans*, 133; Levine, *A. G. Spalding*, 57–58.

25. Seymour, *Baseball: The Early Years*, 128–29, 224; Lowenfish, *Imperfect Diamond*, 27–30; Albert Spalding Scrapbooks, vol. 9, Albert G. Spalding Collection, NBL.

26. Scully, *Business of Major League Baseball*, 61, 64; Heitz, "Rules and Scoring," 2224; Lowenfish, *Imperfect Diamond*, 32–34; Seymour, *Baseball: The Early Years*, 111, 128, 171, 222, 224–25; Voigt, *American Baseball*, 1:145.

27. Voigt, *American Baseball*, 1:117; E. C. Alft, "The Development of Baseball as a Business, 1876–1900," in House Judiciary Committee, *Study of Monopoly Power: Hearings before the Subcommittee on the Study of Monopoly Power of the Committee on the Judiciary*, serial no. 1, pt. 6, Organized Baseball, 82d Cong., 1st sess., July 30–October 24, 1951 (Washington, D.C.: Government Printing Office, 1952), 1439; *Spalding's Base Ball Guide* (1890), 19–21; Scully, *Business of Major League Baseball*, 64; Craig, "Organized Baseball," 41, 112a, tab. 8.

28. *Sporting Life*, September 16, 1889; Voigt, *American Baseball*, 1:293; Lowenfish, *Imperfect Diamond*, 34–35; Seymour, *Baseball: The Early Years*, 225–27; Levine, *A. G. Spalding*, 62.

29. Lowenfish, *Imperfect Diamond*, 35–36; Seymour, *Baseball: The Early Years*, 227–30. For a description of reform unions' fascination with cooperative schemes, see Grob, *Workers and Utopia*, 44.

30. Seymour, *Baseball: The Early Years*, 230–32; Gerald Astor, *The Baseball Hall of Fame 50th Anniversary Book* (New York: Prentice Hall Press, 1988), 29.

31. *Sporting Life*, January 29, February 26, March 19, 1890; Seymour, *Baseball: The Early Years*, 232–33; Lowenfish, *Imperfect Diamond*, 40.

32. Seymour, *Baseball: The Early Years*, 233; Lowenfish, *Imperfect Diamond*, 36; Alexander, *Our Game*, 55.

33. Seymour, *Baseball: The Early Years*, 233–34; Alexander, *Our Game*, 56–57.

34. Seymour, *Baseball: The Early Years*, 235–37; Lowenfish, *Imperfect Diamond*, 41–43.

35. Seymour, *Baseball: The Early Years*, 237–38; Craig, "Organized Baseball," tab. 8; Voigt, *American Baseball*, 1:166.

36. Seymour, *Baseball: The Early Years*, 238–39. Jay Faatz (the only player mentioned in the verse whose name has not come up heretofore) was manager of the Cleveland PL team.

37. Lowenfish, *Imperfect Diamond*, 47–49; Seymour, *Baseball: The Early Years*, 240–43.

38. Seymour, *Baseball: The Early Years*, 243–47.

39. *Sporting News*, November 8, 1890; Lowenfish, *Imperfect Diamond*, 49–51;

Seymour, *Baseball: The Early Years*, 248–49; Voigt, *American Baseball*, 1:218; Alexander, *Our Game*, 58.

CHAPTER FIVE

1. *Spalding's Base Ball Guide* (1890), 44–45.

2. Harold Seymour, *Baseball: The Early Years* (New York: Oxford University Press, 1960), 249–55; Charles C. Alexander, *Our Game: An American Baseball History* (New York: Henry Holt, 1991), 59–60.

3. Seymour, *Baseball: The Early Years*, 256–57; Alexander, *Our Game*, 60.

4. Seymour, *Baseball: The Early Years*, 257–60; Alexander, *Our Game*, 60–62.

5. David Q. Voigt, *American Baseball*, vol. 1: *From Gentlemen's Sport to the Commissioner System* (Norman: University of Oklahoma Press, 1966), 153; Seymour, *Baseball: The Early Years*, 261–62, 266; Gerald W. Scully, *The Business of Major League Baseball* (Chicago: University of Chicago Press, 1989), 3; Alexander, *Our Game*, 62–63.

6. House Judiciary Committee, *Organized Baseball: Report of the Subcommittee on the Study of Monopoly Power of the Committee on the Judiciary*, House Report no. 2002, 82d Cong., 1st sess. (Washington, D.C.: Government Printing Office, 1952), 153; Seymour, *Baseball: The Early Years*, 266, 271.

7. Lee Lowenfish, *The Imperfect Diamond: A History of Baseball's Labor Wars*, rev. ed (New York: Da Capo Press, 1991), 52; Neil J. Sullivan, *The Minors: The Struggles and the Triumph of Baseball's Poor Relation from 1876 to the Present* (New York: St. Martin's Press, 1990), 29.

8. Lowenfish, *Imperfect Diamond*, 50; Peter S. Craig, "Organized Baseball: An Industry Study of a $100 Million Spectator Sport" (B.A. thesis, Oberlin College, 1950), 49, 112a; Seymour, *Baseball: The Early Years*, 267.

9. Seymour, *Baseball: The Early Years*, 267.

10. Ibid., 266, 268–69; Voigt, *American Baseball*, 1:246.

11. Peter S. Craig, "Monopsony in Manpower: Organized Baseball Meets the Anti-Trust Laws," *Yale Law Journal* 62 (March 1953), 605; Voigt, *American Baseball*, 1:233, 283.

12. Seymour, *Baseball: The Early Years*, 270.

13. Ibid., 271–74; Voigt, *American Baseball*, 1:231–32.

14. Voigt, *American Baseball*, 1:80, 247–53, 279–80; Seymour, *Baseball: The Early Years*, 297–98.

15. Craig, "Organized Baseball," 112a; Voigt, *American Baseball*, 1:234–35, 254, 261, 279.

16. Seymour, *Baseball: The Early Years*, 275–77; Bill Felber, "The Changing Game," in *Total Baseball*, ed. John Thorn and Pete Palmer (New York: Warner Books, 1989), 264–65; Voigt, *American Baseball*, 1:208, 287; Scully, *Business of Major League Baseball*, 54, 58, 64, 72; Thomas R. Heitz, "Rules and Scoring," in Thorn and Palmer, *Total Baseball*, 2224, 2246.

17. Felber, "Changing Game," 263; Scully, *Business of Major League Baseball*, 61–62; Heitz, "Rules and Scoring," 2225; Voigt, *America Baseball*, 1:289–91; Seymour, *Baseball: The Early Years*, 274, 276–77, 283–84, 299.

18. Felber, "Changing Game," 265; Seymour, *Baseball: The Early Years*, 278–80; Richard Topp, "Demographics," in Thorn and Palmer, *Total Baseball*, 410.

19. Seymour, *Baseball: The Early Years*, 203–6; Voigt, *American Baseball*, 1:281; Topp, "Demographics," 413.

20. Seymour, *Baseball: The Early Years*, 271, 325, 336; Steven A. Riess, *City Games: The Evolution of American Urban Society and the Rise of Sports* (Urbana: University of Illinois Press, 1989), 70, 112, 224; Lee Allen Notebooks, 1891–99, National Baseball Library, Cooperstown, N.Y. (hereafter, NBL); Bernard Postal, Jesse Silver, and Roy Silver, *Encyclopedia of Jews in Sports* (New York: Bloch Publishing Co., 1965), 27–36.

21. Harold Seymour, *Baseball: The People's Game* (New York: Oxford University Press, 1990), 29, 164, 193–94, 213–14, 259; Voigt, *American Baseball*, 1:280–83.

22. Seymour, *Baseball: The People's Game*, 456, 545–57; Voigt, *American Baseball*, 1:278.

23. Stephen S. Hall, "Scandals and Controversies," in Thorn and Palmer, *Total Baseball*, 440; Voigt, *American Baseball*, 1:230; Seymour, *Baseball: The Early Years*, 291, 295–96, 298; Lowenfish, *Imperfect Diamond*, 60.

24. Voigt, *American Baseball*, 1:104, 192, 236–37; Seymour, *Baseball: The Early Years*, 297, 341; Alexander, *Our Game*, 66–67, 70; Larry R. Gerlach, "Umpires," in Thorn and Palmer, *Total Baseball*, 466.

25. Voigt, *American Baseball*, 1:232; Seymour, *Baseball: The Early Years*, 198–202, 293–94.

26. Seymour, *Baseball: The Early Years*, 193–95; Alexander, *Our Game*, 69–70; Voigt, *American Baseball*, 1:232–33, 297; *Sporting News*, November 12, 1898, 6.

27. Scully, *Business of Major League Baseball*, 89; Seymour, *Baseball: The Early Years*, 298–300; Alexander, *Our Game*, 63.

28. Seymour, *Baseball: The Early Years*, 300–303.

29. Ibid., 307–8; Lowenfish, *Imperfect Diamond*, 58–60; Sullivan, *The Minors*, 25–30. The best biography of Ban Johnson is Eugene C. Murdock, *Ban Johnson: Czar of Baseball* (Westport, Conn.: Greenwood Press, 1983).

30. Seymour, *Baseball: The Early Years*, 304–6; Voigt, *American Baseball*, 1:266.

31. *Sporting Life*, December 28, 1899, March 17, April 7, 1900.

CHAPTER SIX

1. *Sporting Life*, June 9, 16, 1900; Harold Seymour, *Baseball: The Early Years* (New York: Oxford University Press, 1960), 309–10; Charles C. Alexander, *Our Game: An American Baseball History* (New York: Henry Holt, 1991), 77; David Q. Voigt, "Serfs versus Magnates: A Century of Labor Strife in Major League Baseball," in *The Business of Professional Sports*, ed. Paul D. Staudohar and James A. Mangan (Urbana: University of Illinois Press, 1991), 105–6; Lee Lowenfish, *The Imperfect Diamond: A History of Baseball's Labor Wars*, rev. ed (New York: Da Capo Press, 1991), 61–62.

2. Seymour, *Baseball: The Early Years*, 310–11; Lowenfish, *Imperfect Diamond*,

62–63; David Q. Voigt, *American Baseball*, vol. 1: *From Gentlemen's Sport to the Commissioner System* (Norman: University of Oklahoma Press, 1966), 284–86.

3. Seymour, *Baseball: The Early Years*, 311–13; Lowenfish, *Imperfect Diamond*, 63–66; Voigt, "Serfs versus Magnates," 106. Inviting comparison with the emergence of the Protective Association is the description of AFL trade union mobilization in the 1897–1903 period in David Montgomery, *The Fall of the House of Labor: The Workplace, the State, and American Labor Activism, 1865–1925* (New York: Cambridge University Press, 1987), 302, 327.

4. Voigt, "Serfs versus Magnates," 106; Seymour, *Baseball: The Early Years*, 313–14; Alexander, *Our Game*, 77; Voigt, *American Baseball*, 1:278.

5. Seymour, *Baseball: The Early Years*, 275, 314; Alexander, *Our Game*, 78–79; Harold Seymour, *Baseball: The Golden Age* (New York: Oxford University Press, 1971), 7.

6. *Sporting News*, October 19, 1901; Seymour, *Baseball: The Early Years*, 315–17; Neil J. Sullivan, *The Minors: The Struggles and the Triumph of Baseball's Poor Relation from 1876 to the Present* (New York: St. Martin's Press, 1990), 38, 44; Lowenfish, *Imperfect Diamond*, 51.

7. Seymour, *Baseball: The Early Years*, 317–21; Peter Levine, *A. G. Spalding and the Rise of Baseball: The Promise of American Sport* (New York: Oxford University Press, 1985), 66; *Sporting Life*, February 8, 1902; Alexander, *Our Game*, 79; Lowenfish, *Imperfect Diamond*, 67.

8. Seymour, *Baseball: The Early Years*, 314–15; Lowenfish, *Imperfect Diamond*, 67–69.

9. Seymour, *Baseball: The Early Years*, 321–22; Lowenfish, *Imperfect Diamond*, 69; Alexander, *Our Game*, 80–82; Voigt, "Serfs versus Magnates," 107.

10. Seymour, *Baseball: The Early Years*, 322–23; Alexander, *Our Game*, 82–83, 85–86; Lowenfish, *Imperfect Diamond*, 51, 69–70.

11. Seymour, *Baseball: The Early Years*, 323–34; Voigt, "Serfs versus Magnates," 107; Sullivan, *The Minors*, 37, 42; Alexander, *Our Game*, 86.

12. *Sporting News*, October 15, 1904, January 7, February 11, March 4, 1905; Seymour, *Baseball: The Golden Age*, 171–73; Frank deHass Robison to Garry Herrmann, January 18, 1905, August "Garry" Herrmann Papers, National Baseball Library, Cooperstown, N.Y. (hereafter, NBL).

13. *Sporting News*, February 13, 1908; Voigt, *American Baseball*, vol. 2: *From the Commissioners to Continental Expansion* (Norman: University of Oklahoma Press, 1970), 65; Seymour, *Baseball: The Golden Age*, 171–73, 179.

14. Seymour, *Baseball: The Golden Age*, 172–73; Alexander, *Our Game*, 92; Lowenfish, *Imperfect Diamond*, 72.

15. Lawrence S. Ritter, *The Glory of Their Times*, expanded ed. (New York: William Morrow, 1984), 8–9, 23, 38, 93, 139–40, 157; Seymour, *Baseball: The Golden Age*, 174.

16. Voigt, *American Baseball*, 2:78; Seymour, *Baseball: The Golden Age*, 100–121, 127–28, 130–31, 193; Bill Felber, "The Changing Game," in *Total Baseball*, ed. John Thorn and Pete Palmer (New York: Warner Books, 1989), 263.

17. Ted Sullivan to Garry Herrmann, August 29, September 7, 1904, Ban Johnson to Herrmann, December 21, 1904, Herrmann Papers, NBL; House Judiciary Committee, *Organized Baseball: Report of the Subcommittee on the Study of Monopoly*

Power of the Committee on the Judiciary, House Report no. 2002, 82d Cong., 1st sess. (Washington, D.C.: Government Printing Office, 1952), 145.

18. Seymour, *Baseball: The Golden Age,* 178, 180–81; Frank deHass Robison to NL Club Presidents, January 11, 1904, Herrmann Papers, NBL; Ritter, *Glory of Their Times,* 129.

19. Seymour, *Baseball: The Golden Age,* 179, 184–85.

20. Ibid., 183, 186; Ritter, *Glory of Their Times,* 13; Gerald W. Scully, *The Business of Major League Baseball* (Chicago: University of Chicago Press, 1989), 28; Voigt, *American Baseball,* 2:67.

21. Seymour, *Baseball: The Golden Age,* 87; House Judiciary Committee, *Organized Baseball,* 153; Scully, *Business of Major League Baseball,* 28–29, 91.

22. Steven A. Riess, *City Games: The Evolution of American Urban Society and the Rise of Sports* (Urbana: University of Illinois Press, 1989), 194; Seymour, *Baseball: The Golden Age,* 9–11; Montgomery, *Fall of the House of Labor,* 269.

23. Seymour, *Baseball: The Golden Age,* 197–98, 400; Sullivan, *The Minors,* 52–58; Riess, *City Games,* 197.

24. Lowenfish, *Imperfect Diamond,* 51, 71–72; *Annual Report of the National Commission,* January 1905, NBL; Seymour, *Baseball: The Golden Age,* 16–17.

25. *Annual Report of the National Commission,* January 1910, NBL.

26. Peter S. Craig, "Organized Baseball: An Industry Study of a $100 Milton Spectator Sport" (B.A. thesis, Oberlin College, 1950), 234a; Seymour, *Baseball: The Golden Age,* 14–15, 41–42, 58–62, 68–72; Voigt, *American Baseball,* 2:12, 38, 81, 108–9; Riess, *City Games,* 197.

27. Riess, *City Games,* 215–16; Seymour, *Baseball: The Golden Age,* 49–50, 72, 122–23; Alexander, *Our Game,* 88–89; Scully, *Business of Major League Baseball,* 58, 60, 62; Felber, "Changing Game," 260, 268–69; Thomas R. Heitz, "Rules and Scoring," in Thorn and Palmer, *Total Baseball,* 2228; Henry Chadwick, "An Open Letter to the Magnates of Organized Baseball," November 27, 1906, Herrmann Papers, NBL.

28. Lee Allen Notebooks, 1900–1909, NBL; Harold Seymour, *Baseball: The People's Game* (New York: Oxford University Press, 1990), 36, 43–46, 50–64, 112–14, 260–65, 381, 561–73; Riess, *City Games,* 94–104, 160; Seymour, *Baseball: The Golden Age,* 82–83; Bernard Postal, Jesse Silver, and Roy Silver, *Encyclopedia of Jews in Sports* (New York: Bloch Publishing Co., 1965), 27.

29. Seymour, *Baseball: The Golden Age,* 83; Ritter, *Glory of Their Times,* 172; Seymour, *Baseball: The People's Game,* 394, 550, 584–86; Allen Notebooks, 1900–1909, NBL. Steven Riess estimates the proportion of major leaguers active in the period between 1900 and 1919 who had a college background at one-quarter, compared with a national age-group ratio of one out of twenty in the general population. Riess, *City Games,* 87.

30. Felber, "Changing Game," 273; Don Nelson, "Mascots and Superstitions," in Thorn and Palmer, *Total Baseball,* 429–30. For general descriptions of the infiltration of scientific management techniques into Progressive Era workplace routines, see Montgomery, *Fall of the House of Labor,* 236, and especially Samuel Haber, *Efficiency and Uplift: Scientific Management in the Progressive Era, 1890–1920* (Chicago: University of Chicago Press, 1964).

31. Seymour, *Baseball: The Golden Age,* 59, 188–89.

32. Ibid., 24–27; Voigt, *American Baseball,* 2:101–3; Stephen S. Hall, "Scandals and Controversies," in Thorn and Palmer, *Total Baseball,* 440; Larry R. Gerlach, "Umpires," in Thorn and Palmer, *Total Baseball,* 466–67.

33. Seymour, *Baseball: The Golden Age,* 278–85, 288; Alexander, *Our Game,* 117.

CHAPTER SEVEN

1. Charles C. Alexander, *Our Game: An American Baseball History* (New York: Henry Holt, 1991), 91–92; Peter S. Craig, "Organized Baseball: An Industry Study of a $100 Million Spectator Sport" (B.A. thesis, Oberlin College, 1950), 234a; David Q. Voigt, *American Baseball,* vol. 2: *From the Commissioners to Continental Expansion* (Norman: University of Oklahoma Press, 1970), 81; Lee Lowenfish, *The Imperfect Diamond: A History of Baseball's Labor Wars,* rev. ed (New York: Da Capo Press, 1991), 70; Steven A. Riess, *City Games: The Evolution of American Urban Society and the Rise of Sports* (Urbana: University of Illinois Press, 1989), 216; Harold Seymour, *Baseball: The Golden Age* (New York: Oxford University Press, 1971), 28–29, 68; House Judiciary Committee, *Study of Monopoly Power: Hearings before the Subcommittee on the Study of Monopoly Power of the Committee on the Judiciary,* serial No. 1, pt. 6, Organized Baseball, 82d Cong., 1st sess., July 30–October 24, 1951 (Washington, D.C.: Government Printing Office, 1952), 1351, 1612–14.

2. House Judiciary Committee, *Study of Monopoly Power,* 1352, 1612–14.

3. Seymour, *Baseball: The Golden Age,* 13, 172–73; Voigt, *American Baseball,* 2:65–66; Lowenfish, *Imperfect Diamond,* 71–72; Voigt, "Serfs versus Magnates: A Century of Labor Strife in Major League Baseball," in *The Business of Professional Sports,* ed. Paul D. Staudohar and James A. Mangan (Urbana: University of Illinois Press, 1991), 107.

4. Seymour, *Baseball: The Golden Age,* 125–26; Bill Felber, "The Changing Game," in *Total Baseball,* ed. John Thorn and Pete Palmer (New York: Warner Books, 1989), 262, 268–69; Thomas R. Heitz, "Rules and Scoring," in Thorn and Palmer, *Total Baseball,* 2229.

5. Seymour, *Baseball: The Golden Age,* 16, 172, 285–86; Hugh Chalmers to Ren Mulford, Jr., May 12, 1911, August "Garry" Herrmann Papers, National Baseball Library, Cooperstown, N.Y. (hereafter, NBL).

6. Victor Muñoz to Garry Herrmann, June 17, 1911, Herrmann Papers, NBL; Seymour, *Baseball: The Golden Age,* 84–85.

7. *Sporting News,* March 23, April 13, 20, 1911; "Walter Johnson on Baseball Slavery: 'The Great American Principle of Dog-Eat-Dog,'" *Baseball Magazine,* July 1911, 75–76; Seymour, *Baseball: The Golden Age,* 174; Lowenfish, *Imperfect Diamond,* 74–75.

8. Lowenfish, *Imperfect Diamond,* 73–74; Seymour, *Baseball: The Golden Age,* 193–94.

9. Larry R. Gerlach, "Umpires," in Thorn and Palmer, *Total Baseball,* 466; Voigt, *American Baseball,* 2:103; Seymour, *Baseball: The Golden Age,* 184–86; House Judiciary Committee, *Organized Baseball: Report of the Subcommittee on the Study*

of Monopoly Power of the Committee on the Judiciary, House Report no. 2002, 82d Cong., 1st sess. (Washington, D.C.: Government Printing Office, 1952), 145; Charles Comiskey to John E. Bruce, Secretary of National Commission, October 25, 1911, Herrmann Papers, NBL.

10. Seymour, Baseball: The Golden Age, 46–47, 70, 189–92; Annual Report of the National Commission, January 1911, January 1912, NBL.

11. House Judiciary Committee, Organized Baseball, 153; Seymour, Baseball: The Golden Age, 406; House Judiciary Committee, Study of Monopoly Power, 1353.

12. House Judiciary Committee, Study of Monopoly Power, 1612–14; Annual Report of the National Commission, January 1915, 28.

13. David L. Fultz, "What Our Fraternity Really Stands For," Baseball Magazine, February 1913, 29–32, 104, 108, 122, 124; Seymour, Baseball: The Golden Age, 35, 194.

14. Lowenfish, Imperfect Diamond, 76–78; Seymour, Baseball: The Golden Age, 198.

15. Voigt, American Baseball, 2:67; Annual Report of the National Commission, January 1913, NBL; Lowenfish, Imperfect Diamond, 83; Seymour, Baseball: The Golden Age, 31, 181, 187.

16. David L. Fultz, "The Baseball Players' Fraternity and What It Stands For," Baseball Magazine, November 1912, 29–31, 124, 126; Lowenfish, Imperfect Diamond, 78–80, 95; Seymour, Baseball: The Golden Age, 194–95.

17. Sporting Life, November 9, 1912; Fultz, "What Our Fraternity Really Stands For," 29–32, 104, 108, 122, 124; Lowenfish, Imperfect Diamond, 51, 80; Seymour, Baseball: The Golden Age, 176–77.

18. Voigt, American Baseball, 2:65, 81; Thorn and Palmer, Total Baseball, 681; Lowenfish, Imperfect Diamond, 81; New York Yankees Ledger Book, George Weiss Collection, NBL; House Judiciary Committee, Study of Monopoly Power, 1612–14; Baseball Magazine, January 1913, 48, April 1913, 45–62.

19. House Judiciary Committee, Organized Baseball, 145; Seymour, Baseball: The Golden Age, 177, 224; Voigt, American Baseball, 2:79; Lowenfish, Imperfect Diamond, 82.

20. Annual Report of the National Commission, January 1914, NBL; Voigt, American Baseball, 2:66; Seymour, Baseball: The Golden Age, 224; Lowenfish, Imperfect Diamond, 83.

21. Lowenfish, Imperfect Diamond, 80–82; Seymour, Baseball: The Golden Age, 193; Lee Allen Notebooks, 1911, NBL.

22. Seymour, Baseball: The Golden Age, 190–91.

23. Ibid., 199–200; Craig, "Organized Baseball," 234a.

24. Seymour, Baseball: The Golden Age, 200–202; Lowenfish, Imperfect Diamond, 85–86. For a more thorough account of the Federal League war, see Marc Okkonen, The Federal League, 1914–1915: Baseball's Third Major League (Cleveland: Society for American Baseball Research, 1989).

25. Seymour, Baseball: The Golden Age, 225–26; Lowenfish, Imperfect Diamond, 83.

26. Seymour, Baseball: The Golden Age, 33–36, 202–3.

27. Lowenfish, Imperfect Diamond, 82–83; Seymour, Baseball: The Golden Age, 226–27.

28. *Sporting News*, March 5, May 14, 1914; Lowenfish, *Imperfect Diamond*, 84; Seymour, *Baseball: The Golden Age*, 191, 227–28.

29. Seymour, *Baseball: The Golden Age*, 203–5; Lowenfish, *Imperfect Diamond*, 86–87.

30. Seymour, *Baseball: The Golden Age*, 205; Lowenfish, *Imperfect Diamond*, 52.

31. Seymour, *Baseball: The Golden Age*, 209.

32. Ibid., 205–7; Lowenfish, *Imperfect Diamond*, 86–87; Voigt, *American Baseball*, 2:65–66; Craig, "Organized Baseball," 135; Alexander, *Our Game*, 103, 106.

33. Seymour, *Baseball: The Golden Age*, 207–8.

34. Ibid., 209–12; Lowenfish, *Imperfect Diamond*, 87–88.

35. Seymour, *Baseball: The Golden Age*, 219, 416; House Judiciary Committee, *Study of Monopoly Power*, 1354.

36. Voigt, *American Baseball*, 2:79; Seymour, *Baseball: The Golden Age*, 217; *Annual Report of the National Commission*, January 1915, NBL.

37. *Sporting Life*, July 25, August 1, 1914; Seymour, *Baseball: The Golden Age*, 228–29; Lowenfish, *Imperfect Diamond*, 92.

38. Seymour, *Baseball: The Golden Age*, 35–36; Voigt, *American Baseball*, 2:71; Allen Notebooks, 1910–15, NBL; Don Nelson, "Mascots and Superstitions," in Thorn and Palmer, *Total Baseball*, 430; Jules Tygiel, "Black Ball," in Thorn and Palmer, *Total Baseball*, 550–51; Neil J. Sullivan, *The Minors: The Struggles and the Triumph of Baseball's Poor Relation from 1876 to the Present* (New York: St. Martin's Press, 1990), 189.

39. Sullivan, *The Minors*, 60–62; *New York Times*, November 12, December 12, 1914; Seymour, *Baseball: The Golden Age*, 219; House Judiciary Committee, *Study of Monopoly Power*, 1355–56, 1612–14; Steven A. Riess, "Professional Baseball and American Culture in the Progressive Era: Myths and Realities, with Special Emphasis on Atlanta, Chicago, and New York" (Ph.D. dissertation, University of Chicago, 1974), 271.

40. Lowenfish, *Imperfect Diamond*, 82; Seymour, *Baseball: The Golden Age*, 229; *Annual Report of the National Commission*, January 1915, NBL.

41. Seymour, *Baseball: The Golden Age*, 65, 219–22, 234; Voigt, *American Baseball*, 2:81.

42. Seymour, *Baseball: The Golden Age*, 222–23, 230; *Annual Report of the National Commission*, January 1916, NBL.

43. Seymour, *Baseball: The Golden Age*, 212; Lowenfish, *Imperfect Diamond*, 88–90.

44. Voigt, *American Baseball*, 2:21, 81; Craig, "Organized Baseball," 234a; Lowenfish, *Imperfect Diamond*, 90–91; Seymour, *Baseball: The Golden Age*, 230–34, 243; Gerald Astor, *The Baseball Hall of Fame 50th Anniversary Book* (New York: Prentice Hall Press, 1988), 110.

CHAPTER EIGHT

1. Harold Seymour, *Baseball: The Golden Age* (New York: Oxford University Press, 1971), 174–75.

2. Ibid., 175, 235–37; Charles C. Alexander, *Our Game: An American Baseball History* (New York: Henry Holt, 1991), 128; Joseph M. Overfield, "Tragedies and Shortened Careers," in *Total Baseball*, ed. John Thorn and Pete Palmer (New York: Warner Books, 1989), 449; *Annual Report of the National Commission*, January 1917, National Baseball Library, Cooperstown, N.Y. (hereafter, NBL).

3. David Q. Voigt, *American Baseball*, vol. 2: *From the Commissioners to Continental Expansion* (Norman: University of Oklahoma Press, 1970), 81; Peter S. Craig, "Organized Baseball: An Industry Study of a $100 Million Spectator Sport" (B.A. thesis, Oberlin College, 1950), 234a; House Judiciary Committee, *Study of Monopoly Power: Hearings before the Subcommittee on the Study of Monopoly Power of the Committee on the Judiciary*, serial no. 1, pt. 6, Organized Baseball, 82d Cong., 1st sess., July 30–October 24, 1951 (Washington, D.C.: Government Printing Office, 1952), 1612–14; Lee Lowenfish, *The Imperfect Diamond: A History of Baseball's Labor Wars*, rev. ed (New York: Da Capo Press, 1991), 93; *Sporting News*, November 9, 16, 1916; Voigt, "Serfs versus Magnates: A Century of Labor Strife in Major League Baseball," in *The Business of Professional Sports*, ed. Paul D. Staudohar and James A. Mangan (Urbana: University of Illinois Press, 1991), 109–10; Seymour, *Baseball: The Golden Age*, 237.

4. Seymour, *Baseball: The Golden Age*, 239, 242.

5. Ibid., 239–41; Lowenfish, *Imperfect Diamond*, 93; *New York Times*, January 8, 1917.

6. Seymour, *Baseball: The Golden Age*, 240–41; Lowenfish, *Imperfect Diamond*, 93–94.

7. Seymour, *Baseball: The Golden Age*, 236, 241.

8. Ibid., 241–42; F. C. Lane, "The Players' Strike," *Baseball Magazine*, April 1917, 173–78; Lowenfish, *Imperfect Diamond*, 94–95.

9. Seymour, *Baseball: The Golden Age*, 37, 188, 235–36; Alexander, *Our Game*, 111.

10. Seymour, *Baseball: The Golden Age*, 20, 244–46; Alexander, *Our Game*, 108–9.

11. Seymour, *Baseball: The Golden Age*, 247.

12. House Judiciary Committee, *Study of Monopoly Power*, 1357–59, 1612–14.

13. Lowenfish, *Imperfect Diamond*, 96; Seymour, *Baseball: The Golden Age*, 247–49; *Sporting News*, May 9, May 23, June 20, July 4, 1918.

14. Seymour, *Baseball: The Golden Age*, 249–51.

15. Ibid., 251–52; Lowenfish, *Imperfect Diamond*, 96.

16. Neil J. Sullivan, *The Minors: The Struggles and the Triumph of Baseball's Poor Relation from 1876 to the Present* (New York: St. Martin's Press, 1990), 63; Craig, "Organized Baseball," 234a; Seymour, *Baseball: The Golden Age*, 24, 252; Lowenfish, *Imperfect Diamond*, 96; Alexander, *Our Game*, 112.

17. Seymour, *Baseball: The Golden Age*, 253–55; Lowenfish, *Imperfect Diamond*, 96–97; Larry R. Gerlach, "Umpires," in Thorn and Palmer, *Total Baseball*, 467; Voigt, *American Baseball*, 2:104.

18. Lee Allen Notebooks, 1916–20, NBL; Steven A. Riess, *Touching Base: Professional Baseball and American Culture in the Progressive Era* (Westport, Conn.: Greenwood Press, 1980), 185–86; Voigt, *American Baseball*, 2:64.

19. Riess, *Touching Base*, 161–65, 171–80, 237–38; Allen Notebooks, 1916–20, NBL; Steven A. Riess, *City Games: The Evolution of American Urban Society and the Rise of Sports* (Urbana: University of Illinois Press, 1989), 87–91.

20. Riess, *City Games*, 90–91; Steven A. Riess, "Professional Baseball and American Culture in the Progressive Era: Myths and Realities, with Special Emphasis on Atlanta, Chicago, and New York" (Ph.D. dissertation, University of Chicago, 1974), 328.

21. Seymour, *Baseball: The Golden Age*, 255; *Annual Report of the National Commission*, January 1920, NBL; House Judiciary Committee, *Study of Monopoly Power*, 1359–60, 1612–14.

22. Voigt, *American Baseball*, 2:82; Sullivan, *The Minors*, 63; Seymour, *Baseball: The Golden Age*, 68, 262–63, 272; Lowenfish, *Imperfect Diamond*, 97.

23. Seymour, *Baseball: The Golden Age*, 264–71; Lowenfish, *Imperfect Diamond*, 97–98.

24. Seymour, *Baseball: The Golden Age*, 259–61, 272; *Annual Report of the National Commission*, January 1921, NBL.

25. Seymour, *Baseball: The Golden Age*, 68, 423; Voigt, *American Baseball*, 2:67, 81, 109; Craig, "Organized Baseball," 234a; Riess, *City Games*, 197.

26. House Judiciary Committee, *Study of Monopoly Power*, 1361, 1612–14.

27. Overfield, "Tragedies and Shortened Careers," 449; Seymour, *Baseball: The Golden Age*, 424–25; Gerald W. Scully, *The Business of Major League Baseball* (Chicago: University of Chicago Press, 1989), 55, 64, 72; John E. Bruce to National Commission, October 15, 1920, August "Garry" Herrmann Papers, NBL.

28. Seymour, *Baseball: The Golden Age*, 287–91; Alexander, *Our Game*, 117–19.

29. Alexander, *Our Game*, 119; Seymour, *Baseball: The Golden Age*, 292–93.

30. Seymour, *Baseball: The Golden Age*, 297–99, 382–83, 387; Alexander, *Our Game*, 143–45.

31. Seymour, *Baseball: The Golden Age*, 300–305, 384–85. The best study of the Black Sox scandal remains Eliot Asinof, *Eight Men Out: The Black Sox and the 1919 World Series* (New York: Holt, Rinehart and Winston, 1963).

32. Lowenfish, *Imperfect Diamond*, 98–99; Seymour, *Baseball: The Golden Age*, 334–35; Alexander, *Our Game*, 127–28.

33. Seymour, *Baseball: The Golden Age*, 311–12; Alexander, *Our Game*, 125–26.

BIBLIOGRAPHIC ESSAY

The student of baseball's early business history is faced with a dilemma common to the study of nineteenth-century American industry: the scarcity of surviving records from the relevant franchises. Owing to the vagaries of time, haphazard record keeping and storage, the instability of club locations and ownership, and management's penchant for secrecy, few franchises' ledgers or correspondence have survived for the archivist or researcher. For baseball's early development, the most valuable materials are in the New York Public Library's Albert G. Spalding Collection, a microform copy of which is held at the National Baseball Library in Cooperstown, New York. The Spalding Collection includes the records of the Knickerbocker Base Ball Club of the 1840s; scrapbooks of the Cincinnati Red Stockings, the sport's first overtly "all-professional" team (1868–70); the correspondence of manager Harry Wright (1878–85); sportswriter Henry Chadwick's diaries and scrapbooks (1873–88); and Spalding's own scrapbooks, beginning with the year 1874.

Also at Cooperstown are the letters of NL executive Abraham G. Mills, covering the years 1882–96, and the August "Garry" Herrmann Papers, spanning Herrmann's tenure as Cincinnati club president and National Commission chairman during the first two decades of the twentieth century. Also of value are selective records of the Cincinnati American Association club of the 1880s, held by the Historical and Philosophical Society of Ohio at the University of Cincinnati. For demographic and financial records of major league players prior to 1920, the researcher should consult the Lee Allen Notebooks and Vertical Files at the National Baseball Library. The Allen Notebooks, compiled by the renowned baseball librarian and author, are a gold mine of information on the ethnic heritage, educational level, occupation (for the earliest years), and cause of death of major league players since 1871, organized according to the player's year of entry into the big leagues. Information is less comprehensive for the nineteenth-century years but is virtually complete for the 1900–1920 period. The Vertical Files contain alphabetical folders of biographical materials on major leaguers, including, in some cases, actual contracts and other occupational information.

Of organized baseball's published records and official publications, the most valuable are the National Commission's *Record of Proceedings*, compiled in six volumes from 1903 to 1920, and its *Annual Reports*, contained in seventeen yearly volumes. These books constitute the official record of cases filed, heard, and ruled upon by baseball's supreme arbitration panel of the Progressive Era. Also of use in keeping track of the industry's organizational structure, number and names of franchises and leagues, and rules changes are National League of Professional Baseball Clubs,

Constitution and Playing Rules of the National League of Professional Baseball Clubs: Official (Philadelphia: Reach and Johnson, 1876; New York: A. G. Spalding and Bros./American Sports Publishing Co., 1877–1920), and the *Baseball Blue Book* (Ft. Wayne, Ind./St. Petersburg, Fla., 1909–20). Given the paucity of management-generated public records on the details of the industry, however, periodic congressional investigations of the sport have become a central source of documentation for the baseball scholar. In particular, the Judiciary Committee of the U.S. House of Representatives, chaired at the time by New York's Emanuel Celler, generated *Study of Monopoly Power: Hearings before the Subcommittee on the Study of Monopoly Power of the Committee on the Judiciary*, serial no. 1, pt. 6, Organized Baseball, 82d Cong., 1st sess., July 30–October 24, 1951 (Washington, D.C.: Government Printing Office, 1952), and *Organized Baseball: Report of the Subcommittee on the Study of Monopoly Power of the Committee on the Judiciary*, House Report no. 2002, 82d Cong., 1st sess. (Washington, D.C.: Government Printing Office, 1952). The hearings and report provide the most thorough accounting available of the financial position of the industry from 1900 to 1950 and the economic standing of players at all levels during the same span.

Among the various annual guidebooks to the sport are Henry Chadwick, *Beadle's Dime Base Ball Player* (New York: Beadle & Co., 1860–81); *DeWitt's Base Ball Guide* (1868–85); *Reach's Baseball Guide* (Philadelphia: Reach Sporting Goods, 1883–1920); *Spalding's Base Ball Guide* (New York: A. G. Spalding and Bros./American Sports Publishing Co., 1877–1920); and Francis C. Richter, *The Sporting Life's Official Baseball Guide and Handbook of the National Game* (Philadelphia: Sporting Life Publishing Co., 1891). F. H. Brunell issued the *Players' League Guide* (Chicago: n.p., 1890) in the league's sole year of existence, and black baseball's leading promoter published *Sol White's Official Baseball Guide* (Philadelphia: H. Walter Schlichter, 1907; reprint, Camden, N.J.: Camden House, 1983). With newspapers and periodicals of the sporting press a crucial source of primary information on pre-1920 baseball, the leading "national" publications were, for the early years, the New York *Clipper* (from 1853), *Porter's Spirit of the Times* (1856–60), the *Spirit of the Times* (1831–61), and *Wilkes' Spirit of the Times* (1859–72). For the later period, the *Sporting News* (1886–1920), *Sporting Life* (1883–1920), and *Baseball Magazine* (1908–20) are most useful. The *New York Times* provided coverage for the entire time span to 1920, while a long list of other newspapers located in major league cities provided additional information on player-management issues and incidents within individual franchises. During the Progressive Era, the featuring of baseball articles in popular magazines also increased, with *Collier's*, *McClure's Magazine*, and *Lippincott's* the most prominent periodicals offering such space.

Published memoirs and personal accounts include, from the management perspective, A. G. Spalding, *America's National Game* (New York: American Sports Publishing Co., 1911); Ed Barrow, *My Fifty Years in Baseball* (New York: Coward, McCann, 1951); and Connie Mack, *My 66 Years in the Big Leagues* (Philadelphia: John C. Winston, 1950). Among various ballplayers' reminiscences are Adrian C. Anson, *A Ball Player's Career* (Chicago: Era Publishing Co., 1900); Ty Cobb and Al Stump, *My Life in Baseball: The True Record* (New York: Doubleday, 1961); Christy Mathewson with John N. Wheeler, *Pitching in a Pinch* (New York: G. P. Putnam, 1912); and John Montgomery Ward, *Base-Ball: How to Become a Player, with the*

Origin, History and Explanation of the Game (Philadelphia: The Athletic Publishing Co., 1888). The pioneering oral history of pre-1920 players is Lawrence S. Ritter, *The Glory of Their Times* (New York: Macmillan, 1966; expanded ed., New York: William Morrow, 1984), which is full of anecdotal information on player-management contract dealings and double-dealings. Larry R. Gerlach similarly gives the umpires their chance to sound off in *The Men in Blue* (New York: Viking Press, 1980).

Among the many overviews of the game's professional history by historians and other writers, far and away the best are Harold Seymour's *Baseball: The Early Years* (New York: Oxford University Press, 1960) and *Baseball: The Golden Age* (New York: Oxford University Press, 1971). Also good, though less thorough than Seymour's books, are David Q. Voigt's *American Baseball*, vol. 1: *From Gentlemen's Sport to the Commissioner System* (Norman: University of Oklahoma Press, 1966) and *American Baseball*, vol. 2: *From the Commissioners to Continental Expansion* (Norman: University of Oklahoma Press, 1970). The finest one-volume study of baseball is Charles C. Alexander, *Our Game: An American Baseball History* (New York: Henry Holt, 1991). Other general histories include Lee Allen, *One Hundred Years of Baseball* (New York: Bartholomew House, 1950), *The National League Story* (New York: Hill and Wang, 1961), and *The American League Story* (New York: Hill and Wang, 1962); Gerald Astor, *The Baseball Hall of Fame 50th Anniversary Book* (New York: Prentice Hall Press, 1988); James M. DiClerico and Barry J. Pavelec, *The Jersey Game: The History of Modern Baseball from Its Birth to the Big Leagues in the Garden State* (New Brunswick, N.J.: Rutgers University Press, 1991); Joseph Durso, *Baseball and the American Dream* (St. Louis: Sporting News Publishing Co., 1986); Bill James, *Bill James Historical Baseball Abstract* (New York: Villard Books, 1986); Robert Smith, *Baseball* (New York: Simon and Schuster, 1970); and Ted Vincent, *Mudville's Revenge: the Rise and Fall of American Sport* (New York: Seaview Books, 1974).

Earlier overview accounts by contemporary observers and journalists include Seymour Church, *Baseball: The History, Statistics and Romance of the American National Game from Its Inception to the Present Time* (San Francisco: S. R. Church, 1902; reprint, Princeton, N.J.: Pyne Press, 1974); Preston D. Orem, *Baseball: From the Newspaper Accounts, 1848–1891*, 11 vols. (Altadena, Calif., 1961, 1966–67); Francis Richter, *Richter's History and Records of Base Ball* (Philadelphia: Francis Richter Publisher, 1914); and Alfred E. Spink, *The National Game* (St. Louis: The National Game Publishing Co., 1910). For insights into the origins and evolution of baseball language and terminology, see Paul Dickson, ed., *The Dickson Baseball Dictionary* (New York: Facts on File, 1989). Analyses that look into the colonial roots of American baseball, and its participants, include Benjamin G. Rader, *American Sports: From the Age of Folk Games to the Age of Spectators* (Englewood Cliffs, N.J.: Prentice Hall, 1983); Robert Henderson, *Ball, Bat, and Bishop: The Origin of Ball Games* (New York: Rockport Press, 1947); Nancy L. Struna, "Puritans and Sports: The Irretrievable Tide of Change," *Journal of Sport History* 4 (Spring 1977): 1–21; Peter Wagner, "Puritan Attitudes toward Physical Recreation in 17th-Century New England," *Journal of Sport History* 3 (Summer 1976): 139–51; and David Hackett Fischer, *Albion's Seed: Four British Folkways in America* (New York: Oxford University Press, 1989).

Many of the studies of antebellum and late nineteenth-century baseball rely heavily upon modernization or urbanization models. The best of these are Melvin L. Adelman, *A Sporting Time: New York City and the Rise of Modern Athletics, 1820–70* (Urbana: University of Illinois Press, 1986); Stephen Freedman, "The Baseball Fad in Chicago, 1865–1870: An Exploration of the Role of Sport in the Nineteenth-Century City," *Journal of Sport History* 5 (Summer 1978): 42–64; Stephen Hardy, *How Boston Played: Sport, Recreation, and Community, 1865–1915* (Boston: Northeastern University Press, 1982), and "The City and the Rise of American Sport, 1820–1920," *Exercise and Sport Sciences Reviews* 9 (1983): 183–219; George B. Kirsch, *The Creation of American Team Sports: Baseball and Cricket, 1838–72* (Urbana: University of Illinois Press, 1989); Steven A. Riess, "Professional Baseball and American Culture in the Progressive Era: Myths and Realities, with Special Emphasis on Atlanta, Chicago, and New York" (Ph.D. dissertation, University of Chicago, 1974), *Touching Base: Professional Baseball and American Culture in the Progressive Era* (Westport, Conn.: Greenwood Press, 1980), and *City Games: The Evolution of American Urban Society and the Rise of Sports* (Urbana: University of Illinois Press, 1989); Dale A. Somers, *The Rise of Sports in New Orleans, 1850–1900* (Baton Rouge: Louisiana State University Press, 1972); and Ian Tyrrell, "The Emergence of Modern American Baseball, c. 1850–80," in *Sport in History: The Making of Modern Sporting History*, ed. Richard Cashman and Michael McKernan (Queensland: University of Queensland Press, 1979), 205–26.

Offering valuable cultural perspectives are Warren Goldstein, *Playing for Keeps: A History of Early Baseball* (Ithaca, N.Y.: Cornell University Press, 1989); and Steven M. Gelber, "Working at Playing: The Culture of the Workplace and the Rise of Baseball," *Journal of Social History* 16 (Summer 1983): 3–22, and "'Their Hands Are All Out Playing': Business and Amateur Baseball, 1845–1917," *Journal of Sport History* 11 (Spring 1984): 5–27. Providing context for the antebellum separation of club management and on-field playing functions and personnel are Richard L. Bushman, *The Refinement of America: Persons, Houses, Cities* (New York: Alfred A. Knopf, 1992), which notes the Yankee middle class's pursuit of the trappings of respectability and its hostility to "lower" ethnic and economic classes, and Clifford S. Griffin, *Their Brothers' Keepers: Moral Stewardship in the United States, 1800–1855* (New Brunswick, N.J.: Rutgers University Press, 1960), and Paul Boyer, *Urban Masses and Moral Order in America, 1820–1920* (Cambridge, Mass.: Harvard University Press, 1978), which describe the uses of urban voluntary associations as mechanisms of social order. Dale T. Knobel, *Paddy and the Republic: Ethnicity and Nationality in Antebellum America* (Middletown, Conn.: Wesleyan University Press, 1986), demonstrates patterns of popular ethnic working-class stereotypes in the antebellum press.

There are few solid studies of the baseball industry as such. Noteworthy in this regard are Peter S. Craig, "Organized Baseball: An Industry Study of a $100 Million Spectator Sport" (B.A. thesis, Oberlin College, 1950), and "Monopsony in Manpower: Organized Baseball Meets the Anti-Trust Laws," *Yale Law Journal* 62 (March 1953): 576–639; Paul Gregory, *The Baseball Player: An Economic Study* (Washington, D.C.: Public Affairs Press, 1956); and especially Gerald W. Scully, *The Business of Major League Baseball* (Chicago: University of Chicago Press, 1989). Andrew Zimbalist, *Baseball and Billions* (New York: Basic Books, 1992), is excellent, especially on the sport's overall financial situation. General works on the business struggle for market control and its labor consequences in the era of industrialization include Robert H. Wiebe, *The Search for Order, 1877–1920* (New York: Hill and Wang, 1967); David Montgomery, *The Fall of the House of Labor: The Workplace, the State, and American Labor Activism, 1865–1925* (New York: Cambridge University Press, 1987); and Herbert G. Gutman, "Work, Culture, and Society in Industrializing America, 1815–1919," *American Historical Review* 78 (1973): 531–87. For comparative purposes, David Brody's study of the steel industry's labor history, *Steelworkers in America: The Nonunion Era* (Cambridge, Mass.: Harvard University Press, 1960), is excellent.

Good treatments of the labor economics of sports, including baseball, are Robert C. Barry, William B. Gould IV, and Paul D. Staudohar, *Labor Relations in Professional Sports* (Dover, Mass.: Auburn House, 1986), and Paul D. Staudohar and James A. Mangan, eds., *The Business of Professional Sports* (Urbana: University of Illinois Press, 1991), particularly David Q. Voigt's "Serfs versus Magnates: A Century of Labor Strife in Major League Baseball," 95–114. Gerald Grob's study of Gilded Age reform unionism, *Workers and Utopia: A Study of Ideological Conflict in the American Labor Movement, 1865–1900* (Evanston, Ill.: Northwestern University Press, 1961), suggests striking parallels between the Knights of Labor and the baseball brotherhood of the 1880s. The standard treatment of baseball unions and their struggles is Lee Lowenfish, *The Imperfect Diamond: A History of Baseball's Labor Wars*, rev. ed. (New York: Da Capo Press, 1991). Marc Okkonen has given the Federal League the scrutiny it deserves in *The Federal League, 1914–1915: Baseball's Third Major League* (Cleveland: Society for American Baseball Research, 1989). The standard treatment of the impact of Taylorism and scientific management changes upon American industry and workers is Samuel Haber, *Efficiency and Uplift: Scientific Management in the Progressive Era, 1890–1920* (Chicago: University of Chicago Press, 1964).

Among other studies of narrower segments of baseball's economic structure, team histories are plentiful, but most contain little beyond anecdotal information and accounts of each club's on-field glories. The best team studies remain those of the G. P. Putnam series of the late 1940s and early 1950s, written by Lee Allen, Warren Brown, Frank Graham, Harold Kaese, Franklin Lewis, Fred Lieb, and Shirley Povich. Harry Ellard, *Base Ball in Cincinnati* (Cincinnati: Press of Johnson and Hardin, 1907), details the early Reds. The best history of the minor leagues is Neil J. Sullivan, *The Minors: The Struggles and the Triumph of Baseball's Poor Relation from 1876 to the Present* (New York: St. Martin's Press, 1990). Other accounts include John B. Foster, *A History of the National Association of Professional Base Ball Leagues* (Columbus, Ohio: National Association of Professional Base Ball Leagues, 1926); Robert Finch, L. H. Addington, and Ben M. Morgan, eds., *The Story of Minor League Baseball* (Columbus, Ohio: Stoneman Press, 1952); and Robert Obojski, *Bush League: A History of Minor League Baseball* (New York: Macmillan, 1975). Accounts of particular circuits are Fred W. Lange, *History of Baseball in California and Pacific Coast Leagues, 1847–1938* (Oakland, Calif., 1938); Robert French, *Fifty Golden Years in the American Association of Professional Baseball Clubs, 1902–1951* (Minneapolis: Syndicate Publishing Co., 1951); and Bill O'Neal, *The Texas League, 1888–1987* (Austin, Tex.: Eakin Press, 1987).

In addition to material in the general histories of the sport cited above, other secondary accounts provide individual and collective profiles of the participants within baseball's occupational structure. For a look at the sociology of participation outside the ranks of organized baseball in the period before 1920, the essential study is Harold Seymour, *Baseball: The People's Game* (New York: Oxford University Press, 1990). American Jews in baseball receive their due in Bernard Postal, Jesse Silver, and Roy Silver, *Encyclopedia of Jews in Sports* (New York: Bloch Publishing, 1965). The best treatment of African Americans in baseball remains Robert Peterson, *Only the Ball Was White* (Englewood Cliffs, N.J.: Prentice Hall, 1970). Individual biographies of baseball founders, magnates, and managers include Charles C. Alexander, *John McGraw* (New York: Viking Press, 1988); Gustaf W. Axelson, *"Commy": The Life Story of Charles A. Comiskey* (Chicago: Reilly and Lee, 1919); Peter Levine, *A. G. Spalding and the Rise of Baseball: The Promise of American Sport* (New York: Oxford University Press, 1985); Eugene Murdock, *Ban Johnson: Czar of Baseball* (Westport, Conn.: Greenwood Press, 1986); Harold Peterson, *The Man Who Invented Baseball* (New York: Charles Scribner's Sons, 1972), a biography of Alexander Cartwright; and J. G. Taylor Spink, *Judge Landis and 25 Years of Baseball* (New York: Thomas Crowell, 1974). The best scholarly biographies of players active before 1920 are Alexander, *Ty Cobb* (New York: Oxford University Press, 1984); Robert Creamer, *Babe* (New York: Simon and Schuster, 1974); and Donald Gropman, *Say It Ain't So, Joe: The Story of Shoeless Joe Jackson* (New York: Little, Brown, 1979). Eliot Asinof's *Eight Men Out: The Black Sox and the 1919 World Series* (New York: Holt, Rinehart and Winston, 1963), remains the most thorough account of that scandal, but Bill Veeck with Ed Linn, *Hustler's Handbook* (New York: G. P. Putnam, 1965), supplies additional intrigues.

Finally, in recent years a number of new journals and annual compilations of essays have enriched the field of baseball research. For academic articles, the *Journal of Sport History*, as witnessed by the individual citations earlier, has been a major contributor. The Society for American Baseball Research has produced the *Baseball Research Journal* since 1972 and *The National Pastime* since 1981. John Thorn and Pete Palmer, major figures in the society, have edited *Total Baseball* (New York: Warner Books, 1989) and its updates, combining perhaps the best aggregation of playing statistics with fine essays on subjects ranging from labor relations to rules changes to player demographics to scandals. Meckler Publishing of Westport, Connecticut, has offered *Baseball History*, an annual collection of essays edited by Peter Levine, since 1988 and also produces the *Cooperstown Symposium on Baseball and the American Culture*, edited by Al Hall, an annual publication since 1989, which features papers presented at conferences held in Cooperstown each summer.

INDEX

California State League, 82, 167, 187
Canada, baseball clubs in, 58, 61, 82
Canadians, in baseball, 67, 90, 204, 223, 238
Canary Islanders, in baseball, 204
Canton, Ohio, baseball clubs in, 109
Carroll, Cliff, 97
Cartwright, Alexander, 4–5, 22
Caruthers, Bob, 99, 120
"Cat," 2
Caylor, O. P., 69, 73
Cermak, Edward Hugo, 194
Chadwick, Henry, 21, 35, 45, 48, 54, 57, 107, 170–71
Chalmers Award, 181
Chance, Frank, 163, 185
Chapman, Ray, 229
Chase, Hal, 159, 167, 176, 181, 202, 230–32
Chesbro, Jack, 158
Chicago, Ill., baseball clubs in, 14, 30–32, 34, 51, 53, 69, 120–21, 138
Chicago Browns (UA), 74, 80
Chicago Chifeds (Whales) (FL), 195–96, 199, 201–2
Chicago Cubs (White Stockings) (NL), 53–54, 56–57, 59–60, 62–63, 68, 72–73, 76–77, 79, 84, 87–88, 90–93, 97, 100, 102, 108, 117, 124–25, 128, 134, 137, 140, 143–44, 147, 154, 156, 159–60, 163–64, 170, 172–73, 175–76, 185, 187, 196, 209, 211, 222, 231–32
Chicago Pirates (PL), 105, 108, 113
Chicago White Sox (AL), 142–43, 147–48, 150, 154, 156, 170, 175–76, 183, 201–2, 206, 220, 230, 232–35
Chicago White Stockings (NA), 40–41, 44, 46–48, 51
Childs, Clarence "Cupid," 119
Cicotte, Eddie, 232–33
Cincinnati, Ohio, baseball clubs in, 29–31, 34, 54, 69, 98, 195
Cincinnati Outlaw Reds (UA), 74
Cincinnati Reds (Porkers) (AA), 71, 87, 93, 96, 99, 105, 118–20
Cincinnati Reds (Red Stockings) (NL), 57, 59, 68, 111, 120, 122–23, 130, 140, 155–58, 163, 175, 180–81, 185, 196, 201–2, 211, 216, 222, 230, 232, 235
Cincinnati Red Stockings, 36–40
Civil War, baseball in, 24–29, 34
Clarke, Bill, 143
Clarkson, John, 100
Clayton Act, 205
Clements, Jack, 125
Cleveland, Ohio, baseball clubs in, 14, 41, 77, 138, 195
Cleveland Forest Citys (NA), 41
Cleveland Indians (Blues, Bronchos, Naps) (AL), 148, 154, 156, 165, 182, 211, 221, 226, 229, 231–32, 235
Cleveland Infants (PL), 105
Cleveland Spiders (AA), 83
Cleveland Spiders (NL), 62, 73, 79–80, 119, 124, 133, 136–37, 140
Cobb, Ty, 173, 180–82, 185–87, 189, 191, 207, 225, 231–32
Colleges, baseball in, 3–4, 88, 94, 126, 138
Collins, Eddie, 206, 233
Collins, Hub, 130
Collins, Jimmy, 150
Colonial League of New England, 207
Columbus, Ohio, baseball clubs in, 29
Columbus Colts (AA), 112, 119, 121
Comiskey, Charles, 87, 103, 108, 112, 120, 138, 143, 150, 156, 175, 183, 199, 201, 220–21, 232–34
Connecticut League, 152
Craver, William, 61
Crawford, Sam, 156, 191
Creamer, Joseph, 176
Creighton, James, 23–25, 30
Cricket, 18, 22, 36
Croker, Richard, 133
Cross, Lave, 125
Cubans, in baseball, 44, 172, 181–82, 202, 204, 223, 238
Cummings, Candy, 58
Cuthbert, Ned, 46
Czechs, in baseball, 204

rights in, 54–55, 58–59, 73, 75, 80, 140, 156; labor practices in, 55–56, 60, 62–67, 71, 85–86, 90–91, 108, 117, 119–23; gate split in, 55–56, 79, 98, 100, 110, 119, 134–35, 140; profits in, 57, 59, 62, 65, 73, 92–93, 104, 111, 120, 135, 147, 169–70, 206, 228; operating expenses in, 57, 59, 64, 74, 98–99, 103–4, 111, 127, 135–36, 160, 169–70, 210; admission prices in, 57–59, 69, 72, 74, 99–100, 120–21, 135, 218; attendance in, 92, 98, 104, 111, 135–36, 151, 169, 178, 191, 206, 208, 210, 212, 217, 222, 225, 228
Nava, Lou, 132
Navin, Frank, 187, 190–91
Newark, N.J., baseball clubs in, 98, 203–4
Newark Peps (FL), 207, 209
New England, early baseball in, 2–4, 21–22
New England League, 58, 152
New Haven (Conn.) Elm Citys (NA), 47
New Jersey, baseball clubs in, 2, 4, 8, 10–12, 32–33
New Orleans, La., baseball clubs in, 31–32, 89, 99, 164, 203
New York, N.Y., baseball clubs in, 2, 4–5, 8, 11–14, 16, 24, 28–33, 36, 41, 44, 54, 68–69, 83, 89, 98
"New York game," 4, 14, 16
New York Giants (Gothams) (NL), 56, 58, 68, 72, 85, 92, 94, 97, 99, 102–5, 110–11, 113–14, 123–25, 127, 130, 133–35, 137, 140, 144, 152, 155–57, 159–61, 164–65, 169–70, 174–76, 188, 201–2, 204, 207, 227, 229–31
New York Giants (PL), 105, 109, 113–14
New York Knickerbockers, 4–8, 10, 13–14, 16, 27–29, 36, 40
New York Metropolitans (AA), 69–70, 72, 85
New York Mutuals (NA), 41, 44
New York state, baseball clubs in, 4, 13, 16, 20, 31, 33, 39, 41, 44, 82

New York State League, 151
New York Yankees (Highlanders) (AL), 155–57, 169, 176, 185, 192, 212, 214, 220, 226–28
Nichols, Al, 61
North Carolina League, 152
Northwestern League, 62, 68, 72, 79, 88, 99, 117
Norwegians, in baseball, 171

O'Brien, J. Morgan Joseph, 110
O'Connor, Jack "Peach Pie," 181
O'Loughlin, Frank "Silk," 175
O'Mara, Ollie, 164
O'Neill, J. Palmer, 118
O'Neill, James "Tip," 98
O'Rourke, James "Orator," 60
O'Rourke, John, 60
O'Rourke, Tim, 201
Overbeck, Harry, 88
Owners, backgrounds of, 16–17, 21, 26, 28–29, 51, 82, 133, 166

Pacific Coast League, 166–67, 220, 231
Pacific Northwest League, 151
Park, John, 69
Peckinpaugh, Roger, 192
Pennsylvania, baseball clubs in, 20, 33, 35
Peoria, Ill., baseball clubs in, 88
Pepper, George Wharton, 202
Perry, Scott, 226
Pfeffer, Fred, 126
Philadelphia, Pa., baseball clubs in, 4, 8, 14, 27, 30, 35, 48, 54, 68–69, 83, 89, 98
Philadelphia Athletics (AA), 69–72, 114, 117, 121
Philadelphia Athletics (AL), 147–48, 150, 153–54, 156, 173, 188, 193, 206, 226
Philadelphia Athletics (NA), 41, 46–48, 53
Philadelphia Keystones (UA), 74, 80
Philadelphia Phillies (NL), 56, 58, 68, 72, 93, 100, 107, 110–11, 123, 125,